Shakespearean Character

ARDEN SHAKESPEARE STUDIES IN LANGUAGE
AND DIGITAL METHODOLOGIES

Series Editors: Jonathan Hope, Lynne Magnusson and
Michael Witmore

*Arden Shakespeare Studies in Language and Digital
Methodologies* seeks to identify, develop, and publish new
work on Shakespeare and his contemporaries with a focus on
language and/or digital methods.

Shakespeare's Common Language
Alysia Kolentsis
ISBN 978-1-350-00701-7

FORTHCOMING

Reproducing English Renaissance Drama, 1711–2016
Brett Hirsch
ISBN 978-1-350-02186-0

Shakespearean Character

Language in Performance

Jelena Marelj

THE ARDEN SHAKESPEARE
LONDON · NEW YORK · OXFORD · NEW DELHI · SYDNEY

THE ARDEN SHAKESPEARE
Bloomsbury Publishing Plc
50 Bedford Square, London, WC1B 3DP, UK
1385 Broadway, New York, NY 10018, USA

BLOOMSBURY, THE ARDEN SHAKESPEARE and the Arden Shakespeare logo are trademarks of Bloomsbury Publishing Plc

First published in Great Britain 2019
This paperback edition published 2020

Copyright © Jelena Marelj, 2019, 2020

Jelena Marelj has asserted her right under the Copyright, Designs and Patents Act, 1988, to be identified as the author of this work.

For legal purposes the Acknowledgements on pp. viii–ix constitute an extension of this copyright page.

Cover design: Irene Martinez Costa
Cover image: Royal Shakespeare Company's production of William Shakespeare's *Henry IV* © Robbie Jack / Getty images

All rights reserved. No part of this publication may be reproduced or transmitted in any form or by any means, electronic or mechanical, including photocopying, recording, or any information storage or retrieval system, without prior permission in writing from the publishers.

Bloomsbury Publishing Plc does not have any control over, or responsibility for, any third-party websites referred to or in this book. All internet addresses given in this book were correct at the time of going to press. The author and publisher regret any inconvenience caused if addresses have changed or sites have ceased to exist, but can accept no responsibility for any such changes.

A catalogue record for this book is available from the British Library.

Library of Congress Cataloging-in-Publication Data
Names: Marelj, Jelena, author.
Title: Shakespearean character : language in performance / Jelena Marelj.
Description: London, UK ; New York, NY : The Arden Shakespeare, 2019. | Series: Arden Shakespeare studies in language and digital methodologies | Includes bibliographical references and index.
Identifiers: LCCN 2018055714 (print) | LCCN 2018058715 (ebook) | ISBN 9781350061392 (ePub) | ISBN 9781350061408 (ePDF) | ISBN 9781350061385(hardback) | ISBN 9781408134512 (ePDF) | ISBN 9781408145123(eBook)
Subjects: LCSH: Shakespeare, William, 1564-1616–Characters. | English language–Early modern, 1500-1700–Rhetoric. | Characters and characteristics in literature.Classification: LCC PR2989 (ebook) | LCC PR2989. M29 2019 (print) | DDC 822.3/3–dc23
LC record available at https://lccn.loc.gov/2018055714

ISBN:		
	HB:	978-1-350-06138-5
	PB:	978-1-350-17500-6
	ePDF:	978-1-350-06140-8
	ePub:	978-1-350-06139-2

Series: Arden Shakespeare Studies in Language and Digital Methodologies

Typeset by Integra Software Services Pvt. Ltd.

To find out more about our authors and books visit www.bloomsbury.com and sign up for our newsletters.

For my mother Milena,
moje srce i moja duša

CONTENTS

Acknowledgements viii
Series Editors' Preface x

Introduction: Re-Characterizing Shakespearean Character 1

1 Gricean Implicature and Falstaff's Roundness in *1 Henry IV* 21

2 Reported Speech and Cleopatra's Sexual Charisma 59

3 Pragma-Rhetoric and Henry V's Moral Ambivalence 97

4 Kate's Defiant Obedience in *The Taming of the Shrew* 137

Coda: Questioning Anteriority: Hamlet's Undecidability and Pragmatic Failure 169

Notes 191
Bibliography 227
Index 238

ACKNOWLEDGEMENTS

I am immensely indebted to Elizabeth Hanson and Marta Straznicky, my mentors at Queen's University in Kingston, for their steadfast support and guidance over the years. Not only did they readily journey with me into the depths of linguistics but they also penetratingly engaged with my ideas as they urged me to further explore and articulate them. Thanks to their pointed feedback and astute insights, I learned to ask the questions that matter. Many thanks are also due to Katherine Acheson for her sound professional advice and unwaning enthusiasm for the project. I also wish to acknowledge the support of the Social Sciences and Humanities Research Council of Canada (SSHRC) as well as Queen's University for the fellowships that assisted in this research.

My deepest appreciation goes to series editor Jonathan Hope for his probing questions and constructive comments, which have helped give the book greater coherence and clarity. I am likewise grateful to his co-editors, Lynne Magnusson and Michael Witmore, as well as to Mark Dudgeon, the publisher at The Arden Shakespeare, for his attentiveness in all matters and for ensuring a smooth publication process.

Special thanks are also due to Dale Tracy for her publishing advice and support; to my husband, Greg Sipos, for scaling every mountain with me; and to my parents, Dušan and Milena Marelj, for the countless sacrifices that helped to make the impossible possible.

Parts of this book have previously appeared as articles. A version of the Cleopatra chapter was published as 'The "Serpent of Old Nile": Cleopatra and the Pragmatics of

Reported Speech' in *Shakespeare Survey* 68 (2015): 337–52, while a portion of the Henry chapter was first published as 'Pragma-Rhetoric and Henry's "Rabbit-Duck" Effect in Shakespeare's *Henry V*' in *Early Modern Literary Studies* 19, no. 2 (2017): 1–24.

SERIES EDITORS' PREFACE

Arden Shakespeare Studies in Language and Digital Methodologies seeks to identify, develop and publish new work on Shakespeare and his contemporaries which draws on linguistic and/or digital approaches.

While the series is open to work on language which is not primarily digital, and to digital or quantitative work which is not primarily linguistic, we bring them together because they share objects of interest, methodologies and often practitioners, and because their intersection has opened exciting new paths in research.

A characteristic of the series is close engagement between the general editors and authors: we offer hands-on editing and collaborative engagement with ideas and methodology. We believe that the shape of literary studies is changing, and we look forward to working with scholars making that change happen.

Series Editors:
Jonathan Hope, Arizona State University, USA
Lynne Magnusson, University of Toronto, Canada
Michael Witmore, Folger Shakespeare Library, USA

Introduction: Re-Characterizing Shakespearean Character

Shakespeare's dramatis personae are definitively not human, yet the reception history of his plays shows that critics, audiences and actors have nevertheless experienced them as such – as familiar, accessible, yet simultaneously evasive and ultimately unfathomable individuals who seem to exist outside of and prior to their play-texts. Taking firm root in the fervent bardolatry of the Romantic age and reaching its zenith with A. C. Bradley's seminal lectures on Shakespearean tragedy, the tendency to read Shakespeare's characters as if they were real people with occluded core selves prevented both nineteenth-century commentators and twentieth-century critics from recognizing what English music composer William Jackson had so perceptively highlighted back in 1795: that 'Shakespeare's characters, have that appearance of reality which always has the effect of actual life'.[1] Jackson's assertion that dramatic characters produce the 'appearance' of reality – or a certain reality 'effect' without actually possessing ontological reality – leads to a crucial but often overlooked question in Shakespeare scholarship: if a fictional person in a dramatic text produces a reality effect, how is that effect produced?

The answer, I suggest, lies in a character's use of language. One can easily picture Shakespeare carefully selecting and assembling particular words and phrases into units of speech and assigning them to individual speakers in his play-texts who are then brought to life by an actor. Yet even though characters are verbal constructs, they are no less speakers and active users of language who communicate with other characters and with their offstage audiences. Characters' speech and their verbal agency have been neglected by Romantic and Bradleyan critics who, in accordance with their novelistic treatment of dramatic characters as psychologically autonomous persons, assume a character's language to be the fixed external expression of, and index to, a self-contained and interiorized essence that exists prior to language and generates it in the first place.[2] While both New Critics and Post-Structuralist critics hostilely denounced this reification of character, their respective emphases on a text's poetic language and on its socio-historical discourses only served to sideline character and its use of language. Famously dismissing Bradley's psychological realism in his essay 'How Many Children Had Lady Macbeth?' (1933), L. C. Knights promoted instead a scrutiny of poetic language in a New Critical vein and disparaged character as a mental 'abstraction' that threatens to 'impoverish the total response' of the plays as dramatic poems 'in the mind of the reader or spectator'.[3] Positing that poetic language affects the reader with a particular textual meaning or value arising from the coherence of its parts, Knights called for an 'exact and sensitive study of the quality of the verse, of the rhythm and imagery, of the controlled associations of the words and their emotional and intellectual force'.[4] Since meaning, for Knights, is intrinsic to and deductible from poetic language and does not reside in character, he subsumes character within a play's larger poetic structure and disregards the individual traits of a character's speech.

The New Historicist emphasis on discourse as a socio-historical and political force that shapes the speaking subject further stripped character of speech and verbal agency in denying character ontological presence. The New Historicism's post-structuralist conception of reality as always and already a discursive construct with no external points of reference led its practitioners to posit literary characters as mere subjects of discourse and ideology.[5] Given the New Historicism's conflation of characters with real people, both real persons and fictional subjects are denied individual agency and autonomous subjectivity: they are, to use Stephen Greenblatt's terms, 'subjected' to 'the cultural system of meanings' that are fashioned by competing ideologies inherent to discourse.[6] The speaking subject's language thus becomes a de-personalized by-product of these discourses, and its motives, aspirations and intentions are the effects of whatever discourse within which he or she operates. Although, for Greenblatt at least, the subject does have limited agency to fashion himself or herself through language and express 'a distinctive personality ... [a] consistent mode of perceiving and behaving', this 'distinctive personality' is nevertheless a function of how various discourses intersect in his or her speech as well as his or her orientation in discourse rather than any personal qualities inhering in the speaker.[7] As a function of discourse rather than its origin, the subject speaks from its position as a grammatical subject or an 'I' within discourse, whose meaning is determined by the conditions and structures that bring it into being: speech is not self-referential but is rather a function of the speaker's relative place in what Foucault styled an 'enunciative domain'.[8]

Although a number of historicist accounts like those of Karen Newman and Christy Desmet salvaged the subject's individual agency by illustrating that characters possess their own rhetoric and are not merely discursive functions, they nevertheless subordinated characters' use of language to larger discursive and contextual frameworks that purportedly govern their speech. Newman showed that a comic character's rhetoric is contained within and constrained by the linguistic conventions of the soliloquy, while Desmet, examining how a character's dramatic identity is shaped through the rhetorical exercises of the early modern grammar school, deemed that a character's use of rhetoric is circumscribed by and embedded within a moral interpretive framework that structures a reader's ethical evaluation of character.[9]

Despite this New Historicist wave of largely anti-character sentiment, the study of character has nevertheless made a steady comeback in Shakespeare criticism in the past two decades. Heralding the re-emergence of character study in a post-structuralist climate that had all but dispensed with the notion of character as a critical concept, the essay collection *Shakespeare and Character: Theory, History, Performance, and Theatrical Persons* (2009) reasserts the centrality of character to the dramatic action of Shakespeare's plays. In their introduction to the volume, editors Paul Yachnin and Jessica Slights maintain that Shakespeare prioritizes character over the Aristotelian emphasis on plot, and boldly assert that 'character is the organizing principle of Shakespeare's plays – it organizes both the formal and ideological dimensions of the drama and is not organized by them'.[10] Foregrounding character as an agent rather than merely a node or element of dramatic discourse, Yachnin and Slights's bravely branded 'new character criticism' is set into motion by the volume's contributors, who adopt interdisciplinary approaches ranging from analytic philosophy and phenomenology to semiotics and performance criticism to theorize dramatic character.[11] However, only William Dodd's essay stands out among the others in its linguistic approach to Othello's quiddity or his 'effect of character'.[12] Yu Jin Ko and Michael Shurgot's more recently edited collection of essays, *Shakespeare's Sense of Character: On the Page and from the Stage* (2012), similarly participates in this burgeoning new character criticism by harnessing performance studies with literary criticism to chart how performance, rehearsal and theatre practices contribute to our understanding of character. But while the volume features a number of accounts that treat character as a dramatic construct and explore how characters negotiate their roles within their respective play-worlds, none focalize on characters' use of language. I expand the parameters of this new character criticism by approaching character from the field of linguistic pragmatics to examine how our impression of characters' ontological reality is produced.

As a social science, pragmatics operates on the premise that speakers either are or stand in for real people. Its linguistic methods and theories are grounded in empirical investigations into how real people naturally use language, based on which rules and theories are formulated to systematically describe speakers' language behaviour. In pragmatics, a speaker's language behaviour is determined by a pre-existing system of language which the speaker deploys in certain speech contexts that, in turn, shape speaker meaning. Linguistic-oriented Shakespeare critics who have applied pragmatic theories to their readings of character have, nevertheless, subscribed to the assumption that characters *are* real people and, in doing so, have succumbed to the Bradleyan quagmire of attributing psychological essence to dramatic character; some even see characters operating in contexts that are analogous to 'real life' contexts and situations, and thus interpret characters' linguistic behaviour accordingly. These critical pitfalls risk neutralizing characters' complex and idiosyncratic identities, as the literary term 'character' becomes equated with the term 'speaker' in linguistics. Since pragmatics is interested in accounting for universal modes and methods of communication that are relevant and applicable to human beings as a category, speakers are severed from any larger conception of who they are as individuals; lacking personal traits and unique identities, they are largely interchangeable.

Bringing together linguistic pragmatics and character analysis, I posit that dramatic characters are mimetic representations of real people and not actual people or extra-linguistic entities with coherent inner selves. While Shakespeare's dramatic characters are hypothetical speakers, they are clearly not the self-contained and self-willed agents they are in pragmatics since they are partially put into motion by the playwright himself who communicates with his audience through them; their agency, in other words, is partly dependent on the playwright. Moreover, they are differentiated from one another as dramatic speakers by Shakespeare, who selects and assigns habits of linguistic behaviour to individualize his major characters. My purpose in using pragmatics is not to delineate who or what these characters are in terms of their idiosyncratic personalities as determined by their distinctive speaking styles or the pragmatic traits of their speech, for to do so would be to merely sacrifice their multifaceted variety and complexity as dramatic creations. Instead, my purpose is to disclose the pragmatic mechanisms that occasion critics and audiences to comment on the lifelike complexity and variety that Shakespeare's dramatic characters seem to possess. I will demonstrate that the audience's perception of a character's ontological reality is a linguistic effect produced by the conjunction between a character's pragmatic use of language in an interactive context with other characters, and the particular meanings that Shakespeare ascribes to his characters and conveys to his audience by dramatic and meta-dramatic means.

The linguistic turn: Towards a pragmatics of dramatic character

Collapsing the Aristotelian distinction between lexis or verbal expression and praxis or action, language philosopher J. L. Austin's influential treatise on speech act theory, *How to Do Things with Words* (1962), demonstrated that a speaker's verbal utterances are performative: they 'do' things or act upon reality rather than merely reflect it. Within this performative framework, a speaker's agency can be inferred through the illocutionary force and perlocutionary effect of his or her utterances.[13] Austin's seminal treatise established the foundation for the still relatively young field of pragmatics, which is concerned with language use in social contexts.

Developing in the 1970s and 1980s as a subfield of linguistics under Austin's successors, John Searle and H. P. Grice, pragmatics is a reaction against the conceptualization of language as an abstract, self-referential and fixed system as evidenced in both Saussurean structural linguistics and Chomsky's generative grammar. For Ferdinand de Saussure, language (*langue*) is a system of signification constituted by the dynamic relation between signs. These signs, which are comprised of a signifier (the linguistic form of a word) and a signified (the corresponding mental concept evoked by the signifier), relate to other signs to produce meaning. The meaning of the signifier is contingent on its conventional usage, which is to say that even though the signifier is inextricable from the signified, it is ontologically arbitrary. Meaning in structural linguistics is therefore relational since it is determined by the differences, oppositions or combinations both within and between linguistic signs in this language system. Conceived of as a normative system for expressing mental concepts, language for Saussure is a self-enclosed and self-sufficient system that has no reference to extra-linguistic causes, speaker intentions or reality outside of the realm of language; it is wholly divorced from speech (*parole*), or language as it is spoken. Noam Chomsky similarly detaches language from reality and grants it autonomy as a concept. In his model of generative grammar, Chomsky claims that the mind has an innate and unconscious knowledge of the principles or rules of a 'universal grammar', which allows a speaker to formulate grammatically correct sentences. For Chomsky, the grammatical correctness of an utterance is the expression or external manifestation of a mental and universal grammar that delimits the speaker's competence, regardless of his or her intelligence. Chomsky thus construes language as a logical and syntactic framework in which meaning is synonymous with the speaker's innate cognitive ability to properly frame the sentences he or she utters in accordance with the syntactic rules generated by this grammar: meaning becomes a function of grammatically correct and logically valid sentences.

Pragmatics revolts against this structuralist tendency in linguistics to examine the logical laws and principles of language, since doing so forfeits the context of utterances. Pragmatics, 'interested in the process of producing language and in its producers, not just in the end-product, language' as Jacob Mey states, reintroduces the speaker into the linguistic equation and shifts the focus of linguistics from *langue* to *parole* to explore language as it is used by real people.[14] The speaker in pragmatics, who acts upon reality by speaking, is a rational and intentional agent possessing performative agency: the speaker's speech (*parole*) creates meaning in a given context as well as shapes that context, instead of merely reproducing the meaning inscribed onto language-as-system. As Jenny Thomas defines it, pragmatics is '*meaning in interaction*', which is to say that 'making meaning is a dynamic process, involving the negotiation of meaning between speaker and hearer, the context of utterance (physical, social and linguistic) and the meaning potential of an utterance'.[15] Context, a crucial component in determining the speaker's meaning, is not only dialogic but also relative to the speaker's intentions and communicative goals: it is, as Mey explains, a dynamic 'environment that is in steady development, prompted by the continuous interaction of the people engaged in language use'.[16] Under pragmatics, language becomes a constitutive force which personalizes – without essentializing – the speaking subject.

Nevertheless, the application of pragmatics to Shakespeare's plays has proven to be unenlightening with respect to character, since literary critics have tended to override characters' speech in treating it as a function of the language of the play. Using Austin's speech act theory in their respective studies of Coriolanus and Henry V, Stanley Fish and Joseph A. Porter interpret these characters' speeches as allegories of their plays' thematic concerns with language. Examining the illocutionary behaviour of Coriolanus, who repudiates the reciprocal obligations inhering in the speech acts of requesting and accepting, Fish notes that Coriolanus's decision to use the speech acts of promising and rejecting signals his desire to posit an essential and God-like self beyond language. He concludes that Coriolanus's transgressive self-fashioning through performative utterances serves as a meta-dramatic commentary on the proper rehearsal of speech acts and the conditions and consequences of their performance; *Coriolanus*, claims Fish, is a 'Speech Act play' about the impossibility of a speaker standing autonomously outside of language which structures reality.[17] Joseph A. Porter, likewise, reads the characteristic verbal actions of the monarchs in Shakespeare's history plays as an index to the second tetralogy's meta-dramatic concern with the thematic progression of language from its non-dramatic form in *Richard II* to its dramatic expression in the polyglotism of *Henry V*.[18] Since Porter and Fish render speech subservient to thematic development, they do not concern themselves with the meaning of characters' speech in particular linguistic and social contexts. John Kerrigan has, more recently, examined 'binding' speech acts such as oaths, vows, contracts, pledges, promises and curses in Shakespeare's dramatic canon.[19] However, like Fish and Porter, he too disassociates these performative utterances from their speakers and instead contextualizes them within early modern religious, historical, legal and philosophical discourses.

Linguists approaching Shakespeare from the field of pragmatics have, on the other hand, regressed to a Bradleyan essentialism in conflating mimetic representations with real people. This conflation underwrites one of the first pragmatic explorations of dialogue in Shakespeare's plays, linguist Roger Brown and literary critic Albert Gilman's article 'Politeness Theory and Shakespeare's Four Major Tragedies' (1989). Brown and Gilman quantitatively mine the early modern English language of Shakespeare's *Othello*, *King Lear*, *Hamlet* and *Macbeth* for linguistic data in order to uncover the historical dimensions of the pragmatic phenomenon of politeness in early modern English; their method falls under the rubric of what would later become historical pragmatics.[20] In their study of Shakespeare's linguistic corpora, the authors assume that the soliloquy reveals a character's 'true feelings and intentions' and provides 'access to [the speaker's] inner life that is necessary for a proper test of politeness theory'.[21] This supposition of a character's essential interiority also underpins Juhani Rudanko's *Pragmatic Approaches to Shakespeare* (1993), the only book-length study devoted to the practical application of pragmatics to dramatic character. Aspiring to bridge the disciplinary divide between linguistics and literary analysis by enriching the understanding of Shakespeare through pragmatic strategies and vice versa, Rudanko's analysis of Othello, Coriolanus and Iago is premised on the pragmatic assumption that 'man is an essence and not a construct of "special discourses" or of "social context"'.[22] Because of this assumption, Rudanko's reading of character merely champions the applicability of pragmatic tools to Shakespeare without arriving at any novel insights into character. He correlates, for instance, the difference between the 'early' and the 'later' Othello sensed by the audience to the linguistic breakdown in adjacency pairs and Gricean maxims in Othello's speech, which mark his 'lack of self-control and loss of composure'.[23]

What is notably missing in these early, one-dimensional pragmatic explorations of dramatic character is an interactive framework between speakers and hearers and the social context within which speakers operate. It is the embeddedness of the speaker's speech in social and discursive contexts that makes the speaker a character with an idiosyncratic identity and distinctive character effect; the synergy between speech and social and discursive contexts particularizes character and allows the audience to differentiate characters from each other even as they engage in verbal exchange. Although Keir Elam and Andrew Kennedy have accounted for the social context of interpersonal exchange between characters, the concept of character is sidelined and underdeveloped in their work since they treat characters as impersonal speakers or switching points in discourse rather than as origins of speech. Elam's *Shakespeare's Universe of Discourse* (1984), indebted to Austin's speech act theory and to Wittgenstein's language games, interprets the language of Shakespeare's comedies as social discourse: the verbal interaction between characters draws attention to the significance of this social language-in-use. Nevertheless, this social discourse takes on a life of its own as it becomes the central subject of Elam's study and, in turn, strips Shakespeare's speakers of agency by rendering them 'interpersonal forces responsible for carrying forward the narrative dynamic'.[24] The speakers' particular aims and intentions, as they intersect with larger discursive narratives in the plays, go unexplored, as does the way speakers present themselves within this social discourse. Kennedy, demonstrating that the interactive dialogue or 'duologue' between two characters reciprocally transforms their speech and their values, similarly fails to account for characters' *individual* communication strategies apart from these interpersonal 'duologues', whose purpose is usually to accomplish the play's dramatic action.[25]

At issue in the metaphysical debate about character with which these pragmatic approaches overlap is the question of agency, which has been conceptualized either as an extra-personal and collective social force or as unrestrained free will that constitutes the core of individual identity. The pragmatic contributions of Shakespeare critics William Dodd and Lynne Magnusson in the past two decades, as well as Simon Palfrey and Tiffany Stern's theatrical study of cues and part-scripts, all make use of Bakhtinian dialogism to illustrate that Shakespearean character is neither a passive instrument of discourse nor the essential origin of speech but a negotiation of both. Palfrey and Stern conceptualize character as a dynamic process of imminent and 'imaginative "becoming"' borne of the jostling between the actor's 'part' or cue-script (comprising both text and context) and the larger play-script (comprising the other part-texts to which the actor's role responds).[26] They contend that a character's lifelikeness emanates from the conflict between a character's desire to tell his or her story through the cued part while heeding 'cues' and responding to other scripted speeches, narratives and ideological forces in the play-script.[27] Being both a discrete entity and a component of the larger play-text, this cued part reveals the equivocal nature of a character's agency, which is in equal measure activated and enabled by the cue-script as well as determined and restrained by the play-script. This strategic negotiation or jostling that constitutes Palfrey and Stern's understanding of a character's reality effect also features in Dodd's and Magnusson's pragmatic considerations of what a character 'does' with his or her speech in relation to what is theatrically and discursively (Dodd) or historically and discursively (Magnusson) scripted. Both Magnusson and Dodd posit that a 'character effect' issues from the verbal interaction between speakers and hearers and from the intersection between speakers' speeches and plays' dominant discourses.[28] Magnusson, blending together discourse analysis, politeness theory and Bourdieu's economic model of sociolinguistic exchange with sociocultural practices and contexts, shows that even though dramatic speakers are constrained by social and power relations recorded in their speech, they nevertheless shape these relations through their linguistic performances and socially invent themselves in verbal interaction. Suggesting that Catherine of Aragon's 'external forms of politeness' in *Henry VIII* serve as the coordinates of her illusory psychology and establish the character effect of her 'negative politeness', Magnusson argues that 'character "effects" can be shaped by the speech patterns of the speakers' relative social positions, both as given in the present moment of the verbal interaction and as gathering up the cumulative trajectory of accustomed speech positions'.[29] Magnusson's concept of character as the product of a speaker's linguistic negotiation relative to his or her social or historical situatedness is translated into performative terms by William Dodd. For Dodd, the 'character effect' is lodged in a character's 'discourse biography', which is 'produced dynamically in the interplay between a *dramatis persona's* pragmatic behavior (what it "does with words" and how it interacts with others) and its semantic attributes (the social, cultural, and moral identity ascribed to it)'.[30] This cumulative 'discourse biography' is what creates the quiddity of character and our impression of its interiority for Dodd. Both Dodd's and Magnusson's understanding of characters' reality effects is premised on an interpretation of agency as verbal performance, or performative agency: a speaker's agency is evidenced in and inferred from what this speaker pragmatically does with or in his or her speech in an interactive context, as well as how this speech dialogically responds to impersonal discourses within which it is necessarily delimited. Since speakers are 'aware of and respond to transpersonal "discourses", as opposed to being simply voiced or subjugated by them', a speaker's agency, explains Dodd, is consciously willed and underwritten by choice.[31]

Although Dodd and Magnusson discuss character effects, their objective is not to spell out how these effects are produced. Dodd's primary aim is to theorize character in a performative context by examining the interface between fictional characters' 'discourse biograph[ies]' and early modern actors' 'performance biographies', whereas Magnusson's objective is to delineate how Shakespeare's characters are socially constructed through dialogic interaction and how they, in turn, construct social relations.[32] The only critic to focus on how reality effects are constructed in a dialogic context is linguist Jonathan Culpeper, who combines pragmatics with cognitive psychology to explain how readers form an impression of dramatic and non-dramatic character. However, because Culpeper is primarily interested in how readers mentally process fictional characters, his rather broad and not Shakespeare-centric study is positioned in the field of cognitive stylistics to show that fictional character occupies the interface between a reader's psychological schemata and a text's linguistic cues.[33] The goal of my book, by contrast, is to explain how the character effects or the very lifelikeness of Shakespeare's characters are produced pragmatically, by accounting for the role of the audience as interlocutor in a communicative network of speakers and hearers. Since pragmatics is, to reiterate Jenny Thomas, an interactive process comprising 'the negotiation of meaning between speaker and hearer, the context of utterance (physical, social and linguistic) and the meaning potential of an utterance', it becomes necessary to examine not only how a character's pragmatic use of language intersects with his or her scripted roles but also the effect that these utterances have on the audience as hearer.[34]

Characters, as pragmatic speakers in a drama, clearly have verbal agency or the capacity to perform linguistic actions. This agency arises from a character's speech in a dialogic situation; it is an 'agency of intention' to move or act upon others which motivates speech and is evident in the very act of speaking.[35] However, this agency of intention is always and already predetermined, compromised and set into motion by the playwright himself, who frames his characters' utterances to communicate his own meaning to the audience. The theatre audience, like a character's onstage interlocutor, is actively involved in constructing the meaning(s) produced by a character's utterances; it is the auditor or recipient of the message of a speaker's speech. The primary difference between actual conversation and dramatic dialogue, however, as Andrew Kennedy notes, is that the latter issues from onstage actors whose speech is 'always directed outwards to an anonymous or non-conversational auditor or spectator'; dramatic dialogue is always scripted.[36] As Mick Short explains, drama is structured as a series of 'embedded discourses': the discourse between two characters (speaker and hearer) communicating on stage is embedded within a larger discourse between playwright or author (speaker) and audience or reader (hearer), and it is this layering of discourses that enables the playwright to communicate with his audience: 'Character speaks to character, and this discourse is part of what the playwright "tells" the audience.'[37] The presence of an overhearing audience in the theatre is inscribed in the dramatic structure of a play as well as in a dramatic character's 'part': in an onstage dialogue or verbal exchange, the triangular relationship between an onstage speaker, hearer and the theatre audience attunes the audience to messages which may be directed exclusively towards it rather than towards other onstage characters, while also helping constitute the audience's understanding of the play. Shakespeare then, just like his characters, may be said to possess an agency of intention: he takes opportunities to speak to his audience through his characters and pragmatically uses them to communicate a layer of meaning that jostles with the meanings created by characters' speech.

Any mention of intentions with regard to Shakespeare, however, warrants a caveat. While it will never be possible to truly know what Shakespeare 'intended' as a playwright, this epistemic impossibility neither prevents us from ascribing intentionality to him nor discounts the fact that there nevertheless are extant meanings that Shakespeare did intend which the audience or reader, as Duncan Salkeld has rightly noted, can possibly 'negotiate, grasp and misconstrue'.[38] As David Schalkwyk has proposed, intentionality should not be associated with mental events that precede language and determine the meaning of a text but should rather be 'retroactively or retrospectively posited as the purposeful structure of significance of the text'.[39] Schalkwyk acknowledges that Shakespeare wills his plays into being and endows them with purpose but he foregrounds that Shakespeare has no ultimate control over his plays' meanings, since meanings are gleaned by the audience. It is necessary to add that Shakespeare's purpose, plan or design in scripting his plays is not only compromised by the intentions of his character-speakers, who are constantly 'doing things' with and to their words, but also mediated or compounded by actors' performative intentions in interpreting their scripted roles. In communicating with his audience, then, Shakespeare positions this audience as hearer or interlocutor who is capable of inferring or cognitively grasping the possible or potential meanings he conveys. The audience that Shakespeare imagines and implicitly addresses in the play-text are active and responsive participants in the creation of meaning; the audience, to use Peter Rabinowitz's terms, is an idealized or imagined 'authorial audience' rather than a real or 'actual audience' whose expectations and responses the playwright manages and guides.[40] Shakespeare orchestrates audience response not only verbally or through his characters' speech but also dramatically and meta-dramatically through devices such as soliloquies and asides, the juxtaposition of scenes, the commentary of onstage characters and many other techniques identified by critics that allow the playwright to communicate directly with his audience.[41] Shakespeare's craft and agency as a playwright largely contribute to the distinctive and memorable character effects we find in his plays.

By inserting the theatre audience into the pragmatic framework, I underscore that character effects require the presence of an audience who actualizes or brings character to 'life' by inferring the meaning of a character's verbal utterances and Shakespeare's non-verbal cues.

I examine five of Shakespeare's linguistically self-conscious characters who continue to be subjects of extensive critical debate and audience fascination: Falstaff, Cleopatra, Henry V, Katherine in *The Taming of the Shrew* and Hamlet. I account for the way in which the distinctive character effects of Falstaff's vitality, Cleopatra's sexual charisma, Henry V's moral opacity, Katherine's ambiguity and Hamlet's undecidability are produced in a communicative and theatrical context. I argue that the audience's impression of a character's ontological reality and its distinct character effect is produced by the intersection between a character's pragmatic use of language in interaction with other characters, and the particular meaning Shakespeare conveys to his audience through dramatic and meta-dramatic means that underpins the character's speech and structures the play. I propose that Shakespeare's characters possess anteriority – rather than a-historical interiority – which defines their mimetic reality. A character's references to anterior utterances, meanings and discourses with which it is in dialogue creates the impression that characters have lives independent of the play-text and its discourses. This anteriority arises from the tension between a character's pragmatic behaviour (what she or he does with and to his or her speech) and the character's historically or textually scripted role in Shakespeare's sources, which informs character and furnishes it with a historical 'life' that pre-dates its fictional life as dramatic speaker. This scripted role presses up against the distinct meanings that Shakespeare ascribes to his characters and dialogically converges with their speech to create the impression that characters control language and have extra-textual lives of their own.

About the book

The book is divided into four chapters and a coda, each focusing on a particular character's reality effect. The chapters progressively build on one another as they trace speakers' pragmatic techniques from the impeccable (Falstaff) to the questionable (Hamlet) in verbal exchanges with their interlocutors. Chapter 1 makes use of Grice's theory of conversational implicature within the framework of Brown and Levinson's politeness theory to examine the character effect of Falstaff's roundness in *1 Henry IV*. I argue that Falstaff's conversational implicatures in his exchanges with Hal converge with meta-theatrical moments in the play to produce his 'roundness' or exuberant lifelikeness as a character: Falstaff's utterances allow him to embrace his scripted roles in the play as vainglorious braggart, Puritan, hedonist and thief even as he comically undermines or deflates these very roles to indirectly mock the illegitimacy and hypocrisy of the Lancastrian dynasty in which he, ironically, participates. Falstaff's implicit criticism of the Bolingbroke world intersects with the actor's implicatures and with the visual representations staged in key scenes to create the impression that Falstaff transcends his roles and exists prior to the play. In Chapter 2, I adopt a pragmatic approach to Cleopatra's reported speech in *Antony and Cleopatra* to explore how her sexual charisma is generated. I claim that Cleopatra's use of Roman reporting strategies – such as reporting other characters' speech, reporting her personal imaginings and commanding that her own speech and behaviour be reported to the Romans – allows her to glorify her sexual power as an Egyptian sovereign even as she performs her scripted role as an Egyptian courtesan.

Her pragmatic use of report enables Cleopatra to re-script her identity as a sexually powerful and victorious Egyptian in a Roman discursive context that denies her this very power. I demonstrate that Cleopatra's verbal performances are informed by meta-theatrical moments in the play that call attention to the boy actor's performance of Cleopatra, which valorizes her female sexuality and lends her anteriority. In Chapter 3, I adopt a pragma-rhetorical approach to examine how the character effect of Henry V's moral ambivalence as a Christian king and Machiavellian politician is produced. I argue that Henry's attempt to persuade his interlocutors of his ethos as a virtuous Christian monarch and as a plain-speaking and humble soldier conflicts with his logos: the faulty logic permeating Henry's utterances undercuts his ethos and exposes his aggressive political expediency, which gives rise to the audience's impression of his Machiavellianism. I show that Henry's Machiavellian wiliness is not innate but is rather a linguistic effect arising from the way his rhetorical performances counterpoint the dramatic irony produced by the juxtaposition of scenes in the play. The ironic framing of Henry's speech allows Shakespeare to convey to the audience the paradoxical nature of rhetorical kingship. In Chapter 4, I examine how Kate's pragmatic use of rhetoric in *The Taming of the Shrew* creates her ambiguity as a defiant shrew and obedient wife in her final monologue. I demonstrate that Kate transforms her shrewish defiance of Petruccio into a critique of patriarchy discreetly aimed at her female audience. I contend that Kate's argumentative use of comparisons in her monologue buttresses her ethos as a submissive wife and serves to persuade her male audience of her obedience to Petruccio, while the echoic irony, puns and semantic ambiguity peppering her speech give rise to implicatures that allow her to pragmatically convey to her female audience her scorn of the very subordination she endorses. The divergent persuasive and communicative intentions structuring Kate's monologue intersect with the meta-theatrical utterances of the boy actor playing her as well as with the reactions of her onstage audience to produce the impression of Kate's anteriority in the final scene of the play. Finally, the coda explores how Hamlet's utterances in the guise of a madman give rise to his questionable anteriority and undecidability as a character. I claim that Hamlet's conversational implicatures in his exchanges with the Elsinore characters underline his moralistic critique of their hypocrisy and establish his anteriority, at the same time as his utterances betray a blatant misogyny that intrudes upon this critique to effectively cancel the audience's impression of his anteriority. This counterpointing of Hamlet's display of anteriority with its erasure, along with the dramatic framing of Hamlet's conversations and his onstage auditors' failure to comprehend the pragmatic import of his implicatures, creates the impression of Hamlet's undecidability and his ultimate inscrutability as a character. Attending to these five characters' pragmatic use of language reveals that they are more than just the sum of their scripted parts: they possess an agency of intention that allows them to vie with and ultimately exceed their dramatic roles as character-types which are scripted for them both by other characters and by the playwright himself.

A pragmatic approach to Shakespeare's dramatic characters neither exhausts their meanings nor invalidates other interpretations but rather helps to elucidate the multifaceted variety that makes them seem so enticingly human, without needing to revert to anachronistic psychological models. Shakespearean character is neither a fixed and definitive analytical object nor a ready-made product that stands ready for interpretive excavation but, instead, a dynamic, open-ended and collaborative process that involves both onstage speakers and hearers and the offstage audience as interlocutors. Pragmatic theories and principles can yield significant insight into the rich interplay of voices – the character's, the playwright's and the actor's – that structure a play's meanings and its character effects. Indeed, pragmatics illuminates the triangular relationship between playwright, audience and character-actor in a communicative network, and brings to the fore that characters are not autonomous beings, nameless subjects of discourse or receptacles of language conceived thematically but quasi-symbolic personated persons whose idiosyncratic reality effects are contingent on their pragmatic strategies as much as they are on Shakespeare's dramatic strategies. Produced dialogically, Shakespeare's remarkably three-dimensional characters are linguistic effects that can only be fully realized in the presence of an audience.

1

Gricean Implicature and Falstaff's Roundness in *1 Henry IV*

In the preface to his annotated edition of Shakespeare's plays, a mildly bemused Samuel Johnson expressed his difficulty in delineating Falstaff: 'But *Falstaff* unimitated, unimitable *Falstaff*, how shall I describe thee? Thou compound of sense and vice; of sense which may be admired but not esteemed, of vice which may be despised, but hardly detested.'[1] So strongly had Falstaff affected Johnson that he felt compelled to pose his question to the character himself, as if Falstaff were a real person who could respond. Because Falstaff contradicts himself, he exceeds Johnson's rational attempt to comprehend him yet it is this contradiction – which turns on Falstaff's virtuous and vicious behaviour – that, as Johnson suggests, grants Falstaff his 'unimitable' complexity as a real person. Johnson's commentary invites the inference that Falstaff possesses a psychological reality which exceeds words and evades our attempt to logically grasp him.

Johnson's outcry is symptomatic of both past and present critical attempts to define the expansive parameters of the multifaceted and contradictory Falstaff. Falstaff's fatness, manifested by his bulging belly which exceeds his bodily frame, is a metonymy for the roundness or psychological reality that critics have attributed to him.² Exemplifying the tendency to read plump Jack as a real person with an inner self is Maurice Morgann's 1777 essay, which connects the antitheses of sense and vice noted by Johnson specifically to Falstaff's courage and cowardice. Attempting to vindicate Falstaff from claims of 'constitutional cowardice', Morgann advanced that Shakespeare 'contrived to make fecret Impreffions upon us of [Falstaff's] Courage'.³ Morgann attributes Falstaff's roundness as a character – what he calls Falstaff's 'diftinct and feparate fubfiftence' – not to our rational conception of Falstaff's cowardice but to our instinctual 'Impression' of Falstaff's courage which, he deems, 'belonged to his conftitution, and was manifeft in the conduct and practice of his whole life'.⁴ Morgann asserts that cowardice '*is not* the *Impreffion*, which the *whole* character of *Falftaff* is calculated to make' since it is merely the external or 'seen' part of this character and is relative to the unseen or sensed aspect of Falstaff's courage, which lies 'within' and can only be inferred 'from general principles, from latent motives, and from policies not avowed'.⁵ Although Morgann implies that the totality of Falstaff's character is comprised of his external cowardice and his inferred courage, he nevertheless locates the source of Falstaff's roundness in an occluded interiority which the audience must infer. Morgann observes that in spite of Falstaff's resistance to rational conceptualization and verbal explanation, he nevertheless produces in the reader or audience an impression of roundness that is grasped intuitively.⁶

While early character critics from Corbyn Morris to E. K. Chambers treated Falstaff as a real person, it was only in 2001 that Richard A. Levin took up Morgann's quest in an attempt to uncover what exactly Falstaff's verbally unarticulated 'latent motives and policies not avowed' are. In claiming that Falstaff is a schemer with Machiavellian shadings who uses the 'device' of covert or 'secret scheming', Levin clearly structures his reading on the binary of exteriority/interiority that undergirds Morgann's visible part/invisible whole theory of Falstaff: he assumes that Falstaff's public self-presentation through language has recourse to a private self with hidden motives.[7] What is more, he labels Falstaff a schemer and groups him with a host of minor Shakespearean characters who embody this character type. Although Levin lays out in his Appendix the various rhetorical modes or 'oblique prompts' adopted by schemers, such as a rhetoric of court compliment, popular allusions and equivocation, he divorces these rhetorical modes from dramatic speakers' pragmatic use of them in their interactions with other characters.[8] Even though Levin sets out to explain Falstaff's quiddity of being, he ends up reducing Falstaff to a character type and flattens out his roundness or psychological complexity.

Although Shakespeare's Falstaff is one of the most lauded characters in critical history, there is a repeated failure to explain the character effect of his roundness – the impression that he both transcends and exists prior to the play-text – on audiences and readers alike. Twentieth-century critics like Levin, who map specific character types onto Falstaff in an effort to trace his lineage back to historical and literary antecedents, fall short of accounting for the surplus meanings that Falstaff produces as a character. While the jovial knight certainly embodies the character types of a medieval Riot or Vice figure, a Plautine *miles gloriosus*, the braggadocio of Italian comedy, the parodic inversion of a Puritan and the Lord of Misrule in Saturnalian revelry, the sum total of these types does not amount to his roundness since they downplay Falstaff's idiosyncratic lineaments as a character by reducing him to a dramatic function with only allegorical value in the Henriad.[9] Both source study and character-type studies of Falstaff fail to acknowledge the fact that Falstaff not only adopts various dramatic roles but also exceeds them to his advantage.

Even critics who acknowledge Falstaff's agency and his ability to transcend his dramatic roles nevertheless adopt an essentializing view of Falstaff as an actor or, as Mark Van Doren states, a 'universal mimic' or 'parodist [and] artist' with a separate essence who is paradoxically 'so much himself because he is never himself'.[10] Falstaff's idiosyncrasy is assumed to be lodged beneath the fictional roles he inhabits, 'buried under heaps of talk delivered from a hundred assumed personalities, a hundred fictitious identities'.[11] Twentieth-century critics who have noted this paradox have overlooked how Falstaff makes use of the various discourses woven throughout his speech. Roy Battenhouse, for instance, suggests that Falstaff's parodic use of biblical allusion reveals that he is a 'holy fool' at his core and intimates 'the hidden truth about his inner and real self'.[12] Kristen Poole, claiming that Falstaff's verbal satire of extreme Puritanism is also satirized by Shakespeare, provides a New Historicist reading that renders Falstaff both a social representation of Puritanism and an instrument of Puritan discourse.[13] Agreeing with Poole that Falstaff is an agential subject of speech who mocks others, Harry J. Berger additionally asserts that Falstaff's mockeries are self-directed. However, despite portraying Falstaff as a speaker, Berger does not explore how Falstaff uses language but instead demonstrates that his self-representation as both the Puritanical subject and object of his own speech marks his self-audition and endows him with self-consciousness: 'to imagine Falstaff as subject is to imagine the speaker ... performing like the actor (but not as an actor) in that he presents his representation of himself as the object he interprets, and in that he continuously audits and monitors this performance'.[14]

What Berger, Poole, Battenhouse and other twentieth-century critics neglect in looking beyond Falstaff's language to an *a priori* animating agent is Falstaff's linguistic agency or how he pragmatically uses language to communicate with others. For all of the attention granted to Falstaff's language in the last decades of the twentieth century, whether it be identifying the copious discourses operating in his speech or noting the linguistic traits that render his speech distinctive – such as his conditional pseudo-promises, puns, lies or hyperbolic Puritan rhetoric replete with repetition and biblical allusions – critics have failed to acknowledge that Falstaff is not a reified essence with absolute agency that can be expressed through speech but rather a speaker with verbal agency who produces contextually relevant meanings in his speech. Overflowing with surplus meaning, Falstaff's utterances surpass the semantic or conventional meaning of his words to suggest more than he explicitly says.

Pragmatics can help account for the range of meanings produced by Falstaff in an interactive context with his interlocutors.[15] H. P. Grice's theory of conversational implicature, in particular, sheds light on how audiences and critics infer what Falstaff suggests beyond what he explicitly states, and provides a tangible way to account for the excess meanings that underwrite our impression of his roundness in *1 Henry IV*. I argue that Falstaff's conversational implicatures in his exchanges with Hal allow him to uphold his scripted roles as allegorical Vice, braggart, thief, hedonist and Puritan, while simultaneously allowing him to transcend these roles by mocking the illegitimacy and hypocrisy of Hal and the Lancastrian dynasty through his own self-mockery. This mockery or indirect critique of the Lancastrians – which is suggested by Falstaff's puns, wordplay and appositional asides – intersects with moments of meta-theatricality and visual representation in the play to invite the audience to infer that Falstaff transcends as well as exists prior to the play-text. The tectonic jostling between Falstaff's comic self-inflation and self-deflation facilitated by his conversational implicatures creates the distinctively buoyant energy or exuberance that gives him his roundness as a character. What emerges is a character who is much more critical of Hal and the ruling Bolingbrokes than critics allow. Framing Falstaff's speech in pragmatic terms annuls neither source study nor the character-type approach to Falstaff. Instead, it acknowledges that the literary and dramatic types that Falstaff invokes in his speech and actions contribute to his lifelikeness as a character by virtue of what he does with language. A Gricean approach to Falstaff's speech can thus illuminate how Falstaff carefully treads the interface between subverting and upholding the Machiavellian power structure of the play's Lancastrian plot to negotiate his place within it by continually (re)crafting his linguistic performances; it can also explain how Falstaff fulfils the audience's expectations of his vainglorious braggartism while unpredictably exceeding them at the same time. Falstaff's roundness, as I will demonstrate, is an effect of his linguistic performances in a theatrical context.

Gricean implicature and unspoken meaning

Falstaff initiates his opening conversation with Hal by asking him for the time: 'Now, Hal, what time of day is it, lad?' (1.2.1).[16] Instead of logically answering Falstaff with the precise time, Hal launches into a caustic critique of his fat companion:

> Thou art so fat-witted with drinking of old sack,
> and unbuttoning thee after supper, and sleeping upon
> benches after noon, that thou hast forgotten to demand
> that truly which thou wouldst truly know. What a devil
> hast thou to do with the time of the day? Unless hours
> were cups of sack, and minutes capons, and clocks the
> tongues of bawds, and dials the signs of leaping-houses,
> and the blessed sun himself a fair hot wench in flame-
> coloured taffeta, I see no reason why thou shouldst be so
> superfluous to demand the time of day.
>
> (2–11)

Hal's indirect and excessive response, which clearly marks his refusal to cooperatively uphold the conversation, triggers the audience to look for an additional meaning to his words. Hal's response produces a conversational implicature.

According to language philosopher H. P. Grice, conversational implicatures are performative utterances or indirect speech acts produced by speakers when they wish to imply a meaning beyond the merely grammatical or semantic meaning of their words. A conversational implicature is an intentional and responsive act performed by a rational agent or speaker in conversation with an interlocutor; the speaker utters a clause or a sentence whose implied (or implicated) meaning differs from its semantic (or conventional) meaning. Stemming from the verb 'to imply', implicature is, to use Wayne Davis's more explicit formulation, 'the act of meaning or implying something by saying something else', where the meaning implied occurs in addition to, and not instead of, what is said.[17] A conversational implicature thus signals an additional meaning that is independent of, and differs from, the semantic meaning of the utterance, yet a meaning that is nevertheless contextually sensitive and variable since it depends on the discursive features of the conversation.

A conversational implicature occurs when a speaker forgoes what Grice calls the 'Cooperative Principle' structuring the bi-directional exchange between interlocutors. This Cooperative Principle governs conversational exchanges and requires speaker adherence if participants are to communicate efficiently and achieve their conversational goals. A conversation, notes Grice, always has 'a common purpose or set of purposes, or at least a mutually accepted direction' that is recognized by its speakers, even though these speakers' conversational goals may differ from the 'common purpose' of the exchange or even conflict with it.[18] Grice expresses his Cooperative Principle by the axiom 'make your conversational contribution such as is required, at the stage at which it occurs, by the accepted purpose or direction of the talk exchange in which you are engaged', and identifies four maxims or universally held assumptions to which speakers are expected to adhere in their exchanges: the maxim of quantity ('make your contribution as informative as is required [for the current purposes of the exchange]'); the maxim of quality ('try to make your contribution one that is true'), which Grice breaks down into two smaller maxims, 'do not say what you believe to be false' and 'do not say that for which you lack adequate evidence'; the maxim of relation ('be relevant'); and the maxim of manner ('be perspicuous'), which is further broken down into various maxims: 'avoid obscurity of expression', 'avoid ambiguity', 'be brief' and 'be orderly'.[19] The speaker's intentional transgression or infringement of these maxims creates a conversational implicature but only if the speaker adheres to the Cooperative Principle. Once conversational maxims are infringed, violated, opted out of, suspended or 'flouted' by a speaker, or if a speaker 'blatantly fail[s] to fulfill' a maxim, the hearer is forced to infer or rationally deduce the speaker's implied meaning by taking into account the semantic meaning of the speaker's words, the speaker's (non)conformity to the Cooperative Principle and its maxims, linguistic and other utterance contexts, and shared background knowledge.[20] In Grice's model of conversation, the speaker intends for and expects the hearer to recognize an implicature and to thereby contemplate what the speaker had in mind in uttering it. However, the speaker's intention in producing the implicature does not necessarily need to be recognized by the hearer. In spite of the hearer's potential failure to detect or comprehend the conversational implicature, the implicature nevertheless exists and effectively signals that the speaker's implied message has intentionally been '*made [] available*' to the hearer or audience for uptake.[21] Meaning in a verbal exchange, for Grice, is a cooperative and interactive process between speaker and hearer that rests not only on the semantically intelligible utterance of words but also on their pragmatic import as registered and inferred by an audience of hearers.

Conversational implicatures are often motivated and justified by their interlocutors' reciprocal need to maintain 'face' and may thus occur within a politeness framework. Influenced by sociologist Erving Goffman's pioneering use of the term, the concept of 'face' underlies Penelope Brown and Stephen Levinson's linguistic theory of politeness and is defined as both the speaker's and the hearer's 'public self-image', which they cooperatively strive to uphold in a verbal exchange.[22] Brown and Levinson assert that a speaker's 'face' is comprised of two components: negative face wants or desires, such as his or her right to 'freedom of action and freedom from imposition', and positive face wants or desires, or his or her need to be 'appreciated and approved of' or 'ratified, understood ... liked or admired' by others.[23] Given that 'face' is highly vulnerable and can be easily damaged in social interaction, interlocutors must cooperate in upholding, fulfilling or 'attending to' each other's face wants – in recognition of each other's need to do so – by deploying politeness strategies to mitigate face threats that inhere in social interaction. These politeness strategies are speech acts that work to save 'face' or minimize face-threatening acts (FTAs) and are divided into positive and negative politeness strategies. Positive politeness strategies, which signal the speaker's intimacy with and appreciation for the hearer's wants and serve to enhance the hearer's self-esteem, include expressing interest, approval or sympathy with the hearer, using in-group identity markers or forms of address, seeking agreement or joking to put the hearer at ease.[24] Negative politeness strategies are used in the case of high-risk FTAs to protect the hearer's face from imposition: the use of linguistic formality, honorifics, impersonal passives, and linguistic or non-linguistic acts of deference, for instance, are all 'avoidance-based' strategies which reassure the hearer that the speaker 'recognizes and respects the addressee's negative-face wants and will not (or will only minimally) interfere with the addressee's freedom of action'.[25] In addition to these positive and negative strategies, the speaker may also opt to use 'off-record' strategies or indirect linguistic utterances to merely hint at his or her intended meaning without making it explicit. This hinted meaning, as Brown and Levinson note, is 'either more general ... or actually different from what one means (intends to be understood)' and thus requires the hearer to 'make some inference to recover what was in fact intended'.[26] These off-record strategies, which include the use of metaphor, irony, rhetorical questions, understatements/overstatements, contradictions and tautologies, violate Grice's maxim of quality and create implicatures that invite inference.[27] Falstaff uses these off-record strategies to politely disguise his critique and to maintain his and Hal's face.

About face: Falstaff's conversational implicatures

In his opening conversation with Hal in 1.2, Falstaff's request for political immunity is framed as an implicature that serves to maintain Hal's negative face as well as his own positive face. However, the request also exists in ironic service to Falstaff's self-mockery, as Falstaff mocks his self-glorification as a braggart and a thief in order to mock the Lancastrians; Falstaff implies his ridicule of Hal and the illegitimate reign of the Lancastrian dynasty by shamelessly promoting and praising himself as a vainglorious braggart and thief. The opening question that Falstaff poses to Hal in order to ascertain the time of day ('Now, Hal, what time of day is it, lad?' [1.2.1]) acts as an overture to Falstaff's request, formulated more than fifty lines later, that Hal safeguard Falstaff from potential punishment as a thief when he becomes king: 'Do not thou, when thou art king, hang a thief' (1.2.59). The request, taken together with the opening question, forms an implicature: in explicitly asking Hal for the time of day, Falstaff additionally albeit implicitly asks Hal for mercy and does so politely in order to maintain Hal's face. Hal's incredulous response (9–10) signals that there is an additional meaning to Falstaff's question beyond its merely semantic meaning. Falstaff, in calling Hal a 'lad' in his opening question, employs the positive politeness strategy of an in-group identity marker to refrain from imposing on Hal's negative face wants.[28] This strategy is used by Falstaff each time he tries to fully verbalize his request after being interrupted by Hal; he refers to the prince as 'sweet wag' to ingratiate himself with Hal by highlighting his intimacy with him, and he uses 'thou' to the same effect: 'And I prithee, sweet wag, when thou art a king' (15), and again: 'Marry then, sweet wag, when thou art king, let not us that are squires of the night's body be called thieves of the day's beauty' (22–4). The latter quote, which constitutes Falstaff's preliminarily formulated request, contains an additional implicature due to the presence of two metaphors ('squires of the night's body' and 'thieves of the day's beauty') and a pun on beauty/booty which flout the Gricean maxim of quality ('do not say what you believe to be false').[29] While Falstaff uses this additional implicature to comically praise himself as the night's guardian that he knows he is not, he eventually reformulates his request as an explicit command: 'Do not thou, when thou art king, hang a thief' (1.2.59). Since Falstaff's desire to know the time of day ultimately segues into his request for Hal's assurance of his safety as well as his emotional reassurance, this request is an indirect speech act that politely serves to uphold Hal's negative face. In asking Hal for political pardon by asking him the time of day, Falstaff alludes to the passing of time and anticipates Hal's future reign as king who will – like the 'sun' that marks the day – bring crimes and injustices to light for punishment. He thus proleptically lauds Hal for the duties he will, or rather should, perform as monarch.

The politeness-framed implicature that constitutes Falstaff's request and serves to maintain Hal's face, however, contains other implicatures that indirectly damage Hal's face through Falstaff's mockery of his own self-praise. Although Falstaff suggests that he sincerely seeks to be spared a trial so as to persist in his hedonistic ways, the sincerity of his request for pardon is diminished and its politeness is comically exaggerated by an ensuing series of implicatures that puncture his retorts to Hal. Upon posing his opening question to Hal, Falstaff is immediately intercepted by Hal's profuse – and at least partially hollow – and abrasive accusation that Falstaff's question violates the Gricean maxim of relation ('be relevant').[30] Instead of adhering to the Cooperative Principle and logically answering Falstaff with the precise time, Hal launches into a harangue against Falstaff that violates the Gricean maxim of manner ('be brief') and triggers an implicature of his own:[31]

> What a devil hast thou to do with the time of the day? Unless hours were cups of sack, and minutes capons, and clocks the tongues of bawds, and dials the signs of leaping-houses, and the blessed sun himself a fair hot wench in flame-coloured taffeta, I see no reason why thou shouldst be so superfluous to demand the time of day.
>
> (1.2.5–11)

Recognizing the discrepancy between Falstaff's question and his (mis)use of time, Hal suggests that it is out of character for the excessively indulgent and irreverent Falstaff to ask for the time of day. Enumerating Falstaff's defects through a spate of metaphors and personifications that instantiate Falstaff's sexual and gluttonous behaviour, Hal's ironically superfluous words produce an implicature to highlight his superior rhetorical skill in condemning Falstaff. The word 'superfluous' in Hal's speech, however, may also be Shakespeare's way of implicating his own mockery of Hal's verbal excess. Falstaff's retort maintains Hal's face by politely affirming his observation at the same time as it preserves his own comic face as a scripted thief by featuring an implicature: 'Indeed you come near me now, Hal, for we that take purses go by the moon and the seven stars, and not by Phoebus, he – "that wand'ring knight so fair"' (1.2.12–14). Confessing to be a bandit who takes purses under the cover of night and is therefore unconcerned with the time of day, Falstaff uses pleonasm ('the moon and the seven stars') to reference the Pleiades constellation and alludes to a lost ballad in which the sun (Phoebus) is personified as 'that wand'ring knight' to create an implicature that flouts the maxim of manner ('avoid obscurity of expression').[32] If 'the moon and seven stars' is a pun on a tavern or an inn, as Herbert Weil suggests, then Falstaff is underlining that he is indeed a petty and harmless thief who steals from taverns and thereby upholds his public image as a parasite who frequents them.[33] However, since the phrase 'moon and seven stars' additionally refers to the Pleiades, Falstaff is also engaging in mock self-valorization by implicating that his vocation as a thief is noble since theft under the Pleiades is far superior to theft under a 'wand'ring' or inconstant sun. Falstaff comically reverses the symbolic values associated with the sun and the moon by attributing constancy to the notoriously fickle moon in order to justify his criminal actions. In doing so, he offsets Hal's unflattering depiction of him as a gluttonous lout to redress the damage done to his face but only by, ironically, damaging it further: in praising himself as a noble thief, Falstaff mocks his own self-praise.

Falstaff's ironically redressive self-promotion gives way to another implicature, denoted by an apposition, that allows him to take a jab at Hal's illegitimacy and his reprobate behaviour in the process of formulating his request for pardon:

FALSTAFF
  And I prithee, sweet wag, when thou art a king, as God
  save thy grace – 'majesty', I should say, for grace thou
  wilt have none –
PRINCE
  What, none?
FALSTAFF
  No, by my troth, not so much as will serve to
  be prologue to an egg and butter.
PRINCE
  Well, how then? Come roundly, roundly.

(1.2.15–21)

Denoted by editorial dashes (16, 17), the syntactic apposition interrupts and qualifies the positive politeness strategy characterizing Falstaff's utterance ('sweet wag' [15]). The apposition, through Falstaff's pun on 'grace', transgresses Grice's maxim of quantity (be as informative as necessary) and creates an implicature whose implied meaning retracts or cancels the semantic meaning of Falstaff's half-formed request. In line with his politeness strategy, Falstaff uses 'grace' as a monarchical epithet to show his deference as well as to express his wish for the future king's political and spiritual blessedness ('as God save thy grace'), but this wish is quickly undermined by Falstaff's gloss on 'grace' as 'majesty', which implies that Hal will lack grace or Christian salvation ('for grace thou wilt have none') due to his reckless lifestyle in the tavern realm. This meaning is reinforced by the audience's awareness of King Henry's lament of Hal's riotous behaviour in his opening speech (1.1.84–5). However, the pun in the apposition also invites the inference that Hal will lack salvation since his father's usurpation of the Yorkist throne denies Hal the possibility of being a legitimate and divinely appointed king. Although both implicated meanings blend into one another, the first allows Falstaff to deflate the self-righteousness underlying and motivating Hal's implicatures and to thus mar Hal's public face, while the second allows him to indirectly criticize the injustice and illegitimacy of Lancastrian rule. The implicature in the apposition transgresses the tacit agreement structuring polite verbal exchanges identified by Brown and Levinson – namely, that participants work to maintain one another's face through negative or positive face strategies – and registers Falstaff's off-record impoliteness. In his study of impoliteness which, he argues, results from a speaker's intentional performance of FTAs, linguist Derek Bousfield differentiates on-record impoliteness from off-record impoliteness: on-record impoliteness is explicitly conflictive and shows that a speaker deliberately and unambiguously attacks the hearer's face, whereas off-record impoliteness is conveyed by an implicature that discreetly attacks the face of the hearer (and includes sarcasm and the withholding of politeness).[34] Although Falstaff's apposition suggests off-record impoliteness, his impoliteness is an *insincere* form of impoliteness that marks his FTA as a good-humoured jest – rather than a serious threat – which he deploys to counteract Hal's thinly veiled insults.

Perceiving that Hal has either not understood his implicature or that he requires clarification ('What, none?' [18]), Falstaff proceeds to pun on 'grace' to create an additional implicature that violates the maxim of manner ('avoid ambiguity') in order to further mock the future king.[35] In turning the tables on Hal by refusing to answer his question clearly, Falstaff demonstrates to Hal that he can match or even outplay him in his rhetorical game of one-upmanship. Punning on 'grace' as a prayer pronounced before a meal, Falstaff suggests that Hal will not even receive minimal favour from God ('not so much as will serve to be prologue to an egg and butter' [19–20]) or, quite possibly, any blessings from his ruled subjects if he persists in his rascally ways. Pressing up against Falstaff's implicit ridicule of Hal's inept behaviour, however, is his faint warning to Hal that he reform his ways; Falstaff's pun may bring to the forefront of the audience's mind the Reformed interpretation of salvation as achievable through good works rather than through faith alone. Taken in conjunction with his opening question about the time of day, Falstaff's pun additionally signals his adoption of his scripted role as Puritan as he voices his moral concern for Hal's soul and urges the prince to reform his ways through noble deeds. Falstaff's request for pardon, then, may be motivated by his disapproval of Hal's reckless use of time and disguises his cautionary advice to Hal. While Falstaff's implied meaning escapes Hal, who teasingly evokes Falstaff's physical proportions in asking him to clarify what he says ('Well, how then? Come roundly, roundly' [21]), it does not escape the offstage audience who is able to infer and comprehend the meanings of Falstaff's implicatures. Falstaff's apposition and the triple pun on 'grace' suggest that his implicatures are intended to be (over)heard and understood by the audience. The apposition exploits the effect of the dramatic aside in enabling Falstaff to address the audience as recipients of his utterance, while the pun invites the audience to actively participate in inferring a number of implied meanings. As Jeremy Lopez states, an Elizabethan audience was automatically conditioned to 'look for the convergence of literal and figurative levels of meaning in *any* context' when faced with a pun.[36] Since it conjoins different meanings in one word, the pun is a verbal analogue for Falstaff's excess and helps to convey the impression that he is bursting with life at the linguistic seams. The incongruence between Hal's failure of uptake and the audience's successful uptake of Falstaff's implied meaning(s) produces dramatic irony that joins the audience in humorous league with Falstaff against Hal. In experiencing the superfluity of meaning in Falstaff's utterances, the offstage audience perceives how Falstaff exceeds his scripted identity and invites the conjecture that he pre-exists his speech.

Falstaff's second appositional implicature, embedded in his sexual wordplay with Hal, reinforces his ridicule of Hal by way of a pun. Responding to Hal's insinuation that Falstaff is a thief, Falstaff insinuates in turn that the profligate prince is licentious and has repeatedly bedded the Hostess of the Boar's Head tavern by punning on 'reckoning': 'thou hast called her to a reckoning many a time and oft' (1.2.47–8). Hal's subsequent question maintains the bantering tone and sexual wordplay of the exchange even as it suggests a sharp attack on Falstaff for his financial irresponsibility: 'Did I ever call for thee to pay thy part?' (49). While Falstaff admits that Hal has paid all his tavern bills, he continues to sexually pun on 'part' as phallus to reinforce his implicature that the prince has 'paid all' at the tavern ('No, I'll give thee thy due; thou hast paid all there' [50–1]). Hal's statement, which answers his own question and affirms Falstaff's response, serves to gallantly redeem himself from rumours of his dissolute behaviour by suggesting that he is responsible for financially redeeming Falstaff: he claims to have paid the tavern expenses 'so far as [his] coin would stretch, and where it would not [he has] used [his] credit' (1.2.52–3). That Hal is as good as his word and that he fulfils the vow made in his soliloquy to 'pay the debt [he] never promised' (1.2.199) is later evidenced when he promises to repay Falstaff's bill for food ('The money shall be paid back again with advantage' [3.1.533–4]). While Hal cooperatively continues with the sexual punning, his mention of 'credit' –

financial solvency based on his character or good name, which allows him to pay the debts that Falstaff owes – conveys his sense of personal self-worth.

The pun that constitutes Falstaff's appositional implicature undercuts Hal's self-confidence and threatens his face. Punning on 'credit' to mean 'favourable estimation' or 'honour', Falstaff performs an insincere, off-record FTA: 'Yea, and so used it that were it not here apparent that thou art heir apparent – but I prithee, sweet wag, shall there be gallows standing in England when thou art king?' (1.2.54–7).[37] His pun on 'here apparent'/'heir apparent' which opens his utterance admonishes Hal and his misuse of not only his time but also his reputation (his 'credit') to the point where it is no longer recognizable ('apparent') to Falstaff that Hal is the future king. Falstaff says that if it were not obvious or clearly visible ('apparent') that Hal is physically present and palpable ('apparent') to him 'here', or during their conversation, nobody would know that Hal is the 'heir apparent' or next in line to the throne, with the implication that he does not bear himself like a future monarch. In implicating that Hal is recognizable as the future king based only on Falstaff's knowledge of who he is rather than on his name or 'credit', Falstaff deflates Hal's self-aggrandizement as a noble and true prince and thus implicitly damages his face. Moreover, the deictic 'here' in Falstaff's apposition carries meta-dramatic weight in referring not only to the speech situation within the narrative of the play but also to the theatrical space of the stage. Underscoring that Hal is physically present to the theatre audience and not just to Falstaff, Falstaff's use of 'here' dismantles the gist of his implicature by calling attention to the actor's body which legitimates Hal's performance of an illegitimate prince. The discreet meta-dramatic irony allows the offstage audience to witness how Falstaff undoes his own pun by insinuating that it is *not* Hal who is 'here' apparent as the true prince but rather a counterfeit, created by the actor playing him. Falstaff, however, quickly reverts to a positive politeness strategy to diffuse the face threat caused by his admonition as he resumes formulating his request: 'but I prithee, sweet wag, shall there be gallows standing in England when thou art king?' (1.2.55–7). Framed by his polite request for pardon, Falstaff's appositional implicatures allow him to comfortably mock Hal's reprobate behaviour and his illegitimacy in an indirect manner.

Falstaff's comical lambaste of Hal occurs in tandem with his self-mockery as a vainglorious braggart. His shameless self-ennoblement and self-praise as a thief allow Falstaff to implicate his critique not only of Hal but also of the corruption and theft of the Lancastrian dynasty through self-ridicule. This self-ridicule allows Falstaff to fulfil his scripted roles and to uphold his comic face while also dismantling this face in the service of indirectly criticizing the political Bolingbroke world. Fast on the heels of his implicature that Hal will not have grace is Falstaff's attempt to explicitly formulate his request for pardon without being interrupted by Hal. As with his initial attempt to valorize himself as a noble thief who goes 'by the moon and the seven stars' (1.2.13), Falstaff's request comically foregrounds his inflated sense of self-worth as a bandit:

> Marry then, sweet wag, when thou art king, let
> not us that are squires of the night's body be called
> thieves of the day's beauty. Let us be Diana's foresters,
> gentlemen of the shade, minions of the moon, and let
> men say we be men of good government, being
> governed, as the sea is, by our noble and chaste mistress
> the moon, under whose countenance we steal.
>
> (1.2.22–8)

The copious metaphors contained in Falstaff's utterance, which violate the Gricean maxim of manner ('be brief'), alert his hearers to a deeper meaning that rests on the form of his words as much as it does on their content: Falstaff implies his self-praise and undoes the politeness of his request through metaphors that mark his imposition on Hal's negative face wants.[38] Falstaff's enumerative synonymy, which rivals the plethora of metaphors in Hal's opening response that serve to insult and assault him (1.2.2–10), marks him as a braggart or the archetypal *miles gloriosus* of Plautine comedy who, as Hal suggests, embodies vanity.[39] Falstaff seeks to re-constitute the way he is characterized in the corrupt Bolingbroke world. In re-scripting himself as a 'squire of the night's body' who virtuously safeguards the night's chastity, personified by the moon goddess Diana, Falstaff inverts Hal's incrimination that he steals and self-indulgently consumes time in order to valorize himself and his vocation as a thief who protects the night. Nevertheless, the puns constituting the metaphors of Falstaff's self-valorization comically undermine his claim to be a worthy knight. The puns on night's body ('knight's bawdy') and day's beauty (day's 'booty') ironically undercut Falstaff's implied self-ennoblement to suggest that he is a sexually promiscuous thief. In other words, in explicitly asking to be known as a noble knight, Falstaff implies that he is not a noble knight but a thief and thus deflates his own attempt at self-ennoblement. The distinction that Falstaff draws between a knight and a thief collapses in light of this implicature, as he reveals that the morally upright knight is a promiscuous thief who abides by the laws of the notoriously fickle moon: 'let men say we be men of good government, being governed, as the sea is, by our noble and chaste mistress the moon, under whose countenance we steal' (1.2.25–8). The pun on 'government', which connotes personal discipline as well as a political system, further destabilizes what Falstaff says by implicating an additional meaning that constitutes his critique of the Lancastrian regime. Claiming to be politically well-governed by an inconstant moon – which, Jack Sublette has shown, Falstaff associates with the king[40] – Falstaff immediately undercuts the meaning of 'good government' with his simile ('as the sea is'), which implies that good government is as inconstant as the ebb and flow of the sea. Subject to the moon, Falstaff performs his duty ('steals') under the protection ('countenance') of the political regime. In thus suggesting that the Lancastrian government sanctions his theft, Falstaff delivers a moral attack on the corrupt regime by alluding to Henry Bolingbroke's theft of Richard II's crown.

Falstaff's derision, however, is aimed at Hal's anticipated rule as much as it is at Henry Bolingbroke's illegitimate reign: Falstaff's request, which looks forward to a time when Hal will be king (1.2.22), hints at the likelihood that Hal's government, like that of his father, will endorse robbery, given that Hal is complicit in Falstaff's thievery as evidenced in Falstaff's inclusive 'let us be' (24). The pun on 'government' as personal self-discipline also implicates a secondary meaning: that Falstaff is well-disciplined enough to unobtrusively 'steal' under the government's face ('countenance'). In addition to making jabs at the illegitimate and corrupt Lancastrian reign, Falstaff also discreetly asserts his own cunning by insinuating that he can outdo or outcheat the Lancastrian political thieves, including Hal. This secondary meaning, which attests to Falstaff's competitive self-reassertion in the face of Hal's continuous attempts to deflate him during their verbal one-upmanship, allows Falstaff to let the audience in on his attempt to smugly and covertly praise his ability to cheat the Bolingbrokes under the guise of self-praise, even as his feigned self-praise condemns the very theft in which he participates. Falstaff steals under Hal's face while telling the audience that he is doing so and thus becomes the target of his mockery of a Lancastrian rule founded on theft. Falstaff's mock hypocrisy, which reveals that a knight is a thief, serves as a commentary on the hypocritical Bolingbroke whose public image or 'face' as king betrays that he, too, is a Machiavellian thief.[41]

Although Falstaff mocks Hal and the Lancastrians in asking for political immunity, his utterances nevertheless invite the audience to surmise that a serious and moral voice antedates this mockery. Falstaff's opening question about the time of day, serving as an overture to his request for pardon, may also mark his attempt to instruct or at least incite Hal to reform his behaviour and redeem time by reminding him of his moral obligation as king. That Falstaff is conscious of his sinful behaviour in the tavern realm and of the inescapable reckoning that awaits him is intimated in his expression of melancholy following his allusion to a hangman: 'S'blood,

I am as melancholy as a gib cat or a lugged bear' (1.2.70–1). Although this suddenly professed melancholy quickly gives way to a simile contest with Hal (72–5) that detracts from or perhaps temporarily disguises Falstaff's emotion, it nevertheless suggests that Falstaff, for all of his self-indulgent hedonism, may regret his ignoble actions. Falstaff's soliloquy, in which he shamefully confesses that he has accepted bribes to conscript 'tattered prodigals' (4.2.33–4) instead of soldiers into the king's army, allows the audience to perceive his biting conscience: 'I have misused the King's press damnably. I have got, in exchange of a hundred and fifty soldiers, three hundred and odd pounds' (4.2.12–14). If Falstaff urges Hal to redeem time, it is because he knows the dangers of misusing it. Falstaff's detachment from his mockery and self-mockery is heightened by the very fact that he speaks alone on stage and directly to the audience; we can even imagine that he occupies a downstage position close to the audience. His soliloquy substantiates the audience's impression that the spurts of melancholy which intrude upon Falstaff's otherwise humorous linguistic performances are indicative of an anterior moral sense that informs his utterances. That Falstaff quickly reverts to playing the nonchalant hedonist who defends his 'ragamuffins' as 'good enough to toss; food for powder, food for powder. They'll fill a pit as well as better' (4.2.64–6) when Hal enters the scene produces dramatic irony, which allows the audience to see that Falstaff both fulfils his scripted roles and exceeds them in standing apart as the morally conscious spectator of his own actions. In spite of his dishonest behaviour in the scene, it is Falstaff's witty linguistic acrobatics, which dress his knowing transgression of maxims, that kindle the audience's affinity with and admiration of the jovial knight.

The robbery at Gad's Hill provides Falstaff with the ideal opportunity to enact his scripted role as braggart in order to poke fun at Hal's illegitimacy through the implicatures attending his braggadocio. It is in exposing his cowardice and undoing his own face that Falstaff criticizes Hal. Hal and Poins concoct a playful ploy to turn on Falstaff and rob him just as he robs travellers passing by Gad's Hill; their anticipation of the pleasure they will derive from repudiating Falstaff's 'incomprehensible lies' (1.2.176) drives their ploy and sets the audience's expectations for Falstaff's excessive boasting. Falstaff, on cue, fulfils these expectations by enumerating his opponents in order to eulogize his bravery in battle:

> I am a rogue if I were not at half-sword with a
> dozen of them, two hours together. I have scaped by
> miracle. I am eight times thrust through the doublet,
> four through the hose, my buckler cut through and
> through, my sword hacked like a handsaw
>
> (2.4.158–62)

The 'dozen' (159) men who, as Falstaff claims, fell upon him are hyperbolically exaggerated to 'sixteen at least' (171) and then to fifty and more: 'if I fought not with fifty of them, I am a bunch of radish. If there were not two- or three-and-fifty upon poor old Jack, then am I no two-legged creature' (2.4.179–82). The 'two rogues in buckram suits' (2.4.185–6) with whom Falstaff claims to have fought likewise multiply to 'four' (188) and quickly grow to 'seven, by these hilts, or I am a villain else' (199), then to nine (205) and eleven (211). While Hal gloatingly confesses that he duped Falstaff and exposed the latter's lies to be 'like their father that begets them, gross as a mountain, open, palpable' (2.4.218–19), Falstaff punctures Hal's face: he resorts to insincere, off-record impoliteness to mockingly tarnish Hal's reputation by disclosing that Hal is a false prince. It is in comically undermining his own bravery to expose his cowardice that Falstaff ridicules Hal as a counterfeit:

> By the Lord, I knew ye as well as he that made
> ye. Why, hear you, my masters: was it for me to kill the
> heir apparent? Should I turn upon the true prince?
> Why, thou knowest I am as valiant as Hercules, but
> beware instinct. The lion will not touch the true prince;

instinct is a great matter. I was now a coward on instinct.
I shall think the better of myself, and thee, during my
life – I for a valiant lion and thou for a true prince.

(2.4.259–66)

While Falstaff praises himself by drawing comparisons to Hercules and a lion, he also praises Hal by designating him as the 'true' or legitimate prince whom he abstains from killing. However, Falstaff's assertion of his instinctual cowardice comically undermines his professed courage just as the pun on 'true' registers his implied denunciation of Hal's worth: Falstaff's vow that he 'shall think the better of myself, and thee, during my life – I for a valiant lion and thou for a true prince' (2.4.265–6) implies that since Falstaff is not valiant, neither is Hal a true prince. The pun on 'true', signifying both loyal and genuine, creates an implicature that allows Falstaff to criticize Hal for being both disloyal to him and an illegitimate heir to the throne.[42] The double implicature invites the audience to infer that Hal's deception is closely associated with his being a Bolingbroke; his disloyalty towards Falstaff mirrors – or is a direct consequence of – his father's unlawful usurpation of the Yorkist throne. The wordplay in the opening sentence reinforces Falstaff's implicit attack on Hal. Revealing that he was aware of Hal's ruse at Gad's Hill from the outset, Falstaff claims to know Hal and his disingenuous ways as well as his father does: 'By the Lord, I knew ye as well as he that made ye' (2.4.259–60). However, Falstaff's assertion also implies that he knows that Hal and the father who made him are similar, and thus hints at the villainy that Hal shares with the king. Falstaff shows that he can predict Hal's moves. While the jovial knight wishes that the 'true prince may, for recreation sake, prove a false thief' (1.2.147) by participating in the theft at Gad's Hill, his pun on 'true' conveys the realization that Hal is an illegitimate or counterfeit prince who is also a genuine (true) thief. Fulfilling both our and Hal's expectations of his braggartism, Falstaff's stupendous, improvised lies allow him to inhabit and exploit his scripted role as braggart for comic effect. But they also give rise to implicatures that allow Falstaff to substantially exceed his role in exclaiming against Hal and, through him, the Lancastrians' usurpation of the throne. Falstaff's lies ultimately call attention to the king's lie – his authenticity as lawful king.

In addition to enacting his scripted role as braggart, Falstaff also adopts a Puritan role to incriminate the Lancastrians for hypocrisy by way of mocking Hal's corruption. To do so, Falstaff first mocks his own hypocrisy and undermines his Puritan performance. Falstaff terminates his simile competition with Hal by donning the linguistic habit of a Puritan as a way of humorously projecting his own faults onto the prince:[43]

> O, thou hast damnable iteration, and art indeed
> able to corrupt a saint. Thou hast done much harm
> upon me, Hal; God forgive thee for it. Before I knew
> thee, Hal, I knew nothing, and now am I, if a man
> should speak truly, little better than one of the wicked.
> I must give over this life, and I will give it over. By the
> Lord, an I do not, I am a villain. I'll be damned for
> never a king's son in Christendom.
>
> (1.2.87–94)

Falstaff strives to reclaim his innocence by deflecting the role of Vice or Vanity that Hal has scripted for him in his play of a prodigal's reformation onto Hal himself. He turns the tables on Hal by suggesting that he has been seduced and corrupted by the dissolute behaviour and immoral actions of the prince. Falstaff-the-Puritan's intention to repent ('I must give over this life, and I will give it over') is subsequently undercut by his response to Hal's question ('Where shall we take a purse tomorrow, Jack?' [1.2.95]), which exposes his feigned piety: 'Zounds, where thou wilt, lad. I'll make one; an I do not, call me villain and baffle me' (1.2.96–7). The irony arising from the discrepancy between Falstaff's vow to repent and his promise to engage in theft at Hal's beckoning denotes an implicature. Falstaff defies the Gricean maxim of quality ('try to make your contribution one that is true' or 'do not say what you believe to be false'), which deflates his linguistic performance of Puritanism to foreground his hypocrisy.[44] This intentionally divulged hypocrisy implies an attack on the hypocritical piety of King Henry. At the same time, however, Falstaff's flouting can also be enjoyed on a purely linguistic level, as the audience is invited to revel in Falstaff's ingenuity with words as words, separated from their surface or depth meanings. The juxtaposition of this scene with the play's opening scene allows the audience to hold Falstaff's self-parody in counterpoint with King Henry's hollow piety. Henry publicly proclaims his 'holy purpose' (1.1.101) to launch a crusade to the Holy Land, but his speech reveals his purpose to be unholy: Henry's crusade would serve as a means of politically uniting the warring factions at home and distracting them from civil war by pursuing a foreign war in the name of God (1.1.1–9). While the king's purpose may be motivated by his desire to absolve himself of his sinful murder of Richard II and his usurpation of the throne, his possible remorse is only secondary to his main goal. Henry hypocritically uses Christianity in a Machiavellian fashion to serve his political ends and to dispel his own cares (1.1.1–4). If there is 'a good amendment of life' in Falstaff 'from praying to purse-taking' (1.2.98–9), as Hal sarcastically remarks, there is also a 'good amendment' in the king from robbing the Yorkist throne to using religious piety in order to conceal and justify his theft. Falstaff's mockery of his own hypocrisy serves as a commentary on the king's religious hypocrisy.

Falstaff's Puritan mockery, however, may also suggest an incisive critique of Oldcastle's feigned piety. Brewing in the background of the play to which an Elizabethan audience would have been privy is the Oldcastle controversy, which Falstaff's impersonation of Puritanism brings to the surface. If Hal's wordplay in alluding to his fat comrade as 'my old lad of the castle' (1.2.40) reinforces Falstaff's hedonism by associating him with a well-known tavern or brothel called the 'Castle', as editors have noted, it also reinforces the identification of Falstaff with the historical Lollard martyr Sir John Oldcastle. But while Falstaff may echo the historical Oldcastle by virtue of his Puritan speaking style which hints at his moral principles, his implicatures allow him to exceed the role of Oldcastle by enabling a self-mockery that undercuts it. Read within a Catholic context in which Oldcastle is viewed as a hypocrite and a traitor rather than the pious, proto-Puritan martyr of Protestantism, Falstaff's self-mockery highlights Shakespeare's implicit criticism of Oldcastle's feigned piety which disguises his treason. If we laugh with Falstaff in criticizing the king, we also laugh at Falstaff with Shakespeare, who satirizes Oldcastle through the portly knight.[45] Yet in spite of this ridicule, Shakespeare valorizes Falstaff by giving him a moral aspect or voice that underwrites his criticism of Hal and King Henry. This moral voice, however, does not derive from Falstaff's Protestant association with Oldcastle but seems to meld instead with Shakespeare's. This double implicature present in Falstaff's Puritan parody enhances the sense of his anteriority as a choric and moralizing voice that intersects with Shakespeare's moralizing voice to comment on the play.

Falstaff's moralizing voice is even more pronounced in the play extempore he stages with Hal (2.4.366–420). Falstaff's impersonation of the king for comic self-praise enables him to reinforce his scripted role as braggart while his deflation of this self-praise through the implicatures in his speech allows him to incisively deride the king as well as Hal. While Falstaff claims that the reason for the impromptu play is for the cowardly Hal to 'practice' appeasing his scolding father (2.4.365), he unabashedly uses the play to showcase his play-acting skills and to refurbish his reputation as a noble, virtuous and courageous knight. In an attempt to redeem his damaged reputation, Falstaff adopts the king's voice to praise himself. Addressing Hal as his father, Falstaff-as-king deems Falstaff-the-rogue to be '[a] goodly, portly man ... of a cheerful look, a pleasing eye and a most noble carriage .... If that man should be lewdly given, he deceiveth me, for, Harry, I see virtue in his looks'

(2.4.410–15). Falstaff's improvised performance is intended to persuade Hal to keep him in his company and to protect him from punitive banishment ('Him keep with; the rest banish' [2.4.418]). Nevertheless, Falstaff ends up mocking the king's performance of kingship and undercutting his moral authority through rhetorical exaggeration. Falstaff-as-king's speech is riddled with Lylyian euphuisms, biblical allusions, rhetorical questions and comparisons which, instead of conveying the king's wisdom, reveal the faulty reasoning that informs the king's judgement and thus destroy his ethos as a wise and virtuous ruler. Falstaff's tropes and schemes, which violate the maxims of manner ('avoid ambiguity', 'avoid obscurity of expression') and relation ('be relevant'), imply the king's failure to morally instruct his son and showcase his ineptitude as both a king and a father.[46] Falstaff-as-king uses the analogy of a creeping camomile flower as a moral maxim to gently reprove Hal for his reckless behaviour as a youth: 'For though the camomile, the more it is trodden on the faster it grows, so youth, the more it is wasted the sooner it wears' (2.4.389–92). However, the didactic force of the analogy fails for it registers the difference, rather than the similarity, between Hal's wasted youth and the downtrodden yet regenerative flower. In drawing attention to the king's use of the form of words without their substance, Falstaff-as-king comments on the superficiality or hollowness of Henry's illegitimate kingship which lacks moral pith or substance and is built on mere appearances.

The sententious phrases peppering Falstaff's impersonation of the king further serve to ridicule the king and his hypocritical attempt to construct his ethos as a benign and virtuous monarch without essentially being one. Henry's hypocrisy is reinforced not only by Hotspur's comment that the king is a Machiavellian 'king of smiles' (1.3.243) who strategically uses forms of flattery and politeness to deceive others (1.3.248–52), but also by the king's adherence to double standards, as suggested by Falstaff's rhetorical questions: 'Shall the blessed sun of heaven prove a micher and eat blackberries? A question not to be asked. Shall the son of England prove a thief and take purses?

A question to be asked' (2.4.397–400). While it is permissible for the king (the symbolic 'sun') to absent himself from his royal duties in order to indulge himself, it is not permissible for the prince to do the same. Falstaff demonstrates that the king sanctions his own self-indulgence while hypocritically condemning that of his son. The reference to blackberries also evokes the vow made by Falstaff to Hal at Gad's Hill that 'if reasons were as plentiful as blackberries, I would give no man a reason upon compulsion, I' (2.4.232–4). Falstaff here slyly ruptures his performance and draws attention to its theatricality to suggest that he is the 'king' of the Boar's Head tavern who, just like King Henry himself, is not bound by any moral or political laws and should thus not be reprimanded by Hal; he is also comically posing as Hal's father. Moreover, Falstaff's parody of the king reveals that the king is not just a counterfeit but also an inept father who is unable to recognize his own son with certainty: 'That thou art my son I have partly thy mother's word, partly my own opinion, but chiefly a villainous trick of thine eye and a foolish hanging of thy nether lip that doth warrant me' (2.4.392–5). In foregrounding the king's incertitude regarding his son's lineage as well as the trust he puts into appearances to ascertain the truth, such as in Hal's 'villainous' eye and his 'foolish hanging' lip, Falstaff mocks the king as a cuckold or a possible lecher who fathered a number of children since he is only able to recognize Hal as his by, ironically, the sexual and moral depravity suggested by his physiognomy. Falstaff implies that Hal is a copy of his father by showing that Hal is also a copy of him. Falstaff's ridicule of the king thus deflates his own self-praise in the mouth of the personated king: in showing the king's lack of good judgement regarding his son's identity, Falstaff shows the king's assertion of Falstaff's appearance-based virtue to be ironic. Falstaff-as-king mocks and thus deflates himself as a virtuous thief at the same time as he mocks the king's hypocritical façade to which he is clearly heir. Hal's ridicule of Falstaff's amateur performance, in which he notes that Falstaff's joint-stool is his throne, his 'leaden dagger' a 'golden sceptre' and his 'pitiful bald crown' the king's 'precious rich crown' (2.4.370–2), inadvertently highlights the similarity between plump Jack and the king as villainous thieves and counterfeits. Falstaff shows the king to be a counterfeit in counterfeiting the king.

If Falstaff derides the king through his impersonation of him, he similarly derides Hal for his villainy by impersonating the prince. In the role-reversal that ensues, Hal-as-king explicitly attacks Falstaff's jocular face and undercuts his self-praise in hurling insults at him: 'that trunk of humours, that bolting-hutch of beastliness, that swollen parcel of dropsies, that huge bombard of sack, that stuffed cloak-bag of guts, that roasted Manningtree ox with the pudding in his belly, that reverend Vice, that grey Iniquity, that father Ruffian, that Vanity in years' (2.4.437–42). In his pragma-stylistic analysis of the scene, Derek Bousfield deduces that Hal thinly masks his linguistic impoliteness towards Falstaff as banter to sincerely criticize Falstaff under the pretext of play. Hal's impersonation of his father, claims Bousfield, allows him the safety and protection of impolitely attacking Falstaff's face and levelling his criticism at his friend's dissolute behaviour under the guise of insincere or mock impoliteness.[47] Undeterred by Hal's FTAs, Falstaff counters Hal-as-king's insults by adopting Hal's voice to repair his face damage through hyperbolical self-praise in the prince's name (2.4.454–67). It is through this self-praise that Falstaff also implicates Hal's baseness, which he aligns with his own. In response to Hal-as-king's question whether Falstaff-as-Hal knows the 'old white-bearded Satan' (2.4.451), Falstaff states in Hal's voice that 'to say I know more harm in him than in myself were to say more than I know' (454–5). While Falstaff's response registers his wish that Hal defends and preserves him from persecution in the face of punishment – he essentially models a response for Hal *to* him – it also implies Falstaff's criticism of Hal's harmfulness, which is ironically made through his attempt to absolve himself from vice in Hal's voice. Falstaff suggests that Hal is as harmful as he is. While the rest of Falstaff-as-Hal's speech serves to profusely promote Falstaff as 'kind' (463), 'true' (463), and 'valiant Jack Falstaff' (464) and to plead against his banishment by the future king ('Banish plump Jack, and banish all the world' [467]), Hal-as-king's terse retort breaks the illusion of the play extempore. Hal's monosyllabic 'I do; I will' (2.4.468) makes visible the collusion between Hal-as-king's voice and Hal-the-future-king's voice. Hal's promise that he will banish Falstaff – which he fulfils in *2 Henry IV* – intrudes upon Hal-as-king's performative act ('I do') with which he banishes Falstaff in the play extempore. The resoluteness of Hal's promise is redolent of Falstaff's promise as a Puritan that he 'must' and 'will give [] over' his dissolute life (1.2.92), and possibly serves as an echoic critique of Falstaff's feigned intention to repent. While Falstaff's words may be duplicitous, Hal shows that he is as good as his word or least faithful to it.

As close companions and tavern mates, Hal and Falstaff are engaged in cooperative conversations whose common purpose is the mutual pleasure afforded by their playful yet competitive one-upmanship. The conversational implicatures that dominate their exchanges reveal their adherence to Grice's Cooperative Principle rather than their non-observance of it; implicatures 'constitute their rapid-fire banter', as J. McLaverty notes, and 'underscore their intimacy with and dependency on one another'.[48] Yet even though both speakers acknowledge and uphold the common purpose of their exchanges, their conversational goals differ. Hal's goal, as Bousfield has noted, is to sincerely criticize Falstaff while pretending to ridicule him. Hal' s engagement in witty banter is underwritten by his recognition that he must ultimately renounce the tavern sphere to become king. Hal's opening soliloquy (1.2.185–207) reveals to the offstage audience that his decadence and idleness are feigned, and that his participation in the tavern world is a strategic means to his ultimate end of garnering accolades and public admiration – he yearns to 'show more goodly and attract more eyes' (1.2.204) by staging a sudden and 'glittering' 'reformation' (1.2.203) in order to rehabilitate his reputation: 'I'll so offend to make offence a skill, / Redeeming time when men think least I will' (1.2.206–7). Hal hints at his ability to skilfully counterfeit that which he is not, both in his soliloquy ('I know you all, and will awhile uphold / The unyoked humour of your idleness' [1.2.185–6]) and in his boastful statement that 'I am so good a proficient in one quarter of an hour that I can drink with any tinker in his own language during my life' (2.4.17–19). But while Hal's profligate behaviour is a skilfully calculated and self-serving performance and his relationship with Falstaff may only be provisional, this does not necessarily make Hal a hypocrite. Instead, Hal's visible shape-shifting may assist him, as some critics hold, to better know and therefore better relate to the diverse peoples of his future kingdom. While Hal's questionable motives render him an opaque character in *Henry V*, in *1 Henry IV* he seems more cynical than not in making a habit of exercising his linguistic superiority over his comrade and foregrounding his ability to do so. In mocking and caricaturing Falstaff as a self-indulgent and immoral lout, parasite, lecher, thief and coward, Hal is able to assign Falstaff a clear allegorical role as the medieval morality play Vice or Vanity in his scripted play of a prodigal's reformation. Hal's conversational goal is not lost on Falstaff, however. Falstaff's implicatures, which highlight his friendly rapport and camaraderie with Hal, enable him to respond to Hal's sincere ridicule of him by discreetly and politely criticizing Hal and the corrupt Lancastrians. By mocking himself and his enactment of the scripted Vice, braggart and roguish clown of the Bolingbroke world – and thus seeming to undo his own face – Falstaff is able to attenuate the force of his implied critique of Hal's illegitimacy and of Lancastrian theft through the use of humour and to thereby shield himself from punishment. Nevertheless, Falstaff's critical commentaries do not constitute any principled criticism of the Bolingbroke world since he clearly takes advantage of its rampant corruption to hedonistically indulge himself. Amicable though Hal and Falstaff's relationship may be, their differing conversational goals give rise to an undercurrent of tension that the audience can detect. While Hal may miss or intentionally disregard the implicated meanings that drive Falstaff's critique, these meanings are nevertheless recognized and understood by the offstage audience, who is able to posit a moralizing – if not altogether moral – aspect to Falstaff that seems anterior to the meanings he implies.

Falstaff's clever impersonations intersect with the meta-theatricality of the play extempore to foreground the actor's impersonation of Falstaff, which further heightens the audience's impression of his roundness. The play extempore functions as a play-within-a-play or, as Robert Weimann calls it, a 'play within playing' that is 'equally concerned with both the showing and the imaginary meaning of the shown'.[49] The audience is made dually aware of Falstaff's impersonation of the king and Hal as well as the actor's impersonation of the personating Falstaff. Falstaff's part, as Weimann notes, thus invites 'secretly open' playing where the actor bleeds through the character he personates to showcase, in this instance, his superior representational acting ability in an ironically presentational manner. In other words, Falstaff's self-praise has meta-theatrical recourse to the actor playing him who, on the Elizabethan stage, was very likely Will Kemp; the audience would be conscious of how the actor strives to inscribe his own self-praise through Falstaff, or at least tries to make the audience admire the superiority of his acting skills in caricaturing a king and a prince through his impersonation of Falstaff. The play extempore is Kemp's (or any actor's) burlesque of the king's performance of kingship.[50] In mocking King Henry's hypocrisy and illegitimacy as a king through Falstaff-as-king, Kemp draws attention to his superior presentational acting ability which allows him to outdo the king's performance of kingship. Set against the king's 'false' performance, Kemp-as-Falstaff's performance of kingship ironically becomes 'true' or authentic in its very meta-theatricality, which defines it as a presentational performance. Even as he ridicules the king's failed performance of kingship, Kemp draws attention to the success of his own and invites the audience to witness the range and extent of his skill as an actor. This 'double personation' of the actor playing Falstaff and Falstaff playing the king and Hal, as Robert Weimann contends, makes the play-acting in question 'secretly open' or simultaneously presentational and representational for the audience, since the impersonation or the 'disguise serves as a "secret" gear through which openly to display (and enjoy) the "sport" of exuberant role-playing'.[51] Within this meta-theatrical context, Falstaff's advice to Hal that he should 'never call a true piece of gold a counterfeit. Thou art essentially made without seeming so' (2.4.478–80) can also be read as the actor's proclamation that he is an authentic or 'true' impersonator, not a counterfeit, despite counterfeiting the king or 'seeming' to be what he is not; the actor may be gesturing towards his own essence in being 'essentially made'. In implicating the superiority and authenticity of his craft which is anterior to and presses up against Falstaff's implicatures, the actor reinforces the audience's sense of Falstaff's substantiality as a character.

As in the play extempore scene, the meta-theatricality of the Shrewsbury scene intersects with Falstaff's conversational implicatures to reveal the flickering interplay of character and actor. The dramatic irony arising from the wordplay in Falstaff's soliloquy at Shrewsbury intersects with the visual representation provided by the actor-character on stage to strengthen the perception of Falstaff's anteriority. Feigning death in his skirmish with Douglas at Shrewsbury by falling down on stage in order to escape with his life, Falstaff resurrects himself and speaks in a soliloquy addressed to the audience. Although the audience has just witnessed his counterfeited death, Falstaff ironically claims not to be a counterfeit: 'Counterfeit? I lie; I am no counterfeit. To die is to be a counterfeit, for he is but the counterfeit of a man who hath not the life of a man. But to counterfeit dying when a man thereby liveth is to be no counterfeit but the true and perfect image of life indeed' (5.4.114–18). Complementing his previous assertion that he is a 'true piece of gold' rather than a 'counterfeit' (2.4.478–80), Falstaff ironically premises his authenticity on his ability to uphold a deceptive self-image. He affirms that he is not what he appears to be: despite his deceptive imitation of death, he is true or authentic. The irony is redoubled by the audience's awareness that the actor impersonating Falstaff is also denying his counterfeiting of death to suggest that he is truly alive, even as he counterfeits Falstaff on stage. The actor thus punctures his personation of Falstaff impersonating death to tell the audience that he, and not Falstaff, is 'the true and perfect image of life indeed' (118). The actor speaks through Falstaff or, in pragmatic terms, uses Falstaff to implicate to the audience that he is real or 'true' and thereby draws attention to his presentational skill by representing death in a convincing or realistic manner. Falstaff ensures his survival by counterfeiting; the actor lives in – and lives by – counterfeiting Falstaff. As James L. Calderwood suggestively points out, 'The biggest lie of all' in the play is 'the notion of the true anointed king set apart from his lesser fellows by divine distinction'.[52] The wordplay on 'counterfeit' in Falstaff's soliloquy lends itself as a commentary on the king's hypocritical counterfeiting, against which Falstaff's truthful or 'secretly open' acting is ironically juxtaposed and valorized. Nevertheless, Falstaff's claim that he is the 'true and perfect image' of life is ironically undercut by the stage direction '*Falstaff riseth up*', which the actor heeds: in rising or standing up from his prostrate position on the stage, the actor playing Falstaff produces a visual analogue to Falstaff's words that contradicts Falstaff's claim to be real or authentic. Since 'counterfeit' also connotes that which is 'represented by a picture or image', the newly resurrected Falstaff, in standing and speaking on stage and perhaps even hovering over the slain Hotspur, inadvertently becomes for the audience a visual representation or the mere image of life that he claims he is not.[53] If Falstaff has hitherto both boastfully inflated and comically deflated himself through his speech, it is now Shakespeare's turn to deflate Falstaff by making a joke of him to the audience. Through the visual representation he orchestrates on stage, Shakespeare implicates his own meaning and shows the audience that Falstaff's claim to reality is, in fact, a lie: he suggests that Falstaff is a counterfeit (a visual image) or an emblem of life in the play, and that despite Falstaff's attempts to evade his scripted roles, he is already scripted by the playwright himself. Shakespeare ultimately has the last laugh since his dramaturgy allows him to convey his own meaning that Falstaff symbolizes life in the play. Falstaff's implicatures fuse with those of the actor and the playwright to create a dialogical interplay of voices and meanings that give Falstaff his anteriority.

Falstaff's wordplay in his brief exchange with Hal at Shrewsbury works with another visual representation he stages to additionally heighten the impression of his roundness. Taken aback by Falstaff's sudden resurrection, a confounded Hal exclaims: 'Thou art not what thou seem'st' (5.4.137). Falstaff nonchalantly affirms Hal's observation: 'No, that's certain: I am not a double man. But if I be not Jack Falstaff, then I am a jack' (5.4.138–40). Falstaff explicitly concedes that he is not a spirit (a 'double man') and that he is, materially or physically, Jack Falstaff. However, playing on the word 'double', Falstaff additionally implicates that he is not two men (a 'double man') at once, even though his impersonations suggest otherwise. His implied meaning is framed by meta-theatrical irony which undercuts his implicature. His pun on 'jack', a diminutive of his proper name but also a synonym for a knave, creates a secondary implicature that further undercuts his claim and accentuates that Falstaff is indeed a double man. The *non sequitur* in his utterance – 'But if I be not Jack Falstaff, then I am a jack' – collapses since Falstaff has consistently demonstrated that in being himself, he is always and already a knave: the pun on 'jack' hints at Falstaff's double identity even as the wordplay on 'double' comically denies it. Not only do Falstaff's words expose what he denies to be but so does the visual representation of doubleness that is produced by his action. Doubleness is visually evidenced on the stage with Hotspur on Falstaff's back, and this visual representation renders his implicature doubly ironic since what the audience sees affirms precisely what Falstaff denies – that he is two men in one. The image of Falstaff piggybacking Hotspur would moreover bring to the audience's mind Falstaff's association with a devil, who typically whisks Vice away on his back in the medieval morality play.[54] The iconography latent in the scene undermines Falstaff's implied meaning that he is not a double man to show that he is, in fact, both the 'white-bearded Satan' (2.4.451) of Hal's play and an actor in his own. However, Falstaff's implicature is also triply ironic because it is underwritten by the actor, whose impersonation of Falstaff makes him a 'double' man or both himself (an actor) and Falstaff (the person personated). While Falstaff's use of the word 'double' hearkens back to his critique of the Lancastrians' duplicity to emphasize his marked difference from them and evokes his singular authenticity, it is nevertheless predicated on the actor's use of the same. The actor speaks not just as Falstaff but also through Falstaff and, like Falstaff himself, foregrounds his presentational acting that produces the theatrical illusion witnessed by the audience.

Falstaff's doubleness is also, finally, evidenced in his lie to Hal, which constitutes his final act of self-promotion as he tries to salvage his reputation and reinstate his positive face. Claiming to have killed Hotspur, Falstaff strives to earn himself honour as well as the titles of 'either earl or duke' (5.4.142): 'I grant you I was down and out of breath, and so was he; but we rose both at an instant and fought a long hour by Shrewsbury clock. If I may be believed, so; if not, let them that should reward valour bear the sin upon their own heads' (5.4.146–50). Falstaff uses a lie to request that he be rewarded for his courageous act which he has, as the audience knows, clearly counterfeited. As with his instances of self-praise and self-mockery, Falstaff steals under Hal's face to redress the damage done to him at Gad's Hill. Shrewsbury becomes Gad's Hill's dramatic double, where Falstaff not only robs death of his 'due' in saving his own life but also robs Hal of his honour – the same honour Hal had hoped to gain by cropping the 'budding honours' on Hotspur's crest 'to make a garland for [his] head' (5.4.71–2) – in killing Hotspur in order to pay Hal back for stealing his 'earnings' at Gad's Hill. If Hal fulfils his promise to 'pay' what he owes (5.4.41–2) and redeems his reputation at Shrewsbury by courageously saving his father, Falstaff also comically repays his young friend in the hope of receiving the same honour and recognition. Although Falstaff shows honour to be an insubstantial word that is not worth dying for in his 'catechism' or soliloquy on honour (5.1.127–40), he nevertheless implies that it is worth living for. In re-scripting valour as discretion, Falstaff vindicates his cowardice by putting it on a par with the rashness exhibited by the courageous but lifeless Hotspur to ensure his salvation on earth rather than after death; Falstaff's cowardice doubles as courage, and his counterfeiting doubles as redemption. Falstaff's 'lie' that he has killed Hotspur is the comic double of Hal's 'lie' or his counterfeiting of prodigality to redeem himself as prince. Falstaff's lie thus complements the visual metaphor produced by Hotspur on Falstaff's back to undermine his implicatures as Shakespeare signals to the audience that Falstaff is, meta-dramatically, double: Falstaff is himself but he is also Shakespeare's for in being the principal character of the subplot, Falstaff serves as the choric commentary to the main Lancastrian plot. It is the friction arising from the interplay between Falstaff's linguistic performances and the meta-theatricality of the actor's speech as well as the playwright's visual dramaturgy that effectively produces Falstaff's roundness as a character.

The bombastic 'hill of flesh' (2.4.237) that is Falstaff can only ever be the energy or exuberance of life he embodies and exudes. His paunch signals his love of life but also the effect of lifelikeness he produces, which transcends the dramatic and thematic conventions of the play. Falstaff's roundness or our impression of his psychological complexity is a linguistic effect that arises from the conversational implicatures in his exchanges with Hal and with the offstage audience, in conjunction with the dramatic ironies produced by meta-theatrical moments in the play that show Falstaff's meanings to be necessarily compounded with the actor's and the playwright's. This produces Falstaff's anteriority or his reality effect. Violating Grice's conversational maxims to create implicatures, Falstaff upholds his scripted roles as braggart, cowardly knight and Puritan even as he undercuts these roles to mock the Lancastrians for their hypocrisy, theft and illegitimacy as rulers. By masking his incisive critique through self-mockery and by laughing at himself, Falstaff is able to take witty jabs at Hal and damage his face under the pretence of expertly maintaining it. His ability to criticize the hypocrisy of which he is inextricably a part indicates that Falstaff possesses a moralizing voice that fuses with, and is largely borne of, the actor's and the playwright's voices which pre-date and dialogue with his own. We laugh at Falstaff not only with him but also with Shakespeare and with the actor personating him, who imply additional meanings through Falstaff that evade Hal and, occasionally, Falstaff himself. Nevertheless, it is still the roguish clown who inevitably gets the last laugh as he teasingly lures us into trying to peer through his linguistic performances to an essential self that is, essentially, insubstantial.

2

Reported Speech and Cleopatra's Sexual Charisma

Upon Antony's return to Rome following the news of Fulvia's death, an agitated Cleopatra asks her female attendants to inform her of Antony's dealings in Rome: 'See where he is, who's with him, what he does' (1.3.3).[1] Anxious at the prospect of losing her power over Antony while he is with Caesar, Cleopatra orders her attendants to report her hypothetical behaviour to Antony: 'If you find him sad, / Say I am dancing; if in mirth, report / That I am sudden sick' (1.3.4–6). In having her reported behaviour contradict Antony's emotional state, Cleopatra strives to affectively control his response in order to ensure Antony's loyalty towards her. She uses report to retain her sexual power over him.

Cleopatra exudes a sexuality that defines her transcendent greatness as a character. However, critics approaching Cleopatra exclusively as a woman in love have overlooked her political role and the sexual power she wields as a queen. Moralistic critics adopting the Roman values expressed in *Antony and Cleopatra* have condemned Cleopatra as a devious Eve and Circe-like temptress who sexually enslaves Antony, while feminist critics, heeding L. T. Fitz's cry against the sexist bias of male critics who reduce Cleopatra 'from the position of co-protagonist to the position of antagonist at best, [or] nonentity at worst', have championed the play's Egyptian values to extol Cleopatra's noble femininity which counters the corruption of Rome.²

Valorizing Cleopatra's agency and her sexual diplomacy as an Egyptian sovereign, politically inclined critics in the 1990s realized that Shakespeare's Cleopatra deftly employs sexual strategies as Julius Caesar's, Gnaeus Pompey's and Mark Antony's seductress and concubine to retain her political power and her kingdom. Nevertheless, in endowing Cleopatra with autonomous political agency, these critics failed to acknowledge that Cleopatra is always and already a subject of, and hence subjected to, the Roman Empire: Theodora Jankowski claimed that Cleopatra strategically unites her bodies 'natural' and 'politic' to maintain her power on the Egyptian throne; Mary Ann Bushman contended that Cleopatra's role-playing allows her to maintain her idiosyncratic and autonomous identity, which is predicated on performance; Linda Charnes contended that Cleopatra's '*histrionic* constitution' enables her to subvert Roman voyeurism in order to safeguard her sovereignty; and Catherine Belsey claimed that Cleopatra's strategic seduction-by-deferral endows her with power, for her self-representations masquerade absence as presence while allowing her to be 'inconsistently *elsewhere*'.³ While it is now a critical commonplace that Cleopatra's political manoeuvring is inextricably intertwined with and dependent on her strategies of seduction, her sexuality does not grant Cleopatra absolute political power as these critics imply. As Cristina León Alfar notes, the highly optimistic view of Cleopatra as 'an agent of events, as a woman in control of her body and her own representation' fails to account for Cleopatra's political subordination to patriarchal Roman rule, which not only instigates but also constrains her reactions.⁴ Egypt's non-violent colonization, to quote Alfar, makes Cleopatra's 'celebrated sexuality both an effect of imperial domination – rather than an erotically motivated act on her part – and a practical mode of national preservation'.⁵

Given her political subordination to Rome, how is the effect of Cleopatra's sexual greatness produced? While critics have noted Cleopatra's use of histrionic strategies to consolidate her sexual power, they have neglected to examine her use of linguistic strategies. Aside from Russ MacDonald's vague assertion that Cleopatra is 'the play's main figure ... of verbal prowess and ambiguity' and David Schalkwyk's brief exploration of how Cleopatra and Antony theatrically perform their performative utterances, discussions of Cleopatra's speech have been limited to identifying rhetorical figures like paradox and hyperbole that characterize her utterances and underwrite the thematic and poetic structure of the play.[6] However, in a play like *Antony and Cleopatra* which infamously trades in reports and messages, as critics have noted,[7] investigating how Cleopatra pragmatically reports other characters' speech as well as her own speech vis-à-vis what is reported about her by the Romans is as crucial in accounting for her political agency and her sexual greatness as examining her theatricality is. Cleopatra's linguistic acts not only complement but also constitute her histrionic performances.

I will demonstrate that Cleopatra's ambivalence – her capacity to produce sexual greatness within the context of her subordination – is an effect of her use of report as a particular linguistic strategy. The Egyptian queen's character is determined not so much by the gender and imperial relations depicted in the play as by the type of speech acts that populate the play. I contend that Cleopatra's instances of reportage – her reporting other characters' speech, reporting her personal imaginings, and commanding that her own responses and behaviour be reported – illustrate her powerless submission and adherence to Roman authority as a pretext for asserting her superiority and sexual dominance over the Romans. This oscillation between Cleopatra's sexual power and her revelations of political powerlessness – or rather, her ability to fulfil her powerless Roman role while simultaneously exceeding it by turning it into a source of sexual self-empowerment – intersects with meta-theatrical moments in the play that foreground the boy actor's presentational skills which contribute to Cleopatra's sexual charisma and produce her ultimate power as a character. An examination of Cleopatra's linguistic performances within a pragmatic framework of reported speech can silence the critical debate about whether Cleopatra is the play's Roman victim or Egyptian victor by demonstrating that Cleopatra's victorious sexuality is predicated on the enactment and transformation of her victimization.

Shakespeare's Cleopatra as reporter

The conception of Cleopatra as a morally depraved, politically ambitious and threatening Other in Shakespeare's time was informed by the imperially biased reports and records of Roman and Greek historians, which depict the Egyptian monarch in an exclusively condemnatory light.[8] Horace and Virgil, for instance, portray Cleopatra as a sexually powerful and politically threatening woman who emasculates men by turning them into her servants, while Flavius Josephus proclaims Cleopatra to be a wicked, covetous and self-centred woman who is enslaved 'to her owne desires' and uses her lust as an excuse to vengefully 'intrap' men such as Herod.[9] Lucan similarly notes that Cleopatra is a 'vicious' woman who seeks to gain control over Rome and lead 'Caesar captive in a Pharian Triumph'.[10] However, Lucan compares Cleopatra to Helen of Troy to stress that her verbal seduction of Caesar would not have been effective were it not for the 'balefull charm' of her physical appearance: 'Her trial of Caesar's stern ear would have been fruitless, but her face entered her plea, her tainted beauty summed up'.[11] Lucan suggestively highlights that what makes Cleopatra powerful is not her speech but her use of physical beauty in the service of her seductive speech. In his *Parallel Lives*, Plutarch similarly emphasizes Cleopatra's physical allure but suggests instead that it is the 'sweetness of her tongue' or her discursive ability that plays the dominant role in her seduction:

And besides her beauty, the good grace she had to talk and discourse, her courteous nature that tempered her words and deeds, was a spur that pricked to the quick. Furthermore, besides all these, her voice and words were marvellous pleasant: for her tongue was an instrument of music to divers sports and pastimes, the which she easily turned to any language that pleased her.[12]

For Plutarch, the wily and circumspect Cleopatra is a gifted conversationalist who uses her speech to discourse on a variety of subjects or in a variety of languages ('any language'). Her linguistic skill is her primary tool for flattery, deceit and seduction.

Countering these highly critical historical depictions of the Egyptian queen, Mary Sidney's translated play *The Tragedie of Antonie* (1595) and Samuel Daniel's play *The Tragedie of Cleopatra* (1594) redress Cleopatra's reputation by valorizing her femininity and heroism. Sidney portrays Cleopatra sympathetically as a heroic and self-sacrificial woman who is undyingly devoted to her Antony.[13] Although Sidney takes after Plutarch in emphasizing 'th'enchaunting skilles' (2.719) of Cleopatra's speech and her polyglotism, or versatile use of diverse discourses, to answer ambassadors 'each in his owne language' (2.724), Cleopatra's speech is depicted as being sincere rather than manipulative.[14] In a series of confessional monologues, Cleopatra discloses her patience and virtue: she accepts her responsibility for Antony's death and renounces her duties as a monarch and a mother in order to atone for his death and reciprocate his love by committing suicide. Samuel Daniel's Cleopatra, by contrast, is not an infatuated woman but a strong and self-conscious queen whose heroism lies in her determination to retain her honour and her freedom by taking her own life. She famously vows 'I must not be, unlesse I be mine owne' (1.73).[15] Acutely aware of the disparity between her public image and her powerless condition following Antony's suicide, Daniel's ambitious Cleopatra carefully contemplates her suicide in her opening monologue.

She acknowledges that her love for Antony was insincere and plans to use her death to trump Caesar.

While traces of Daniel's deceitful and proud Cleopatra can certainly be found in Shakespeare's Cleopatra, the latter is nevertheless more enigmatic and complex than her dramatic predecessors. Shakespeare's Cleopatra is markedly undecipherable: the audience cannot access the internal workings of her mind either through her soliloquies or her monologues since she is never alone and does not introspectively address herself. In foregrounding Cleopatra's verbal interaction with Romans and Egyptians, Shakespeare firmly locates Cleopatra in the sphere of public performance where she is a master of discourse and a speaker of reports rather than the mere subject of Roman report. The titular protagonist of his play is attended to and heard. Shakespeare thus shifts the focus away from Plutarch's and Sidney's report of Cleopatra's pleasing manner of speaking – whether it be speaking courteously, musically, or in different languages – towards the content of her speech. Shakespeare reinvents Cleopatra as a reporter and self-conscious user of language.

The pragmatics of reported speech

Addressing his consorts Maecenas and Agrippa, Caesar discloses to them Antony's defiance of him and Rome by recounting the verbal charges that Antony has laid against him. According to Caesar, Antony accuses Caesar of

> not rat[ing] him
> His part o'th' isle. Then does he say he lent me
> Some shipping, unrestored. Lastly, he frets
> That Lepidus of the triumvirate
> Should be deposed and, being, that we detain
> All his revenue.

(3.6.26–30)

Caesar's account of the words spoken by Antony instantiates his use of reported speech.

Reported speech, also known as direct and indirect quotation, is an interdisciplinary subject of study that has enjoyed particular prominence in linguistics, where it is usually synonymous with indirect speech (speech that is quoted indirectly).[16] Although reported speech has long been approached syntactically as an object of formal analysis in linguistics, it has been gaining increasing acceptance as 'a category of discourse analysis rather than syntax'.[17] The syntactic approach, which examines the speech units of reported speech to determine the grammatical difference in meaning between the speech's manifestation as indirect and direct quotation is, to quote Daniel Collins, 'chiefly concerned with positing rules for converting one RS [reported speech] construction into another'.[18] Criticized for being reductionistic, the syntactic approach does not account for the context or utterance frame of the report which, to borrow Duranti and Goodwin's phrasing, 'provides resources for its appropriate interpretation' such as 'cultural setting, speech situation, shared background assumptions' as well as participant perception.[19] The meaning of reported speech, in other words, is not determined exclusively by abstract grammatical and syntactical rules but is, rather, shaped by the reporter's linguistic performance within a given discourse context involving speaker intention and hearer reception. A discourse pragmatic approach takes into account the variability between the reported speech and the reporting context as well as the intentionality of the reporter who, as Collins states, shapes and presents the reported speech 'to interpreters in a specific context, for his own communicative purposes'.[20] Reacting against the structuralist foundations of Saussurean-based linguistics, the pragmatic approach holds that meaning is actively produced between speakers and hearers in a given discourse context.

The pragmatic approach to reported speech is heavily indebted to Mikhail Bakhtin's and Valentin Vološinov's dialogical and heteroglossic theory of language, in which utterances are evocative of and responsive to prior utterances. Defining reported speech as 'speech within speech, utterance within utterance, and at the same time also *speech about speech, utterance about utterance*', Vološinov explains that reported speech is a discursive category which emphasizes the 'dynamic interrelationship of ... the speech being reported (the other person's speech) and the speech doing the reporting (the author's speech)', or between the reporter and the original speaker's speech.[21] Since the '"authorial" context surrounding the reported speech' is comprised of reply and commentary, the act of reporting is never neutral nor can it transmit the original utterance verbatim.[22] Rather, reporting is an interpretive or, to use Austin's term, a performative act that renders the reporter an active participant in the construction of meaning rather than a passive instrument of its use.[23] The reported speech thus conveys not only the form and content of the original utterance but also registers the reporter's stylistic, syntactic, or compositional adaptation of the speech to suit his or her communicative intentions.[24] An intentional and creative act, reportage thus inscribes the reporter's commentary or response onto the utterance that the reporter purports to report within his or her reporting context.

Report in Roman discourse

In *Antony and Cleopatra*, reportage is a trademark of Roman discourse and a measure of its political power. The continual presence of Roman messengers and reports in the play illustrates the geographical extent of the Roman Empire as well as Caesar's governance and control over it. Since Rome, as Linda Charnes claims, is the locus of the 'narrative imperative' or the 'authoritative (and authoritarian) representational institution of epic and narrative history' that 'drives imperialist historiography', this narrative imperative is instantiated in the use of report, which is a tool for conquest and imperial domination as much as it is a reflection of them.²⁵ If Caesar's use of report and reported speech serve as a means of verbally appropriating or territorializing the foreign Other and absorbing its contours into a politically sanctioned, standardized Roman narrative, they also serve as a means of public self-display and play a crucial role in shaping Roman public opinion.²⁶ In exercising the 'narrative imperative' through his use of report to discursively construct a mighty Roman Empire, Caesar fashions himself for the Roman public as a powerful and exemplary emperor at its helm.²⁷ Caesar not only commands and receives reports from his messengers but also acts as a reporter who broadcasts other characters' speeches, written words and actions to consolidate his power in a threatening environment where not only reports but also, as Andrew Hiscock claims, his '*grand imperial narrative*' is constantly 'exceeded, overtaken by new narratives formulated by interpreting subjects across the empire'.²⁸ In a Rome rife with political competition where messages can be easily compromised, miscommunicated, or distorted, Caesar strategically uses report and reported speech to memorialize himself as a powerful ruler for the historical record – and does so by discreetly belittling his rivals, Antony and Cleopatra.

Caesar's tribute to Antony's past greatness as a stoic general at Modena (1.4.57–72) exemplifies this use of report to promulgate his desired public image. Although Caesar laments Antony's loss of his heroic Roman nature as well as his self-indulgence in Egypt where 'he fishes, drinks, and wastes / The lamps of night in revel' (1.4.4–5), his tribute to Antony's past glory is a calculated rhetorical performance that merely masquerades as praise. Caesar uses report to degrade and criticize Antony under the pretext of praising him in order to reinforce his public image as a righteous ruler who displays no ill will towards his rival. His oral report of Antony is framed by the written report he receives from Alexandria (1.4.1–9), which he reads aloud to Lepidus so as to dispel his rumoured distaste towards Antony: 'You may see, Lepidus, and henceforth know, / It is not Caesar's natural vice to hate / Our great competitor' (1.4.1–3). In referring to himself in the third person, Caesar betrays an acute awareness of his public role and of the need to display his exemplariness to an audience of potential reporters in order to condition public opinion.[29] His report or tribute to Antony is orchestrated to display his admiration of Antony's Roman qualities. However, just as Caesar praises Antony's temperance and stoic abstinence from proper nourishment at Modena, he discreetly undercuts this tribute by his use of degrading imagery which de-mythologizes Antony's heroism: 'Thou didst drink / The stale of horses and the gilded puddle / Which beasts would cough at' (1.4.62–4).[30] 'Gilded', if construed to mean golden rather than yellow, also ironically underscores Caesar's ridicule of Antony. Moreover, instead of praising a victorious soldier at Modena, Caesar praises a defeated Antony who is 'beaten from Modena' (1.4.58) by the Roman senate; Antony's heroism is depicted in a personal war with famine for survival (59–69) rather than in a political battle for the Roman state. As Heather James points out, Caesar's description of the famished Antony in a desolate landscape is intended to critique Antony as an inept and anachronistic leader for 'the emerging bureaucracy of the Roman empire' by highlighting Antony's association with 'Rome's myths of rugged origins'.[31]

Along with images of depravity, Caesar's use of reported speech in his tribute serves to undermine his praise of Antony's heroism and turns his tribute into a critique of the Triumvir. Caesar's eight instances of reportage in the play all, significantly, typify indirect reported speech. Indirect report, or what Vološinov calls the '*pictorial*' style of speech, is structured on a reporting context that 'strives to break down the self-contained compactness of the reported speech, to resolve it, to obliterate its boundaries': by 'infiltrating [the] reported speech with authorial retort and commentary', the report is subordinated to the reporter.[32] Indirect reported speech thus suppresses the original speaker's voice to reframe and convey only the content of the speech in the reporter's reporting context so as to make it appear objective and official. In this manner, indirect report allows Caesar to control the imperial narrative over which he presides by manipulating, to quote Hiscock, 'the textual remains of the past, to re-create history and to delimit its meaning' in order to 're-invent himself so that he too may become part of the Roman narratives of heroic lineage which are greeted with awe by the city-state'.[33] An example of Caesar's use of indirect report, broadly defined, occurs in his confrontation with Antony: 'You / Did pocket up my letters, and with taunts / Did gibe my missive out of audience' (2.2.78–80). Although Caesar does not report the exact words spoken by Antony, he nevertheless recounts the manner of Antony's speech ('gibe', 'taunts') to portray him antagonistically. Nevertheless, the report contained in Caesar's tribute to Antony is not an indirect report of Antony's speech. Rather, the report is what Caesar has *indirectly heard reported* about Antony: 'On the Alps, / It is reported, thou didst eat strange flesh / Which some did die to look on' (1.4.67–9). This unofficial word-of-mouth that Caesar hears at second hand is made into official public record. While it may sound Caesar's wonder or incredulousness at Antony's hardiness and his heroic endurance, the report nevertheless belittles Antony by underlining his uncontrolled appetite, which urges him to consume 'strange flesh' in lieu of the praiseworthy berries and bark that befit a hardy soldier. Caesar may even be attributing a particular savagery to Antony which he had just, ironically, claimed Antony's stoicism allows him to transcend (Antony fights famine 'with patience more / Than savages could suffer' [61–2]). Although Caesar's report admirably illustrates that Antony's physical form does not diminish after his 'strange' feast (his 'cheek / So much as lanked not' [71–2]), his note of admiration covertly registers his implicit criticism of the Triumvir's intemperance and self-indulgence as he sexually feasts on Cleopatra's uncoincidentally strange Egyptian flesh and loses his physical shape as a result.[34] The comparison is subtle yet it registers Caesar's haughtiness and superiority as a virtuous leader – even as the passive voice of the report ('It is reported') distances him from owning his critique – by altering the referential context of Antony's heroism in order to ridicule it. Contained within a reporting context in which Caesar laments the loss of Antony's past heroism and urges him to return to Rome, Caesar's indirectly heard report renders Antony's past heroism questionable. Under the pretext of singing of Antony's past greatness at Modena, Caesar deflates Antony's heroism and tarnishes his reputation 'in the world's report' (2.3.5) in a discreet attempt to promote his own greatness as a ruler and 'earn[] a place i'th' story' (3.13.47) of Rome.

Cleopatra's reports and reported speech

Although report and reportage delimit Rome as the locus of the 'narrative imperative' and distinguish it from Cleopatra's Egypt as the realm of 'mimetic improvisation', to use Linda Charnes's terms, Cleopatra nevertheless adopts Roman reportage to re-script her social and political power within a Roman discursive context.[35] Charnes juxtaposes Cleopatra's 'mimetic improvisation' or 'subversion' against this Roman narrative imperative with which it competes without recognizing that not only are Cleopatra's verbal acts and histrionic deeds mutually constitutive but also that Cleopatra, as Charnes implies, does not merely exemplify 'the subjection, and resistance, to the narrative imperative' – she also embraces and transcends it.[36]

Unlike Caesar who celebrates Antony's past stoic greatness at Modena and laments his present condition, Cleopatra celebrates Antony's present greatness as her war-like lover and laments his absence in Egypt. While Cleopatra's monologue competitively counters Caesar's tribute to Antony, it nevertheless proves to be as self-serving as Caesar's tribute. As a means of combating her political and emotional vulnerability after Antony is summoned back to Rome, Cleopatra's direct report of Antony's words in her monologue marks her self-glorification and sexual dominance over Antony under the pretext of glorifying Antony as a hero and acknowledging his Mars-like power over her. The direct reported speech allows Cleopatra to turn her political powerlessness as a mere woman and sexualized Roman object into a sexual power that she can memorialize. Addressing Charmian and Iras, a seemingly melancholic Cleopatra makes Antony the subject of her ruminations:

> O, Charmian,
> Where think'st thou he is now? Stands he, or sits he?
> Or does he walk? Or is he on his horse?
> O happy horse, to bear the weight of Antony!
> Do bravely, horse, for wot'st thou whom thou mov'st?
> The demi-Atlas of this earth, the arm
> And burgonet of men! He's speaking now,
> Or murmuring 'Where's my serpent of old Nile?'
> For so he calls me. Now I feed myself
> With most delicious poison. Think on me
> That am with Phoebus' amorous pinches black
> And wrinkled deep in time? Broad-fronted Caesar,
> When thou wast here above the ground, I was
> A morsel for a monarch; and great Pompey
> Would stand and make his eyes grow in my brow;
> There would he anchor his aspect, and die
> With looking on his life.
>
> (1.5.19–35)

In littering her monologue with rhetorical questions and an apostrophe that hyperbolically dramatizes her arguably feigned longing for Antony and her fantasizing over his quotidian actions, Cleopatra depicts herself as an enamoured woman who laments her lover's absence and obsessively pines for his presence. Alluding to Antony as a 'demi-Atlas' and metonymically referring to him as the 'arm / And burgonet of men' (24–5), the smitten Cleopatra praises Antony's heroic magnanimity and military prowess as she pictures him mounted on a horse in preparation for battle. Extending her praise of Antony's heroism, Cleopatra imagines Antony speaking and directly reports his epithet for her: '"Where's my serpent of old Nile?" / For so he calls me' (26–7). This instance of direct reported speech creates the impression of her homage to and admiration of Antony, who takes centre stage in her fantasizing. Even though Cleopatra's report of Antony's speech is not circumscribed by quotation marks in the Folio, modern editors have often chosen to place the speech within quotes. However, it is worth noting that quotation marks, or a lack thereof, do not necessarily signify direct or indirect reported speech. As sociolinguist Patricia Mayes explains, if the deictic centre of the reported speech 'is that of the original utterance' and the report 'gives the illusion that the incident is presently occurring', as is the case with Cleopatra's report of Antony's speech, then the reported speech is direct.[37] Indirect reported speech, by contrast, is syntactically restricted by or partially absorbed into the reporting context; an indirect report of Antony's words would read 'Antony is speaking or murmuring, and asking where his serpent of old Nile is'.[38] Direct reported speech – or what Vološinov calls the *'linear'* style of reported speech – is an imitative act underwritten by the desire to maintain the original speech's 'integrity and authenticity' by 'demarcat[ing]' and 'screen[ing] it from penetration by the author's [read: reporter's] intonations' or syntactic reformulations.[39] In thus granting authority to the original speaker of the utterance, direct reported speech underscores the reporter's concession to and acknowledgement of the utterance's encoded authority. It also allows the reporter or speaker to use this reported speech, as Mayes notes, 'as evidence ... to present a more believable story'.[40] In thus casting herself into a subordinate role as a longing, passive beloved by putting a chivalric Antony on a pedestal, Cleopatra underlines the social distance between her and Antony by adopting the 'deference or self-suppression' attendant on direct report to present a seemingly more believable story of her love for Antony to her female audience.[41]

It is in performing this role as a powerless woman in love that Cleopatra is able to turn her apparent deference to Antony to her sexual advantage. Even though Cleopatra, as Ania Loomba claims, 'plays the Egyptian flamboyantly, thus appropriating, and flaunting the difference that Rome assigns to her', her performances do not necessarily imply that her love for Antony is feigned.[42] While the Egyptian queen certainly loves Antony, her love for him is closely intertwined with self-interest. In hyperbolizing her love for Antony by turning it into a spectacle worthy of public admiration and report, both in her monologue and in the play's opening scene, Cleopatra clearly subordinates love to her political agenda of self-promotion in order to stave off complete Roman colonization. As a result, her deference to Antony proves to be self-serving, for her direct report of Antony's speech ('"Where's my serpent of old Nile?"') registers not just the extent of her obsessive preoccupation with Antony but significantly depicts an Antony longing for *her* presence. She transforms his simple question into an emotionally inflected rhetorical question. In glossing Antony's act of speaking as murmuring ('He's speaking now, / Or murmuring' [25–6]) in the very act of pronouncing it, Cleopatra portrays Antony as a man in love who privately guards his passions, is emotionally dependent on her and longs for her as much as she pines for him. Direct reported speech, as Anna Wierzbicka explains, is 'theatrical' or 'playful': it is an act of ventriloquism that allows the reporter to 'temporarily assume[] the role of that other person, [to] "play[] his part", that is to say, imagine[] himself as the other person' or to dramatize another speaker's reported words in order to affectively involve the audience in the inference of meaning, for the speech is 'shown' rather than explicitly told as it is in indirect reported speech.[43] Rather than solely convey the content of Antony's speech, direct reported speech allows Cleopatra to additionally communicate the *affective* aspects of meaning that are associated with, and conveyed through, the wording, 'modality or prosody of the utterance' in order to persuade her audience of Antony's sentiments as well as to highlight her applause-worthy impersonation of him.[44]

In showing her onstage audience that Antony is emotionally bound to her, Cleopatra shows that Antony's greatness is due to her and thereby valorizes her sexual power. The military associations of Antony's horse quickly give way to erotic associations. The horse, symbolizing 'the unreined lust of concupiscence' according to Plutarch, doubles as a sexual self-reference to Cleopatra who literally and physically 'bear[s] the weight of Antony' (22) and makes him 'move' in bed, but also 'bears' the weight of Antony in her memory as she performs her report.[45] Antony's heroism, Cleopatra reveals, is premised on his Egyptian sexuality which is (laboriously) brought to life and praised by Cleopatra, who urges herself to 'do bravely' (23) and depict him in a chivalric light: *she* is the agent or source of *his* greatness and his greatness, Cleopatra implies, is not defined by Roman abstinence or austere measures. Antony is great because of Cleopatra's sexual performance but he is also great because of her theatrical performance of his words, with which she ironically re-enacts his 'greatness' as a chivalric lover. While the horse reference thus seems to undermine Cleopatra's authority by associating her with the ardent lust of Egyptian femininity that the Romans ascribe to her, she nevertheless uses it self-servingly to construct her sexual authority.[46] Moreover, her laudatory allusion to Antony as a heroic 'demi-Atlas' (24) is similarly self-serving: it is spoken ironically to register her belittlement of an Antony who is unable to embody a complete Atlas. As Janet Adelman claims, the allusion registers an ambivalence of praise and criticism to remind the audience 'of the degree to which Antony has dwindled from the heroic stature of his great ancestor [Hercules]' at the same time as it 'emphasizes [the] grandeur' of Antony's ventures.[47] In labelling Antony a 'demi' Atlas, Cleopatra may be implying that she is the other half-Atlas, or perhaps even a complete and self-contained Atlas, who grants Antony his greatness and acts as the standard against which she measures him. In thus 'praising' an Antony who reportedly longs for her, Cleopatra indirectly praises herself by putting words into the mouth of a heroic Antony to show that she is the cause of his heroic greatness. Nevertheless, being subjected to Rome as she is, Cleopatra also needs Antony to gain a political foothold in Rome in order to become 'great' herself. Her verbal sleight-of-hand allows Cleopatra to refashion her dependence on Antony as Antony's dependence on her as a means of combating her political vulnerability during his absence from Egypt. Cleopatra pleases herself by imagining that Antony imagines her as having seductive power over him; her report rebounds back to flatter the reporter.

While Cleopatra's direct report of Antony's epithet sounds her self-praise and sexual dominance by implying that Antony's heroism is not entirely his own, it also subtly ridicules Antony for condemning *her* as he adheres to possible Roman connotations in calling her a serpent. That Antony employs Roman words to call Cleopatra his 'serpent of old Nile' offstage is not questionable; what is questionable is Antony's intention in pragmatically using the epithet, which renders Cleopatra's contention that Antony spoke the words in a state of amorous longing for her (as she imagines him doing) suspect. Given that 'murmuring' also connotes 'to complain in low muttered tones' or 'to give voice to an inarticulate discontent', it may suggest that Antony is complicit in Cleopatra's power games and is dissatisfied with – or bemoaning – Cleopatra's control over him. Alternately, it may suggest that Antony himself is using flattery in a self-serving manner to disguise his one-upmanship with Cleopatra.[48] Cleopatra's report of Antony's 'murmur' is contextualized by a negative tissue of allusion to, and repetition of, the word 'serpent' in the play, which allows Antony's Roman rather than his Egyptian sympathies to emerge. Connoting Satanic wiliness and postlapsarian deceit in the Roman lexis, 'serpent' is used by Antony to characterize Pompey's impending invasion of Rome (1.2.199–201) as the latter 'creeps apace' (1.3.51). Although Antony does not explicitly refer to Cleopatra as a devious snake, the metaphorical connection between the serpent and Cleopatra is implied by Pompey's association with the snake. Just as Pompey 'creeps' quietly and stealthily into the idle hearts of Romans to win their favour and poison their loyalties towards the state, Cleopatra 'creeps' into liking with Antony to win his love and disempower him by poisoning him with sexual overindulgence. Like the Romans, whose idleness is partially at fault for inviting the pestilential invasion that is Pompey, Antony's self-acknowledged idleness and his complicity in his bondage to Cleopatra are similarly at fault: 'Ten thousand harms, more than the ills I know, / My idleness doth hatch' (1.2.136–7).[49] Antony's reference to Cleopatra as 'this enchanting queen' (1.2.135) who is 'cunning past man's thought' (1.2.152) and employs 'strong Egyptian fetters' (1.2.123) and crocodile 'tears' (2.7.50) to ensnare him illustrates his awareness of Cleopatra's duplicity and her manipulative strategies. The possible pun on 'queen' (quean) registers his simultaneous admiration and denigration of his Egyptian lover to suggest that Antony may be just as wily as Cleopatra is.[50]

The wily Egyptian not only reinterprets Antony's epithet in a self-flattering manner but also parenthetically draws attention to her act of reporting it ('For so he calls me' [27]) to mock Antony's possible Roman use of 'serpent'. In a monologue saturated with mid-line prosodic switches for the actor that, as Simon Palfrey and Tiffany Stern demonstrate, indicate 'actable shifts in voice, gesture, or attitude', these mid-line switches serve to illustrate that 'power is truly at work – minds at a cusp, fates undecided, fear and anxiety afoot'.[51] The switches that occur after and also possibly before Cleopatra's parenthetical 'For so he calls me' suggest a change in tone or attitude: 'And burgonet of men! [switch] He's speaking now, / Or murmuring "Where's my serpent of old Nile?" / [switch?] For so he calls me. [switch] Now I feed myself' (25–7). The mid-line switch between 'men' and 'He's speaking' in line 25 marks Cleopatra's movement away from performing the role of a gushing beloved for it attunes her audience to hear the words that Antony speaks and she reports. The switch in line 27 between 'me' and 'Now' (and possibly also before 'for') marks

Cleopatra's distance from reporting his words; she undercuts her praise with a pause pregnant with ironic commentary that serves to mock or condemn Antony's potentially negative use of the epithet as she addresses her female attendants. As Dan Sperber and Deirdre Wilson illustrate, irony is created when the speaker expresses a 'belief ABOUT his utterance, rather than BY MEANS OF it'.[52] Irony is denoted through echoic 'mention' rather than the 'use' of certain words.[53] Cleopatra's ironic mention of Antony's speech, which is evidenced by her parenthetical 'For so he calls me', draws attention to Antony speaking or, as Sperber and Wilson would say, to 'the expression itself' rather than 'to what the expression refers to'.[54] The combination of prosodic switches and the ironic mention present in Cleopatra's report of Antony's epithet may highlight her teasing contempt of Antony and detract from the praise she initially lends him. Irony allows Cleopatra to condemn an Antony who has deserted her for Caesar and to instate her self-praise comfortably.

Despite the possibility of Antony's insinuated belittlement of and domineering Roman attitude towards Cleopatra, Cleopatra adroitly reinterprets his epithet in an Egyptian context to turn her political disempowerment – suggested by the negative Roman connotations of the word 'serpent' – into a valorizing self-reference that showcases her erotic power and dominance as she recollects her sexual conquests of Julius Caesar and Gnaeus Pompey. In an Egyptian context, the serpent carries positive connotations. As Egypt's preeminent mythical creature, the serpent is spontaneously born of the mud of the ebbing Nile 'by the operation of [the] sun' (2.7.27) and symbolizes fertility, renewal and resurrection. As figured in the ancient symbol of the ouroboros, the serpent additionally encompasses antitheses such as mortality and eternity and thus instantiates a cyclicality that Cleopatra's seduction of both Caesar and Pompey embodies as she renews – or re-scripts – herself as a sexually powerful sovereign.[55] Just as she performs the role of a woman in love for Antony, Cleopatra performs her scripted role as a denigrated courtesan for Caesar and Pompey only to valorize this sexual role in an Egyptian context and to assert her sexual power over the Triumvirs. Employing her feminine wiles to seduce Caesar and Pompey, Cleopatra embraces her role as a subjugated Egyptian: she is a 'morsel' (1.5.32) of food that serves to satisfy Caesar's sexual appetite, as well as a woman-mirror that subserviently reflects Pompey's image back to him (1.5.32–5). However, Cleopatra's mention of 'morsel', like her mention of 'serpent', suggests her awareness of its negative Roman connotation as she restructures its meaning in an Egyptian context. In the Roman lexis, 'morsel' is used in a derogatory fashion by the Romans to belittle Cleopatra as a worthless leftover, as an irate Antony's use of the word following the defeat at Actium demonstrates (3.13.121). In the Egyptian lexis, however, 'morsel' evokes Egyptian feasting and may refer 'to the folk tradition that if one ate the food of a supernatural realm one could never leave', as Adelman notes.[56] Although it is not an example of reported speech proper, Cleopatra's mention of 'morsel' is an implicit and ironic report that serves to undermine Roman power. Reinterpreted in an Egyptian context where it signifies the inescapable bondage to which Cleopatra subjects her rivals through her erotic ploys, 'morsel' underlines that Cleopatra not only feeds others' appetites but also feeds her own appetite by making her opponents subservient to her. Playing Caesar's sexual game, as Agrippa reports (2.2.237–9), Cleopatra wields sexual power and politically outwits Caesar by bearing him an heir, Caesarion, through whom she can lay claim to the Roman throne.

Cleopatra's self-dramatization as Pompey's narcissistic mirror of 'self-contemplation' similarly underlines her inferior status as an object of consumption even as she performatively reinterprets herself in an Egyptian context as a consuming subject to valorize her sexual power. Alluding to herself as the power-wielding Gorgon Medusa whose stony gaze makes Pompey 'anchor his aspect, and die / With looking on his life' (34–5), Cleopatra overturns the desiring male gaze as she had done on Cydnus to become, as Heather James notes, 'the bearer of the desiring gaze, not its Petrarchan object'.[57] The pun on 'die', which indicates Pompey's sexual fulfilment in a Roman context, is utilized by Cleopatra to suggest Pompey's political destruction at Cleopatra's hands in an Egyptian context following their sexual tryst. Cleopatra uses the pun to performatively valorize herself as a powerful ruler who ironically grants Pompey 'life' in her report as *her* powerless political subject in Egypt following his Roman 'death'. In thus turning the Triumvirs' sexual surrender and loss into self-gain in the same manner that she turns her lack of youth and a dark complexion (29–30) into a desirable vitality to bait her men, Cleopatra embodies the renewal of the Egyptian serpent and glories in her conquests. The oxymoronic 'delicious poison' (28) with which Cleopatra 'feed[s]' herself (27) in a self-congratulatory manner in her monologue underscores her ouroboric self-identity as she mythologizes herself as a self-sustained, self-sufficient and self-begetting serpent. Her claim to superiority rests on her being her own beginning and her own end.[58] Cleopatra's poison, or the pleasurable reminiscence of her triumph over the three Triumvirs, enables her to valorize herself as a great and sexually powerful monarch while also foreshadowing her suicide with the asp that she maternally 'feeds' with her poison rather than vice-versa. This self-generated poison grants Cleopatra immortality in report and ensures that she is memorialized for posterity. In the face of patriarchal Roman power, Cleopatra's recontextualization of Antony's 'serpent' comes to symbolize her phallic power which enables her to vie with Caesar.

Not only does Cleopatra's direct report of Antony's epithet sound a self-congratulatory note of praise, but it also urges her female attendants – as well as the offstage theatre audience – to praise and applaud her performance. Due to its inherent theatricality, direct reported speech, as Collins notes, 'allows the audience to participate both in the new event (the re-creation) and, vicariously, in the prior event, real or imagined, that is being represented'.[59] In reporting Antony's epithet, Cleopatra speaks as Antony to indirectly *tell* her audience of her sexual power as well as impeccably performs her role as a passive beloved to directly *show* and thus affectively persuade her audience – through prosody, physical enactment, or both – of this power by involving them in the interpretive process. Cleopatra's apostrophe to Antony's horse (1.5.23) and to the absent Caesar (1.5.30) clearly indicate that she stages her speech as a spectacle. Embedding her direct report of Antony's epithet in a monologue that opens with the verbal performance of a smitten beloved and closes with an account of her sexual conquests, Cleopatra directs her audience to honour not only her conquest of the Triumvirs but also her past and current improvisational performance of a powerless Roman subject that is prerequisite to her to triumph. Cleopatra's imperative injunction to her onstage and offstage audiences to 'Think on me / That am with Phoebus' amorous pinches black / And wrinkled deep in time' (28–30), accompanied by mid-line switches which both introduce and conclude the injunction, is a public request that her audiences glorify her sexuality and hold her in the same awe-full esteem in which she holds herself. In desiring to hear others speak of her and in imagining others (particularly Antony) speaking while ironically controlling this speech, Cleopatra wishes to be ever-present in others' speech and thoughts and thus publicly memorialized as a sexually noble and absolute female monarch. Like Caesar, Cleopatra uses report as a means of self-flattery to condition public opinion and to publish her magnanimity to posterity by re-styling her homage to Antony as self-homage. But while Caesar seeks to consolidate his power as a Triumvir under the guise of paying tribute to a lustreless Antony through report, Cleopatra stages her political powerlessness as a smitten beloved and sexualized object *as* sexual power through her use of report. Cleopatra yearns to negotiate an identity that is ironically self-empowering while inevitably being subjugated to imperial Roman authority. Her monologue highlights her sexual charisma and her performative greatness, which allow her to transcend her Roman script and exhibit herself as the director, actor and spectator of her own show.

If Cleopatra aspires to condition her onstage audience's response by directly reporting Antony's epithet, she also attempts to control Antony's emotional response by directly reporting Caesar's hypothetical words to him.[60] In an attempt to turn her powerlessness into power, Cleopatra mocks Caesar through direct report. Her theatrical performance of the words she imagines Caesar uttering serves to manipulate Antony into craving Cleopatra's command over that of Caesar in order to render Antony subservient to her. In the play's opening scene, Cleopatra shames Antony and exposes Caesar's emasculation of him even as she urges him to hear the messengers from Rome:

> Nay, hear them, Antony.
> Fulvia perchance is angry, or who knows
> If the scarce-bearded Caesar have not sent
> His powerful mandate to you: 'Do this, or this;
> Take in that kingdom and enfranchise that.
> Perform't, or else we damn thee.'
>
> (1.1.20–5)

In urging Antony to attend to the messengers, Cleopatra performs her role as an obedient subject who respects and adheres to Caesar's authority: 'your dismission / Is come from Caesar; therefore hear it, Antony' (1.1.27–8). Nevertheless, this urging is quickly undercut by Cleopatra's effeminizing reference to Caesar as a 'scarce-bearded' (22) pubescent boy while she possibly, as Marvin Rosenberg suggests, 'boys' or parodies Caesar's tone and 'youthful gestures' in performing her report.[61] As María Luisa Dañobeitia Fernández claims, Cleopatra hopes to stir up Antony's 'profound animosity' towards Caesar 'by making him *feel* like a foolish servant ready to jump at "[Caesar's] powerful mandate"'.[62] Manipulating Antony through the perlocutionary force of Caesar's hypothetical speech is Cleopatra's way of persuading Antony to stay in Egypt. In addition to her mockery of Caesar, Cleopatra's unflattering description of Fulvia as 'angry' (21) and 'shrill-tongued' (33) is further meant to shame Antony by hinting at his emasculation – which results from his submission to his wife – under the pretext of endorsing his submission. Cleopatra hopes to persuade Antony to redirect his loyalties towards her by making him desire a freedom and a reciprocal relationship that are characteristically Egyptian. However, the freedom and reciprocity implied are illusions since Cleopatra ironically exposes her performance of Fulvia's and Caesar's modes of speaking as a means of gaining power over Antony. In reporting how 'shrill-tongued Fulvia scolds' (33), Cleopatra uses Fulvia's shrillness as a pretext for her own scolding of Antony, which she implicitly performs in the very act of ridiculing Caesar and exposing Antony's shame. She shames Antony for not heeding what she craves to know: the content of the Roman messengers' report. Moreover, as her opening imperatives attest, Cleopatra adopts what Paul Yachnin calls Caesar's '"Roman" language of command' and does so in a Lear-like fashion to challenge Antony to quantify his love for her ('If it be love indeed, tell me how much' [1.1.14]) as she commands Antony on three different occasions to hear the messengers from Rome (lines 20, 28 and 49).[63] In proclaiming that she will 'set a bourn how far to be beloved' (1.1.16), Cleopatra adopts the Roman values of calculation and order and thus directly competes with Caesar to secure Antony's faithfulness to her and to Egypt by making Antony desire exactly what she later warns him against desiring: control and subservience. Performing the role of a calculating monarch, Cleopatra theatrically directs Antony to display his love for her verbally so that she can showcase, and thus boast of, his submission to her as well as her power over him not only to her audience but also to the voyeuristic Romans in Egypt who would report this as a challenge to Caesar. Cleopatra directly reports Caesar's hypothetical speech in an attempt to reinforce her affective control and command over Antony under the pretext of, paradoxically, showcasing her inability to command Antony *to* him, even as she attempts to stage this command for her audience. By impersonating Caesar and his imperiousness at the same time as showing how undesirable it is to be subject to Caesar, Cleopatra draws attention to her performative abilities which allow her to exceed her containment in Philo's and Demetrius's report of her as a 'gipsy' (10) and a 'strumpet' (13) that frames the play's opening scene.

Cleopatra's direct report of Caesar's imaginary words also meta-dramatically foregrounds the boy actor's impersonation of Cleopatra and underlines her greatness. Cleopatra's description of Caesar as 'scarce-bearded' is a self-reflexive reference to the boy actor playing Cleopatra who, ironically, ridicules Caesar for being a 'boy' in order to competitively highlight his superior acting skills over the rival actor playing Caesar. The boy actor 'boys' Caesar and thus exceeds the limitations of his own boyhood by calling attention to his presentational acting abilities. Just as Cleopatra's mocking enactment of Caesar's command reveals her use of this command to outdo Caesar and win over Antony, so too does the boy actor's presentational acting purposefully expose his skilful, representational performance of Cleopatra to outdo or belittle the adult actor's performance of Caesar in order to 'win' over the audience. In both performing and drawing attention to his performance, the boy actor shows that his acting – his performative greatness – valorizes Cleopatra's greatness and her sexual charisma.

In addition to reporting other characters' speech, the actions and behaviour that Cleopatra commands her messengers to report to Antony also serve to secure his political allegiance and emotional loyalty towards her. While Cleopatra's commands clearly bear illocutionary force for her messengers since she orders them to speak on her behalf, she desires and intends this illocutionary force to have a perlocutionary effect on Antony. Fearing that Antony's re-alliance with Caesar will spell Egypt's demise, Cleopatra attempts to sidetrack Antony from his 'Roman thought[s]' (1.2.87) by ordering Charmian to report her feigned emotional state to him in response to his emotional state: '*If* you find him sad, / Say I am dancing; *if* in mirth, report / That I am sudden sick' (1.3.4–6, italics mine). Cleopatra's conditional and unobtrusive commands are effectively calculated to persuade Antony to return to her of his own will. Divulging Cleopatra's strategy of reinvention through performance, the report highlights how Cleopatra embraces the stereotypical role of a fickle woman to subvert Antony's expectations and condition his response; she shows that she is consistently inconsistent by virtue of her 'infinite variety' (2.2.246). Her contradictory actions, disguised here as potential *re*actions in report, are orchestrated to render Antony subservient to her as well as to test where his loyalties lie. By making Antony's reactions dependent on her 'reactions', Cleopatra hopes to emasculate Antony and make him incapable of acting without her supervision. Cleopatra puts her strategy of opposing Antony into practice when, upon his return from Rome, she notices the 'good news' in his eye (1.3.20). She pretends to be 'sick and sullen' (14) and tells Antony to return to Fulvia (1.3.21–4) so as to make him divulge his love to her. Antony's eventual return to Rome similarly triggers an emotionally and politically vulnerable Cleopatra to summon Antony back to her by dispatching messages: she vows that 'He shall have every day a several greeting / Or I'll unpeople Egypt!' (1.5.80–1). In line with her performance as an infatuated beloved, the excessive messages with which Cleopatra vows to shower Antony are intended to flatter him by proving to him how great her love for him is. At the same time, however, these messages serve the more practical purpose of distracting Antony from his political dealings with Caesar so as to prevent the Triumvirs from forming a league against her.

Cleopatra's final test of Antony's loyalty similarly occurs through report: she commands that her impersonation of a love-sick beloved on her deathbed be reported to Antony. Enclosing herself in her pyramid to escape Antony's rage following their defeat at Actium, a powerless Cleopatra orders Mardian to 'go tell [Antony] I have slain myself. / Say that the last I spoke was "Antony", / And word it, prithee, piteously' (4.13.7–9). Dramatizing the degree of her love for, and reliance on, Antony by having it reported that his name was the last word she spoke, Cleopatra flatters Antony by signalling to him the extent of his power over her. She attempts to move Antony to pity and guilt by making him feel partially responsible for her death – which she, reportedly, performs in grievance at the thought that he blames her for their defeat and urges Mardian to tragically ('piteously') report. Serving as both a political 'test of [Antony's] love' and a 'testimony of her love', as Jan Blits states, the report of Cleopatra's feigned suicide is deployed to incite Antony as well as her onstage audience to commemorate her as Antony's noble and faithful beloved, to the same extent that she has just (reportedly) modelled the nobility of her love for Antony by committing suicide.[64] Like a true serpent that daily sheds its skin only to renew it, Cleopatra plays and thus maintains her scripted role as a fickle, weak, powerless and love-struck yet devoted Egyptian while discreetly shedding or exceeding these roles to wield affective power over Antony. Cleopatra strives to emasculate and disempower Antony through the affective force of her reports so that she can use him as a pawn in her contest with Rome.

As she does with Antony, Cleopatra strives to disarm Dolabella by affectively overpowering him with her greatness. Akin to her report of Antony's epithet, her dream-vision report of Antony (5.2.81–91) allows her to glorify herself under the pretext of praising Antony. Cleopatra seeks to affectively control Dolabella by moving him to awe in order to gain his loyalty so that she may sound Caesar's intentions. Signalling her commemoration of Antony's magnificent heroism, Cleopatra's grandiose and ekphrastic description of a deceased Antony serves to pay homage to her greatness. Her description of Antony consists of self-description as well as other characters' reports about her real or imagined traits, including Enobarbus's reports about her. Cleopatra's account of an Antony whose legs straddle the ocean and 'reared arm / Crest[s] the world' (81–2) is an allusion to the Colossus of Rhodes, the sun god Helios, who has lovingly kissed her and made her a tawny Egyptian: she is, as she claims, 'with Phoebus' amorous pinches black' (1.5.29). Antony's voice, composed of both the harmonious music of the spheres (82–3) and the 'rattling thunder' (85) of rage which bears resemblance to Cleopatra's own Fulvia-like 'shrilling tongue', typifies the oxymoronic binaries that characterize Cleopatra as an ouroboric serpent. Antony is, just like Cleopatra or, more precisely, *because* of Cleopatra, a macrocosmic force of nature, as Enobarbus makes clear: 'We cannot call her winds and waters sighs and tears; they are greater storms and tempests than almanacs can report' (1.2.154–6). Enobarbus indicates that Cleopatra's hyperbolic passions exceed human expression ('sighs and tears') and have cosmic ramifications. Nevertheless, these passions are 'made of nothing but the finest part of pure love .... This cannot be cunning in her. If it be, she makes a shower of rain as well as Jove' (1.2.153–8). Even though Cleopatra's hyperbolic passions are genuine, they can be mistaken for being feigned but this feigning is so convincingly performed that it seems authentic. In attributing this all-encompassing greatness to Antony, Cleopatra – or rather, the boy actor playing Cleopatra – points out his own Jove-like performance which allows him to cunningly impersonate Cleopatra but also to 'make' a new Antony out of the materials of his own performance. Finally, Cleopatra's comparison of Antony's bounty to an autumn 'That grew the more by reaping' (5.2.87) recalls not only Enobarbus's observation of her paradoxical, self-regenerating ability to 'make[] hungry / Where most she satisfies' (2.2.247–8) but also Egypt as the realm of renewal and surplus. By reconstituting Antony's fragmented, heroic masculinity, Cleopatra re-authors Antony as a great Egyptian and valorizes Egyptian values in the process of reinventing herself. Cleopatra re-scripts Egypt as the realm of generosity, abundance and liberality which does not corrupt Antony as the Romans claim but rather turns him into an altruistic force who lavishly drops a wealth of 'realms and islands' (89) from his pockets.

Cleopatra's dream-vision report of Antony evokes Enobarbus's notorious barge-scene description of Cleopatra and shares with it the reporter's self-flattery through report.

Enobarbus, concerned with 'earn[ing] a place i'th' story' (3.13.47) of official Roman narrative, attempts to inscribe himself in his report in order to glorify himself under the guise of praising Cleopatra. His report of Cleopatra's transcendent greatness aspires to move his Roman auditors to awe by affecting them with her power, to the same extent that Cleopatra's praise of Antony's paradoxical self-renewal is intended to inspire her Roman auditor with awe at her own reconstitution through her report of Antony. As critics often note, Enobarbus's ekphrastic description of Cleopatra's appearance on Cydnus (2.2.200–14, 2.2.216–28) is notable for the absence of Cleopatra herself. Using hyperbole, metaphor and simile, Enobarbus describes not Cleopatra's physical appearance but her barge, her eunuchs and attendants in a manner that attests to her powers of seduction: the oars of her barge, for instance, make the water of Cydnus 'follow faster, / As amorous of their strokes' (206–7); the winds are 'love-sick' with her perfumed sails (204); and the 'pretty dimpled boys' are 'smiling Cupids' (212) or her instruments of allurement.[65] Cleopatra, Enobarbus claims, 'beggar[s] all description' (208) and thus exceeds any attempt to contain her within report. What Enobarbus transmits to Maecenas and Agrippa instead is the perlocutionary effect produced by her presence on him as he lures his auditors into imaginatively picturing Cleopatra through the seductive rhetoric of his report. Attempting to describe a Cleopatra that 'O'erpictur[es] that Venus where we see / The fancy outwork nature' (2.2.210–11), Enobarbus's report of Cleopatra's greatness rebounds back to flatter the reporter, who imaginatively conveys and commemorates Cleopatra's greatness in his report.

Like Enobarbus, Cleopatra lures Dolabella into imaginatively witnessing the mythical presence of an absent Antony through a description that is self-flattering and self-referential, even as she suggests that his magnanimity exceeds the very possibility of describing him. Cleopatra demonstrates her ability to imaginatively depict a supreme Antony who 'over-pictures' nature: 'Nature wants stuff / To vie strange forms with fancy'

(5.2.96–7). However, she also claims that her depiction of Antony is not just imaginative but brings him to life or makes him a part of the natural realm: 'yet t'imagine / An Antony were nature's piece 'gainst fancy, / Condemning shadows quite' (5.2.97–9). In equating herself with nature while also paradoxically suggesting that she exceeds nature in giving imaginative birth to a 'real' Antony that outdoes her very ability to imagine an even more superior Antony, Cleopatra discreetly turns her tribute to him into an encomium of her life-giving capacity and unfettered verbal performativity. Her report, in other words, has the illocutionary force to make illusions real. In claiming that her performative language allows her to condemn 'shadows', Cleopatra underlines her linguistic superiority in (re)creating Antony's, as well as her own, identity, instead of merely imitating or following a script as stage actors (or 'shadows') are wont to do. The metadramatic reference to actors as 'shadows' attunes the offstage audience to the boy actor playing Cleopatra, whose self-praise underwrites that of the queen. The boy praises himself as an exquisite actor who can 'naturally' bring forth an Antony that exceeds ('condemns') other actors ('shadows') in their capacity to perform Antony's greatness on stage; the boy actor, in a self-congratulatory manner, claims that his performative skill overshadows that of other adult actors. Cleopatra's dream-vision report successfully achieves its intended perlocutionary effect as Dolabella acknowledges her greatness and is moved to sympathize with her great loss of a great Antony: 'Your loss is as yourself, great, and you bear it / As answering to the weight' (5.2.100–1). Having verbally emasculated Dolabella by cutting off his speech and his ability to do anything with his words – witness lines 78, 80 and 91 – Cleopatra successfully transforms Dolabella from a Roman reporter and Caesar's agent into her loyal attendant who reveals Caesar's plans to her (5.2.106–9).[66] He effectively becomes a member of her onstage audience.

While Enobarbus's report succeeds in mythologizing Cleopatra but fails at 'crafting a social performance that will elevate his own status', to borrow Linda Charnes's words, Cleopatra's dream-vision report both mythologizes Antony and succeeds in delivering a powerful social performance where she is both reporter-actor and spectator of her own show.[67] If Enobarbus needs Cleopatra to ennoble himself through verbal performance, Cleopatra needs Antony for the same reason. In recomposing a mythical and heroic Antony in an Egyptian manner that fulfils his desire to display his reputed greatness to the Romans, Cleopatra makes herself out to be greater than the Antony she reports in giving performative 'birth' to him. In performing her scripted role as an Egyptian lover whose flattering tribute to her beloved registers the degree of her love for him, Cleopatra exceeds this role by showing herself to be greater than it: she implies her own magnanimity as reporter. In a play world where 'the nature of the [] news infects the teller' (1.2.101) and where a reporter is coloured by the content of his or her report (1.5.37–9), Cleopatra's dream-vision report rebounds back to flatter her as the charismatic and heroic subject of her speech. Juxtaposed against Enobarbus's barge-scene report, Cleopatra's dream-vision report allows her to assert affective power over the Romans in order to countervail their power over her under the pretext of praising Antony. Cleopatra's pragmatic use of Antony in her speech becomes a powerful phallic weapon in her verbal war against Caesar.

Under the pretext of respectfully paying homage to Caesar and acknowledging his superiority, the words that Cleopatra commands to be reported to him instantiate her pride and self-glorification as an Egyptian monarch as she challenges his power. In keeping with her personal philosophy that news should flatter the hearer rather than report the 'honest' truth (2.5.85), Cleopatra's encomium of Caesar is accompanied by a rhetoric of submission that is consistent with her performance of a submissive and loyal Roman subject. Following her defeat at Actium, Cleopatra uses deference to flatter Caesar and to sue for political favour, as the Roman ambassador reports to him: 'Cleopatra does confess thy greatness, / Submits her to thy might, and of thee craves / The circle of the Ptolemies for her heirs' (3.12.16–18). As suggested by the verbs 'confess', 'submit' and 'crave', Cleopatra's obedience to Caesar registers her acknowledgement of his greatness. However, in her conference with Thidias who is sent by Caesar to 'win' (3.12.27) Cleopatra from Antony through manipulative rhetoric (3.12.26–9), Cleopatra overturns her obsequiousness and asserts her superiority through a pun. She commands Thidias to

> Say to great Caesar this in deputation:
> I kiss his conqu'ring hand. Tell him I am prompt
> To lay my crown at's feet, and there to kneel
> Till from his all-obeying breath I hear
> The doom of Egypt.
>
> (3.13.77–82)

The pun on 'crown', signifying diadem but also head, undermines Cleopatra's proclaimed submission and turns her obsequiousness into a challenge intended to obstruct Caesar's quest for absolute domination. Insinuating that she will fully obey Caesar only when she is decapitated and her 'crown' lies at his feet, the pun reveals that Cleopatra's death – her anticipated suicide – is a precondition for her subservience. Masquerading as powerless obedience, Cleopatra's speech offers a powerful challenge to Caesar's own obsequiousness, as reported by Thidias to her ('For he partly begs / To be desired to give. It much would please him / That of his fortunes you should make a staff' [3.13.70–2]). Cleopatra snidely shows Caesar that she is capable of playing his game through the performative use of language in her report. Moreover, in response to Proculeius's request that Cleopatra flatter Caesar by allowing him to report her 'sweet dependency' (5.2.26) on Caesar to him, Cleopatra prays Proculeius to 'tell [Caesar] / I am his fortune's vassal and I send him / The greatness he has got' (5.2.28–30). Even as she foregrounds her humble submission and accepts her fate at his hands, Cleopatra coyly hints that she is the agent of Caesar's greatness. She not only 'sends' or pays homage to Caesar's greatness as his subject, but also equivocates on 'send' to imply that *she* grants Caesar his greatness by giving him Egypt. If Antony is a heroic warrior of colossal proportions thanks to Cleopatra, then Caesar is also a great ruler thanks to the great Cleopatra who has bestowed her own greatness upon him. In 'sending' Caesar her greatness, Cleopatra glorifies herself as the origin or agent of his greatness while embracing her vassalage. By 'wording' Caesar who 'words' her to 'not / Be noble to [her]self' (5.2.190–1) in an endless game of one-upmanship, Cleopatra transforms her political powerlessness into power in order to challenge Caesar's might.

Cleopatra not only resists containment in Roman report but also resists being appropriated on the Roman political stage and subjected to voyeurism. Learning of Caesar's victory parade, which would showcase her captivity as well as Caesar's political power and his 'nobleness well acted' (5.2.43), Cleopatra imaginatively reports how an actor would impersonate her and her female attendants on the Roman stage:

> Saucy lictors
> Will catch at us like strumpets, and scald rhymers
> Ballad us out o'tune. The quick comedians
> Extemporally will stage us and present
> Our Alexandrian revels; Antony
> Shall be brought drunken forth; and I shall see
> Some squeaking Cleopatra boy my greatness
> I'th' posture of a whore.
>
> (5.2.213–19)

Cleopatra foresees that she would be reduced to her scripted role as prostitute and thus subjected to scorn and ridicule, while Antony would be reduced from a noble and heroic soldier to a hedonistic Egyptian. The meta-dramatic irony attending Cleopatra's imaginative report, however, illustrates that Cleopatra already is a 'squeaking Cleopatra':

she is impersonated by a boy actor who 'squeaks' because his voice has not yet broken. Cleopatra's sexual greatness, in other words, is already 'boyed': she is, always and already, a theatrical representation whose illusory ontology is informed and largely produced by the boy actor playing her. Anticipating the ineptitude of 'Roman' actors who would caricature the Egyptian queen with their parodic impersonations, the boy actor draws attention to his skilful portrayal of Cleopatra and implies the superiority of his own acting abilities; he praises his own performative greatness in bringing to life a mimetic representation of the Egyptian queen on stage. Anterior to the boy actor, however, is the playwright who speaks through the boy-as-Cleopatra to foreground the superiority of his own dramatic creation to his audience. Even though he has already appropriated Cleopatra and entrapped her as the subject of his play, Shakespeare underscores that he has not 'boyed' or reduced her to the Roman strumpet of historical report. Instead, just as the boy discreetly praises his acting skills, Shakespeare draws attention to the superiority of the theatre but also to his dramatic skills, which facilitate a dialogical interplay of voices that underwrite Cleopatra's greatness. The playwright, like the actor and the character, praises his own theatrical art as he 'reports' or reveals to his offstage audience how he re-mythologizes the Egyptian monarch. Like Cleopatra herself, Shakespeare is a masterful reporter who adopts, challenges and re-scripts authoritarian Roman narrative to publicize his work in a dramatic medium that affectively moves his audience and invites them to participate in (re)constructing a mighty and glorious queen.

The final act of the play presents a politically astute monarch whose verbal and visual self-ennoblement successfully transform her into a praiseworthy object of report. In imagining an Antony who beckons her and commends her imminent suicide, Cleopatra achieves the public recognition she had so passionately sought as she is praised by an Antony on whom she had conferred heroic greatness:

> Methinks I hear
> Antony call. I see him rouse himself
> To praise my noble act. I hear him mock
> The luck of Caesar, which the gods give men
> To excuse their after wrath.
>
> (5.2.282–6)

This official tribute to the Egyptian monarch, imagined and reported by Cleopatra herself, not only validates her intended suicide and conveys her self-satisfaction at the thought that Antony is hers, but also enjoins her onstage and offstage audiences to praise her after Antony's honourable fashion. Responding to Antony's praise with 'Husband, I come!' (5.2.286), a declarative utterance akin to Austin's matrimonial 'I do', Cleopatra's performative speech act instantly turns her into Antony's wife and grants her a new life-in-death as his spouse. In thus proclaiming her marital status and verbally completing the visual family portrait she staged in Alexandria's marketplace as a matriarchal Isis (3.6.1–11), Cleopatra underlines her authoritative sexual power which enables her to not only woo, but also win over, Antony as a husband. This verbal self-ennoblement is complemented by and reified in the act of Roman suicide, which constitutes Cleopatra's final theatrical performance. Exemplifying a 'nobleness in record' (4.14.100), suicide allows Cleopatra to commemoratively fix her sexual power and self-proclaimed greatness as a political figure and to show herself 'like a queen' (5.2.226) instead of as a spouse or a promiscuous lover. In declaring 'I am again for Cydnus / To meet Mark Antony' (5.2.227–8), Cleopatra stages her sexual power to seduce Antony as a means of affectively overpowering and verbally emasculating the Romans-as-reporters by turning them into awe-filled spectators who cannot 'boy' her greatness in report.[68] Her suicide is the final opportunity for Cleopatra to control her audience's response.

The juxtaposition of Caesar's report against the spectacle of Cleopatra's sexual charisma only further heightens Cleopatra's greatness as a character. Adamantly striving to diminish Cleopatra's glory, Caesar indirectly reports to his fellow Romans her physician's words in an attempt to belittle Cleopatra by re-scripting her nobility as cowardice: 'for her physician tells me / She hath pursued conclusions infinite / Of easy ways to die' (5.2.353–5). Caesar thus depicts Cleopatra as a weak and irresolute woman whose flight from pain impels her to find release in death. His de-mythologizing of Cleopatra is further evidenced in his attempt to strip her of her power by romanticizing Cleopatra and Antony exclusively as lovers. In publicly proclaiming that Cleopatra 'shall be buried by her Antony / No grave upon the earth shall clip in it / A pair so famous' (5.2.353–5), Caesar delimits Cleopatra as a smitten woman and implies that her suicide is motivated by her undying love for Antony rather than by any political cause. By doing so, Caesar is able to gloriously publicize himself as a magnanimous ruler who, in a self-congratulatory manner, demonstrates a greatness of heart which compels him to honour the deviant lovers:

> High events as these
> Strike those that make them, and their story is
> No less in pity than his glory which
> Brought them to be lamented.
>
> (5.2.359–62)

Although Caesar promotes himself as a noble-hearted reporter who has the affective power to beget his audience's lament, his report is diminished by Cleopatra's spectacle of a powerful sovereignty premised on a seductive Egyptian sexuality. Cleopatra's Egyptian performance of Roman suicide trumps Caesar's report. Both her onstage and offstage audiences witness the superiority of Cleopatra's reportage, which seamlessly ties her verbal performance together with a theatrical performance that allows her to transcend the reductive parameters of Roman report and make her infinitely greater than Caesar. While Caesar may have the last word, Cleopatra upstages him.

Cleopatra's instances of reportage in *Antony and Cleopatra* reveal a diplomatic female monarch who uses her sexual power to offset the total loss of an already politically compromised identity. In a play-world where she is reported as a 'gipsy[]' (1.1.9), 'strumpet[]' (1.1.13), 'slave' (1.4.19) and 'whore' (3.6.68) by the Romans, Cleopatra's adoption of Roman report allows her to re-script herself in an Egyptian context while 'seem[ing] the fool [she is] not' (1.1.44). In reporting Caesar's and Antony's speech as well as her dream-vision report of Antony, and in having her own behaviour and speech reported to them, Cleopatra praises herself and glorifies her sexuality to counteract the political power she does not possess while performing her Roman-scripted role as a submissive, weak and inconstant Egyptian paramour. Under the guise of adhering to Roman authority as a Roman subject, the wily Egyptian turns her powerless subordination into a powerful sexual dominance over the Romans while using the affective power of report to urge her audience to memorialize her sexual greatness, even though her idiosyncratic sexuality is an effect of Rome's imperial domination. Cleopatra's pragmatic use of report intersects with meta-dramatic moments in the play that call attention to the boy actor's performance of female sexual greatness. His performance valorizes Cleopatra's sexuality and invites the offstage audience to posit an anteriority to the character that makes it seem as if Cleopatra exceeds the denigrated sexual role scripted for her by Rome. Cleopatra's strategic manoeuvring in report allows her to straddle both Egypt and Rome as she re-scripts her Roman identity in an Egyptian context and theatrical medium that invite her audiences to (re)construct a mighty and glorious monarch on stage. If the geographical extent and political mightiness of the Roman Empire are made present through continual acts of reportage, then the transcendent greatness of Cleopatra as a character is similarly generated through her acts of reportage which demonstrate a female sovereign who is expansive in her variety and able to contain others in her linguistic performances instead of being contained by them.

3

Pragma-Rhetoric and Henry V's Moral Ambivalence

In the opening scenes of *Henry V*, the audience witnesses a virtuous Christian monarch who appeals to his holy council for advice. Henry, urging the Archbishop of Canterbury to explain whether a war against France would be legally justified, warns the Archbishop of the sinfulness of an illegal and immoral war. He then promises him that 'we will hear, note, and believe in heart / That what you speak is in your conscience washed / As pure as sin with baptism' (1.2.30–2).[1] The disconcerting simile 'as pure as sin', however, seems to undo his Christian image and throws a suspicious light on Henry's intentions. The comparison, violently yoking together sinfulness and purity, is a paradox that gestures towards Henry's possible hypocrisy as a monarch.

Ever since Gerald Gould challenged the univocally patriotic interpretations of *Henry V* by revealing the dramatic ironies in the play that expose Henry's hypocrisy, twentieth-century critical responses to the play's monarch have been largely polarized: critics have either celebrated Henry as a virtuous Christian monarch whose glorious deeds are performed in service to the English commonweal or they have touted Henry as a conniving and self-interested Machiavel whose seemingly virtuous façade belies his ambition for power and political self-aggrandizement.[2] Striving to transcend these bifurcated critical responses, Norman Rabkin proposed that the play 'dar[es]' its readers 'to choose one of the two opposed interpretations' of Henry even as it demonstrates the coexistence – albeit the impossible simultaneity – of these antithetical interpretations.[3] Henry, as Rabkin claimed, is an ambiguous 'rabbit-duck' who leaves audiences and readers in a limbo of uncertainty by asking them to hold in equilibrium Henry's seemingly incompatible qualities of Christian king and Machiavellian politician. The audience's ability to see a rabbit or a duck, Rabkin notes, is contingent on whether they interpret the play as an extension of *1 Henry IV* or of *2 Henry IV*. While Rabkin accounts for the ambiguous impression made by Henry on the audience, he attributes this effect to the conflict between Henry's 'private' self and his 'public' role as king. In asserting that Henry trades his idiosyncratic 'inwardness for the sake of power', Rabkin appeals to an anachronistic notion of a character as a psychologically real person with interiority and falls into the predicament symptomatic of Bradleyan critics.[4] Henry's sincerity, however, is not at issue in the play. Given that Henry is a polyvocal 'chameleon linguist' who 'reflects in his speech not himself, but the expectations of those to whom he speaks', as P. K. Ayers has aptly noted, it is more relevant to the debate about his indeterminacy as a character to examine Henry's use of rhetoric and what he does with it.[5]

New Historicist critics and their heirs, however, have disregarded Henry's rhetorical performances and his linguistic agency. By displacing the question of Henry's moral ambivalence onto issues of power and ideology in the play, these critics made Henry the impersonal mouthpiece for a dominant English language that contains the subversion instigated by the multiple dialects and linguistic groups in the play: Paola Pugliatti, framing her argument in terms of Bakhtinian dialogism, claimed that Henry 'submit[s], disfigur[es], or turn[s] ... into some form of "English"' the polyphony of those voices or 'strange tongues' in the play that offer a subversive 'form of resistance to cultural integration', while critics like Michael Neill, who concentrate on the play's construction of English nationhood, similarly deemed Henry's speech to be synonymous with a conquering English tongue that domesticates and appropriates the 'other' languages in the play which challenge its hegemonic power.[6] Although a few critics like Stephen Greenblatt and Claire McEachern have attended to Henry's rhetoric, they have nevertheless denied the self-referentiality of his speech: Greenblatt deemed that Prince Hal's imitation of his subjects' speech in *1 Henry IV* is emblematic of the monarch's power to contain subversive elements within his kingdom, while McEachern observed that Henry's St Crispin's Day speech, which expresses his simultaneous fantasy of social union and the desire for social hierarchy, instantiates the 'fellowship and hegemony' inhering in the Elizabethan discourse of corporate identity that he personifies as monarch.[7]

While critics have, in the past two decades, refocused their attention on Henry's rhetorical performance of kingship, they have tended to exclude from their analyses the tension inherent to Henry's linguistic manoeuvring and his strategic self-fashioning in discourse.[8] Acknowledging that Henry uses language to instrumentally negotiate his identity as a monarch, critics have failed to recognize that it is this particular use of language – which encodes Henry's struggle with negotiating an identity – that not only succeeds but also fails. Despite the praise that critics have liberally bestowed on Henry as a masterful rhetorician, there has been a dearth of discussion concerning how Henry pragmatically *uses* rhetoric to negotiate his power in discourse: calling Henry a 'communicative king', linguist and literary critic Roger D. Sell explains how the monarch tries to adapt himself to his audience rhetorically but does not address how Henry uses rhetoric to adapt himself to his audience pragmatically; Urszula Kizelbach examines Henry's pragmatic use of (im)politeness strategies to maintain his power as king but does not apply them to Henry as a rhetorician; and David Schalkwyk, foregrounding the persuasive function of Henry's rhetoric, reveals that Henry displaces the illocutionary force of his performative utterances onto performance itself.[9] Schalkwyk argues that, due to his father's usurpation of the Yorkist throne, Henry's 'speech acts of right' become 'mere performance' and it is this 'movement between performative and performance' that accounts for Henry's oscillation between a rabbit and a duck.[10] While Schalkwyk's reading of Henry's verbal displacements may underscore Henry's inability to translate words into deeds and thus signal his failure as a king, it need not necessarily register his failure as a rhetorician or orator.

What these critics overlook is that Henry is not preeminently a king but a skilful public speaker or orator who pragmatically uses persuasive language to construct his ethos as king. Focusing on Henry as an orator, I explore Henry's rhetorical performances through a pragmatic lens to ascertain how Henry's use of language gives rise to his moral indeterminacy as a character. I adopt a pragma-rhetorical approach to Henry's speech in his exchanges with Canterbury, his lords, his soldiers and the French princess Katherine to examine how Henry's overt statements which build his ethos – what J. L. Austin would call his 'constative' use of language – contradict what his words 'do' or his performative use of language.[11] In other words, I examine how Henry's use of rhetoric undercuts the ethos that his constative utterances proclaim he has. I argue that Henry's logos or argumentative use of rhetoric in the Folio[12] inadvertently undermines his ethos as a virtuous Christian monarch and as a plain-speaking, honest soldier which he strives to construct, and thus generates the suspicion of his Machiavellianism. This variance between Henry's logos or logic and his ethos or moral character – two complementary rhetorical appeals – intersects with the dramatic irony framing his encounters with his interlocutors to produce our impression of his moral ambivalence. It is by reading Henry as a consummate orator whose ethos is not pre-discursive but rhetorically constructed through language that we can effectively avoid the ontological quandary stemming from the misguided critical assumption that Henry harbours an inner and *a priori* self. I first discuss Shakespeare's depiction of Henry as an orator in relation to his historical and dramatic sources before explaining the theory of pragma-rhetoric and launching into an analysis of Henry's exchanges with his lords, bishops, soldiers and future wife using this pragma-rhetorical paradigm.

Shakespeare's 'doing': Henry as orator

Shakespeare's emphasis on Henry as an orator can be traced to the divergent portrayals of the monarch and his speech in historical and dramatic sources of the play. In the historical chronicles of Hall and Holinshed, which feature providential interpretations of history, Henry V is depicted as a pious monarch and a just warrior-king who renounces his riotous past to become a virtuous ruler. In Edward Hall's *The Union of the Two Noble and Illustrious Families of Lancaster and York* (1548), the morally reformed Henry is heralded as an 'Arabicall Phenix'.[13] Hall lauds Henry's desire to 'shewe hymself a synguler mirror and manifest example of moral vertues and good qualities to his comen people and louing subiectes' by submitting to the tutelage of his counsellors and becoming a scholar; Henry engages in 'daily study' and does not 'delight in wor[l]dly pleasures'.[14] In his *Chronicles of England, Scotland, and Ireland* (1587), Raphael Holinshed similarly praises Henry for his wisdom and virtue but also commends his military prowess. Holinshed portrays Henry as the paragon of a warrior who is 'of courage inuincible, of purpose vnmutable; so wisehardie alwaies, as feare was banist from him' but a warrior, no less, who is also a just leader: 'a capteine against whome fortune neuer frowned, nor mischance once spurned; whose people him so seuere a iusticer both loued and obeied, (and so humane withall)'.[15] Henry's speech reflects his idealized portrayal as a soldier and pious king with *gravitas*, and is an expression of his spiritual devoutness: 'Eloquent and graue was his speech, and of great grace and power to persuade'.[16]

By contrast, the anonymous play *The Famous Victories of Henry the Fifth* (c. 1598) interrogates the historically idealized portrait of Henry by representing an impetuous and stubbornly ambitious monarch whose self-interest usurps the virtue he is purported to have. While the dramatization of Henry's reformation in *The Famous Victories* is meant to highlight Henry's accomplishments as a warrior and a king, the play nevertheless reveals Henry in a less flattering light as an arrogant aggressor. Despite the fact that Henry changes from a dissolute and lewd rascal who disrespects authority in the first half of the play to a sedate and obedient king who takes his role and responsibilities seriously in the second half of the play, he retains his peremptoriness and haughty manner. His callous indifference to and disregard for others carries over into his role as king; both before and after he is crowned king, Henry's speech reveals a peremptoriness that accompanies his undeterred ambition to achieve his goals. Young Henry's aggressive command to his father's servant that he 'go and tell my father that I must, and will, speak with him' (5.67–8), for instance, resurfaces in his unabashedly authoritarian retort to the French king that he will take the throne: 'Thus I have set it down, and thus it shall be!' (18.21–2).[17] Even Henry's aside quickly transitions from a sentimental longing for Catherine to an ambitious resoluteness to possess her: 'Ay, but I love her, and must crave her – / Nay, I love her, and will have her!' (18.47–8). But while the plethora of modal verbs in Henry's speech certainly conveys his aggressive determination and supercilious manner of speaking, this rather critical view of Henry rests on the audience's ability to sympathize with the scenes of low comedy in the play, which expose monarchy's 'corruption, egocentricity, and militaristic monomania' as Larry S. Champion describes, and alternate with the high scenes of history that glorify the monarchy and laud Henry's aggressive determination as warrior-king.[18] Those who endorse a critical view of the monarch would question the sincerity of his reformation. As Champion claims, the episodic structure of *The Famous Victories* offers the audience an ambivalent perspective on Henry as a representative of the monarchy: 'Hal, from one perspective the mirror of Christian kings, is from another an impetuous upstart reflecting the worst of aristocratic disdain for his common subjects.'[19] Despite the play's episodic structure, which promotes a dialectical view of history and of the monarch himself, Henry's speech in *The Famous Victories* nevertheless bears the mark of violence springing from personal initiative and political and military prowess. It is by foregrounding this violence that the anonymous playwright interrogates the providential view of history.

Shakespeare combines the 'grace' and graceful eloquence of Henry's speech noted by Holinshed with the communicative intentionality suggested by Henry's aggressive use of modals in *The Famous Victories* to re-script Henry as an orator whose speech becomes the locus of his moral complexity. As orator, Henry has the power not only to persuasively affect his audience but also to perform verbal actions. Shakespeare makes Henry's language a site where the spiritual virtues of a Christian king converge with the personal audacity and political expediency animating this public role.

Reviving Aristotle: Rhetoric as pragma-rhetoric

While classical rhetoric has traditionally been conceived of as a mode of persuasion, contemporary philosophical theories of rhetoric employ pragmatics to re-conceptualize rhetoric as a cognitive art of interpretation grounded in inference.[20] In the 1950s, language philosophers Chaïm Perelman and Lucie Olbrechts-Tyteca revived Aristotle's notion of rhetoric as 'a practical discipline that aims ... at exerting through speech a *persuasive action* on an audience'; the orator or speaker, they claim, seeks not only to persuade but also to convey an argument.[21] Resuscitating Aristotle's notion of rhetoric as the counterpart or *antistrophos* to dialectic (i.e. logic), neo-Aristotelians Perelman and Olbrechts-Tyteca abandoned the reductive, Ramist conception of rhetoric as an ornamental 'art of expression' or 'style' to reconceive rhetoric as a theory of argumentation.[22] Their so-called 'New Rhetoric' is predicated on discursive logic or argumentation rather than on deduction and abstraction which characterize formal logic. Formal logic involves extracting a hypothesis already present in the premise(s) and formulating a conclusion that has general truth value. Discursive logic, however, presents an argument whose truth value is subjective since it is contingent on the audience's belief or interpretation.[23] Argumentation, as 'the domain of ... the credible, the plausible, the probable', is dialogic: it rests on the interaction between the orator (speaker) who seeks to persuade and the audience (hearer) who is disposed to listen, with the aim of 'obtaining or reinforcing the adherence of the audience to ... [the orator's] thesis'.[24] Audience-oriented for the purpose of achieving 'adherence' – and ultimate assent – to the orator's thesis, argumentation relies on the orator's discursive use of rhetoric to both induce this adherence and respond to the audience's psychological expectations, exigencies and desires; rhetorical tropes and schemes, situated as they are beyond the realm of demonstrable proof, hence involve inference on the audience's part. For Perelman and Olbrechts-Tyteca, the success of the orator's argumentation thus rests neither on the argument's deductive or inductive correctness nor on an abstract standard of truth in accordance with which the truth or falsity of the thesis may be judged, but on the argument's rhetorical effectiveness – in pragmatic terms, its perlocutionary effect – as measured by the degree of the audience's adherence to the thesis. The speaker's rhetorical persuasiveness, then, is contingent on a flawless deployment of discursive logic which undergirds his use of tropes and schemes and serves to compel the audience to believe his thesis. Embedded within a dialogic network of speakers and hearers, Perelman and Olbrechts-Tyteca's 'New Rhetoric' is a cognitive theory of rhetoric in which tropes and schemes have argumentative-persuasive force instead of a merely expressive function.[25]

Nevertheless, the assumption underlying Perelman and Olbrechts-Tyteca's rhetorical theory of argumentation is that the orator's intention to persuade his audience necessarily coheres with his intention to communicate his argument, through discursive logic, to his audience. As language philosophers Jésus Larrazabal and Kepa Korta have pointed out, even though persuasive and communicative intentions may be 'distinguish[ed] and combin[ed]' in persuasive discourse, they coexist on different levels: while the intention to communicate is overt, the intention to persuade tends to be covert.[26] Proposing a 'pragma-rhetorical' approach to persuasive discourse, Larrazabal and Korta build on the work of Marcelo Dascal and Alan Gross. Dascal and Gross, fusing Gricean pragmatics with Aristotelian rhetoric, agree with Perelman and Olbrechts-Tyteca that persuasion is 'a kind of communicative interaction' premised on the audience's ability to infer the intent behind the speaker's utterances.[27] However, they extend Perelman and Olbrechts-Tyteca's theory by assessing not only the speaker's performative action but also the hearer's ability to grasp the meaning behind the speaker's utterance as well as the perlocutionary effect of the utterance on the hearer's actions or beliefs.[28] While Dascal and Gross agree that effective persuasion is premised on the audience's ability to correctly infer the speaker's intention, they also recognize the 'possibility of misdirection and deception' in persuasive discourse.[29] Whereas successful communication is premised on the hearer's recognition of the speaker's intention, persuasion 'may depend on the [hearer's] *lack* of recognition' of the speaker's intent to deceive.[30] As an example of the possible incongruence between a speaker's covert and overt intentions, Dascal and Gross cite Searle's Second World War scenario of a British soldier held hostage by an Italian. The British soldier, whose goal is to be released, speaks to his Italian interrogator (hearer) in German to persuade him that he is German 'by means of [the hearer's] *not* understanding [the speaker's] intention to do so'; in doing so, the British soldier induces 'a false belief as to his true intention' in order to gain his freedom.[31] The interrogator's belief that the British soldier is German rests on his recognition of the soldier's overt intention to communicate his nationality to him, even though he remains oblivious to the soldier's covert intention to deceive him.

Although I adopt the 'pragma-rhetorical' method propounded by Perelman and Olbrechts-Tyteca and coined by Larrazabal and Korta, I do not interpret Henry in light of Dascal and Gross's overt and covert intentions, for to do so would be to posit that Henry's Machiavellianism secretly motivates his speech and constitutes his inner core as a character. The stock character of the Machiavel, a manipulative schemer with self-serving goals, employs realpolitik *virtù* – commonly glossed as prowess, martial strength or ruthlessness – to achieve and maintain power.[32] Henry, however, is not the innately evil or ruthless deceiver that Richard III or even Iago are. While Henry's intention to persuade his audience of his ethos as a Christian monarch is certainly overt, his proclivity to rhetorically perform an ethos he does not yet possess in order to legitimate his actions is what gives rise to our belief in his Machiavellian nature. Henry's Machiavellianism, as I will demonstrate, is an effect of his verbal behaviour in tandem with the dramatic irony evoked by the juxtaposition of scenes in the play. The pragma-rhetorical conception of rhetoric I adopt is congenial to Shakespeare's own understanding of rhetoric as a persuasive art that is, broadly construed, a performative discourse informed by and inhering in the argumentation structuring the pedagogical exercise of *disputatio in utramque partem*, which enables speakers to rhetorically construct and logically convey verbal actions.[33]

Rhetorical ethos and its discontents

As an orator who seeks to persuade his audience, Henry consummately employs Aristotle's three rhetorical appeals in his speech: ethos (moral character), pathos (emotion) and logos (logic or rational argumentation). Ethos, which for Aristotle denotes the orator's personal character or his moral and intellectual qualities, is established discursively without recourse to the orator's past actions or behaviour; the orator's speech does not reveal character but instead rhetorically constructs an image of character.[34] Although the Aristotelian orator should *appear* to be a good and trustworthy person, he need not necessarily be so; it is only crucial that the orator establishes the impression of trustworthiness and credibility in order to gain the audience's confidence and compel their belief in the truthfulness of his speech.[35] The grounds for establishing the orator's credibility are good moral character or virtue (*arete*), good will (*eunoia*), and good sense or prudence (*phronesis*), which are all intricately intertwined: virtue, according to James Kinneavy and Susan Warshauer, is grounded in the orator's ability to 'gauge society's values', such as 'courage, justice, temperance', and 'display them' in his speech; good will rests on the speaker's ability to relate to his audience by exhibiting and affirming the prejudices, values, aspirations and emotions he shares with them which thus bespeaks his 'good intentions toward his ... audience'; and prudence, or 'moral knowledge, a knowledge of right action', is the ability to deliberate and 'make practical decisions', which is buttressed by the speaker's moral character that directs his practical thinking to select an appropriate means 'to achieve an [appropriate] end'.[36] These three modes of ethical appeal can be produced either directly through statements or anecdotes, or indirectly though pathos, logical proofs or even style.[37] While ethos differs from speech-oriented logos and audience-oriented pathos in being exclusively focused on the speaker, it nevertheless relies on both logos and pathos for its persuasive force.[38] Ethos and logos in particular, as Eugene Garver notes, share an inextricable bond. If ethos is, for Aristotle, the most powerful mode of appeal, then logos – typically manifested by an *enthymeme* or a truncated syllogism[39] – is 'the primary evidence for [being persuaded by] the speech's *ēthos*' for 'if the enthymeme is the body of proof, *ēthos* is its soul'.[40] Not only must the orator's ethos be consistent with logos but it must also be consistently presented and upheld in the orator's speech in order to maintain his image. However, Henry's ethos as a Christian monarch, as we will see, is notably inconsistent since it is constantly destabilized by his deviant logos which neither reinforces nor complements the ethos he presents.[41]

In the opening scene with Ely and Canterbury, Henry discursively presents himself as a pious, peace-loving and honest Christian king who abides by Christian principles. However, his ethos is undercut by his performative use of modal verbs which reveal a mode of reasoning that is dissonant with his assumed Christian virtue; the modal verbs communicate Henry's intent to wage war against France under the pretext of persuading Canterbury and Ely of his virtuous disdain for the same. Henry establishes his ethos directly in his opening monologue. In soliciting the advice of his 'learned' (1.2.9) and religious counsellors before making a decision about war, Henry exhibits his *phronesis* as he invokes God in his warning to Canterbury that the latter speak the 'truth' in 'justly and religiously' (1.2.10) unfolding the reasoning behind the Salic Law so as to prevent the outbreak of war:

> And God forbid, my dear and faithful lord,
> That you should fashion, wrest or bow your reading
> Or nicely charge your understanding soul
> With opening titles miscreate, whose right
> Suits not in native colours with the truth.
> For God doth know how many now in health
> Shall drop their blood in approbation
> Of what your reverence shall incite us to.

Therefore take heed how you impawn our person,
How you awake our sleeping sword of war:
We charge you in the name of God take heed.
For never two such kingdoms did contend
Without much fall of blood, whose guiltless drops
Are every one a woe, a sore complaint
'Gainst him whose wrongs gives edge unto the swords
That makes such waste in brief mortality.
Under this conjuration speak, my lord,
For we will hear, note, and believe in heart
That what you speak is in your conscience washed
As pure as sin with baptism.

(1.2.13–32)

In calling for an ethical and Neoplatonic correspondence between word (*verba*) and thing (*res*) or between 'right' (16) and 'truth' (17), Henry implies his allegiance and obedience to a higher moral authority, which accentuates his *arete* or virtue; a legal right to the French crown should correspond to a moral right.[42] In further warning Canterbury not to 'awake our sleeping sword of war' (22) and not to make 'such waste in brief mortality' (28) that would spill the 'guiltless drops' (25) of blood of both the English and French forces, Henry foregrounds his peace-loving character, morality and good will as he proclaims the innocence of both the French and the English and recognizes the brevity and sacredness of a life that should tend towards virtuous ends. However, Henry's performative use of modals undermines this carefully constructed ethos by calling into question his very prudence, virtue and good will. Henry's urging Canterbury to tell the truth – a virtuous warning in God's name – immediately segues into his anticipation of a hypothetical war by way of rhetorical *descriptio*: 'For God doth know how many now in health / Shall drop their blood in approbation / Of what your reverence shall incite us to' (1.2.18–20). This brief *descriptio*, notable for the double presence of the modal verb 'shall', eerily colours Henry's virtuous request or warning to Canterbury as a promise of war. Modality, defined as the speaker's attitude towards the content of his utterance, is commonly expressed by verbs such as 'will', 'shall', 'may', 'can' or 'must', which can be either epistemic or deontic. Epistemic modals express the speaker's knowledge, belief or opinion about a proposition, while deontic modals are 'concerned with duty, obligation and permission', as Lynne Magnusson states, and signal what John Lyons calls 'the necessity or possibility of acts performed by morally responsible agents'.[43] In other words, epistemic modality informs while deontic modality is *performative*; the latter bears traces of the speaker's illocutionary intentions.[44] Henry's first modal verb 'shall' (19) is epistemic as well as predictive and suggests his belief that only God will know the consequences of the action that Canterbury will urge; only God will know 'how many' or how few will die and whether Canterbury's urging is just or unjust.[45] However, Henry's second 'shall' in 'Of what your reverence shall incite us to' (20) bears a deontic modality that signifies an obligation or a promise, which indirectly underlines Henry's intention to go to war. According to Leslie K. Arnovick, the Wallis Rules, formulated by Bishop John Wallis in 1653 to teach native English speakers the proper usage of 'will' and 'shall' in future tense constructions, encode speaker modality or express 'the speaker's attitude of volition and expectation' in interrogative or declarative sentences.[46] These normative rules indicate that the verb 'will' in the first person and 'shall' in the second and third person (singular and plural) should be used to signify a threat, promise or command. Inversely, 'shall' in the first person and 'will' in the second and third person (singular and plural) should be used to signify prediction or expectation. Instead of using the predictive 'will' as his second modal verb, as prescribed by the Wallis Rules, Henry uses the deontic 'shall', which suggests that he is either *promising* Canterbury that the latter's counsel will be staunchly adhered to and that his countrymen will be obliged to 'drop their blood' in war, or obliquely *commanding* Canterbury to urge war as he unfolds the prohibitive measures of the Salic Law. Henry thus gives his word to Canterbury that war will occur as a necessary consequence of what Canterbury commands, under the pretext of warning or asking Canterbury that war be avoided at all costs through the *descriptio* overseen by God. The ambiguity or 'double register of meanings' that modal verbs invite, as Lynne Magnusson has illustrated, is exploited by characters who engage in 'modal punning', which requires audiences to participate in inferring the pragmatic import of their speech.[47] Regardless of whether Henry's second 'shall' (20) is read as a promise or a command, the indeterminacy of his modal verbs suggests that he has already made his decision to invade France, despite the counsel he is about to receive from Canterbury.

The suspicion of Henry's Machiavellianism elicited by the deontic 'shall' is heightened by the dramatic irony framing the scene to suggest that war is a foregone conclusion. In the opening scene of the play, the conversation between the devious Ely and Canterbury indicates that Henry has accepted the bishops' bribe to not pass a parliamentary bill in exchange for their financial support for his war (1.1.73–81). The possibility of Henry's complicity with the clergy not only renders his sudden 'reformation' (1.1.33) questionable and Canterbury's claim that he is a 'true lover of the holy Church' (1.1.23) ironic, but also makes Henry's anti-war rhetoric in his speech to Canterbury seem like a deceptive form of public display used for the purpose of promoting his Christian ethos. The dramatic irony may easily bring to the audience's mind the Machiavellian principles embraced by Henry's father, who advises his son in 2 *Henry IV* 'to busy giddy minds / With foreign quarrels, that action hence borne out / May waste the memory of the former days' (4.5.213–15).[48] Juxtaposed against Canterbury's revelations in the opening scene, Henry's deontic 'shall' thus invites the audience to infer that Henry's logical reasoning is self-serving as he relegates the responsibility for war onto Canterbury in order to absolve himself of guilt and justify his inadvertently revealed goal to invade France.[49] The unchristian logic underpinning Henry's pragmatic use of modals, framed as it is by Henry's possible complicity with the bishops, undermines the virtue, prudence and good will that serve as pillars of his ethos and throws a Machiavellian shadow over this ethos by showing that Henry's intent to persuade his men against war belies his decision to wage war.

In a similar vein, the modal verb 'will', which signals Henry's promise to Canterbury that 'we will hear, note, and believe in heart / That what you speak is in your conscience washed / As pure as sin with baptism' (1.2.30–2), works with the analogy it introduces ('As pure as sin with baptism') to persuade Henry's auditors of his ethos even as the modal and the analogy fracture this ethos by implying Henry's political praxis.[50] Although Henry uses the modal 'will' in accordance with the Wallis Rules to make a promise to Canterbury, the promise nevertheless fails to be a true promise because it fails to fulfil the 'preparatory' condition formulated by Searle. Searle identifies four conditions that must be fulfilled in order for a promise to be 'felicitous' or to qualify as a true promise: the propositional condition (in uttering the promise, the speaker predicates his or her future action), the preparatory condition (the hearer prefers, and the speaker believes that the hearer prefers, that the speaker carries out this promise, plus the promise is uttered only if it is not obvious that the speaker will carry out his or her action), the sincerity condition (the promise is uttered if the speaker fully intends to carry out the future action), and the essential condition (in uttering the promise, the speaker puts himself or herself under the obligation of carrying out the future action). Henry's promise, however, violates Searle's preparatory condition, which requires that the hearer wishes or *'prefer[s] [the speaker's] doing A to his not doing A*' (and the speaker is aware of this wish), and that the promise be made only if it is 'not obvious to both [the speaker] and [the hearer] that [the speaker] will do A in the normal course of events'.[51] It is clearly not the case that Canterbury would prefer Henry to 'believe in heart' Canterbury's pronouncement since the war with France, as the opening scene suggests (1.1.73–81), is inevitable and Canterbury has nothing to gain from this impending pronouncement. Moreover, given that Henry is the devout and prudent Christian king he claims to be, it would be obvious to both Henry and Canterbury that Henry will do 'A' (wisely heed the Archbishop's counsel) 'in the normal course of events' without the need of making explicit his intention to do so. Henry's promise comes across as superfluous and unnecessary. Rather than serve to assure Canterbury that he will heed his counsel, Henry's 'promise' instead serves to flatter Canterbury by paying homage to his greatness for the purpose of indirectly buoying up Henry's humility and *eunoia* (good will).

The analogy coupled with this 'promise' demolishes Henry's image of piety and beneficence even as it is intended to shore it up, since the ambiguity of the analogy constitutes a verbal fallacy that detracts from its argumentative weight.[52] Ambiguity is a verbal fallacy denoting the improper use of words.[53] Although 'as pure as sin with baptism' refers to the sacrament of baptism – which is a nod towards Henry's virtue and religiousness as it indicates Henry's obligation to or recognition of Canterbury's ethos, to which he appeals as a precondition for acting on Canterbury's word – it misfires. Henry affirms that he will believe that Canterbury's speech is a sober and direct reflection of his innermost thoughts, which are subservient to his conscience, and that these thoughts are cleansed ('baptised') by the dictates of moral wisdom. However, the contradiction in the comparison 'in your conscience washed / as pure as sin with baptism' gives rise to a deviant meaning to suggest that Henry may be urging Canterbury to make the case for a sinful war that Henry, as Canterbury's 'conscience', promises to authorize ('baptise'); untruthful speech may *become* 'good', Henry seems to suggest, when justified and overseen by 'conscience' (Henry himself). These discrepant meanings play off of the bifurcated connotations of conscience. As Camille Wells Slights reveals, conscience in Shakespeare's history plays is a locus where 'internal self-awareness and external political action, the obligations of obedience and the authority of personal judgment converge'.[54] Thus, although Henry promises Canterbury that he will believe the matter of his speech since the Archbishop obeys a transcendent moral authority (God) that is incarnated in his personal conscience, Henry may also be insinuating that Canterbury should follow the dictates of a personal judgement that owes allegiance to Henry, rather than to God, as the supreme ruler and 'conscience' of the commonweal. The ambiguous analogy, employed by Henry to persuade his interlocutors of his Christian ethos, is undermined by its argumentative force which substitutes God's authority for Henry's and thus countermands rather than reinforces the persuasive efficacy of Henry's ethos. Serving as a silent behest to Canterbury, Henry's promise strengthens the impression of a Machiavellian deviousness that resembles Ely's and Canterbury's.

Henry's second analogy further undercuts the direct statements with which he builds his ethos to suggest his Machiavellian cruelty and aggression. The sudden appearance of the French ambassador in his court prompts Henry to urge him to divulge the Dauphin's message. Henry uses an analogy that highlights his Christian clemency, temperance and self-restraint so as to persuade the ambassador to deliver his news plainly and frankly (1.2.245) without the fear of incurring Henry's wrath: 'We are no tyrant but a Christian king, / Unto whose grace our passion is as subject / As are our wretches fettered in our prisons' (1.2.242–4). While making his 'passions' subservient to his 'grace' may be virtuous, the vehicle of Henry's analogy ('our wretches fettered in our prisons') underlines the action of a tyrant who is anything but temperate and benign. In comparing his passions to 'wretches' who are fettered in the 'prisons' of his grace, Henry ironically presupposes an equivalence between his subjection of the wretches and his ability to control his passions, but the comparison between 'prison' and 'grace' fails for grace denotes 'favourable or benignant regard or its manifestation ... favour or goodwill' as well as 'pardon or forgiveness'.[55] True grace thus does not 'fetter' but liberates; Henry's illiberal grace, however, contradicts this spiritual conception of grace as divine favour to reveal his equivocation. The illocutionary force of Henry's analogy hence overturns rather than complements Henry's constative statement that he is a merciful and benevolent Christian king by revealing his tyrannous exercise of power to expediently justify a rule that lacks divinely sanctioned authority. This illogical coupling between tenor and vehicle destabilizes Henry's self-proclaimed *eunoia* or good will and undoes his persuasion by accentuating instead his power, to which all must submit if he is to 'win' his right.

The irony of Henry's analogy is further underlined by Canterbury's praise of Henry in the opening scene, which compounds the impression that a Machiavellian undercurrent of force and violence inhere in his character. Commending Henry's political savvy, Canterbury boasts to Ely that Henry is superior to Alexander the Great: 'Turn him to any cause of policy, / The Gordian knot of it he will unloose, / Familiar as his garter' (1.1.45–7). Canterbury's allusion to the Gordian knot may be intended as indirect praise of Henry's virtue and his political skilfulness in undoing the knot that Alexander could not and hence, as Judith Mossman notes, showcase Henry as 'morally superior' to Alexander since the latter resorted to cheating.[56] However, the allusion also inadvertently implies Henry's craftiness and ruthlessness as a ruler by associating him with the proverbially cruel Alexander who, as Janet M. Spencer explains, either violently cuts through the Gordian knot or cunningly removes the shaft around it.[57] The physical violence latent in Canterbury's allusion, which is later reinforced by the vow explicitly made by Henry following the French ambassador's departure that he will either 'bend [France] to our awe / Or break it all to pieces' (1.2.225–6), underscores Henry's aggression and desire for domination. This aggression, in turn, makes his claim to not be a 'tyrant' highly ironic and his Christian clemency questionable.

Henry's aggression is made even more manifest upon receiving the tun of tennis balls from the Dauphin. Peppered with threats and promises of revenge, Henry's speech undercuts his image as a Christian king as much as his seemingly virtuous promises do. Henry tells the French ambassador that he will 'rise … with so full a glory / That [he] will dazzle all the eyes of

France, / Yea, strike the Dauphin blind to look on us' (1.2.279–81). Henry's promise, conforming to the Wallis Rules, mirrors the scintillating promise that young Hal made to himself in *1 Henry IV* that he will 'imitate the sun' (1.2.187) and break 'through the foul and ugly mists / Of vapours' (1.2.192–3) to redeem himself. This time, however, Henry will not only incite admiration but also inflict harm: turning the Dauphin's tennis balls into 'gun-stones' (283), Henry warns the Dauphin that 'his soul / Shall stand sore charged for the wasteful vengeance / That shall fly' from these cannonballs (283–5). Even though this threat foregrounds his ferocity, Henry thrusts responsibility for war onto the Dauphin by suggesting that the Dauphin will be punished for the ensuing violence that Henry will incite. As in his discussion with Canterbury, Henry seeks to absolve himself of responsibility in the war by implying that his vengeful action is only a reaction to the French king's provocation. What is more, Henry dilutes the force of the violent vengeance he vows to exact by making his threats conditional on God's grace: 'But this lies all within the will of God, / To whom I do appeal, and in whose name / Tell you the Dauphin I am coming on' (290–2).[58] Henry reinforces his ethos of piety in deferring his militancy to moral rectitude: it is in showing his subservience to God that Henry makes his actions seem divinely sanctioned. Nevertheless, it is his drive to requite mockery with revenge rather than show Christian clemency that makes Henry undermine his own claim to be a merciful monarch. His speech to the ambassador suggests an impetuousness or uncontrollable rage which contradicts the temperance and self-restraint that his analogy preaches. Henry shows that his 'passion' is not 'subject' to his will but instrumental to revenge rather than pardon.

In spite of the discrepancy between his ethos and his logos, Henry nevertheless succeeds in persuading Scroop, Cambridge and Grey of his Christian ethos as he accuses them of treason. Henry's use of biblical allusion and his continued use of analogy in his speech to his three lords (2.2.79–144) indirectly reassert his ethos as a divinely anointed sovereign and serve to convince the lords of his piety, even as the series of logical fallacies following his speech ironically dismantle his image as a pious monarch. Since Henry is already acquainted with his lords' plot to overthrow him, as Bedford indicates (2.2.6–7), the goal of his speech is not to urge the lords' confession but to impel them to admire his devoutness as a divinely anointed monarch and to thereby incite their repentance. His speech successfully achieves both the illocutionary force of condemnation and the complementary perlocutionary effect of moving the lords to pitifully repent for their crime (2.2.151–4, 160, 165). Henry presents himself to his lords as an honest Christian king who embodies *eunoia* and *arete*. In underlining his disbelief of Scroop's betrayal by asking him a rhetorical question ('May it be possible that foreign hire / Could out of thee extract one spark of evil / That might annoy my finger?' [2.2.100–2]) and confessing his incomprehension of the betrayal ("Tis so strange / That though the truth of it stands off as gross / As black on white, my eye will scarcely see it' [2.2.102–4]), Henry foregrounds the degree of his faith and the extent of his trust in Scroop's 'white' character, the virtue and purity of which metaphorically blind Henry to the 'black' news of treason that sullies it. Henry's use of anaphora moreover serves to highlight his astonishment and his difficulty or unwillingness in coming to terms with the crime: 'Thou that didst bear the key of all my counsels, / That knewst the very bottom of my soul, / That almost mightst have coined me into gold' (96–8). The foregoing rhetorical strategies all underscore Henry's benevolence or good will towards his men, whom he has taken into his bosom and for whose sins he promises to 'weep' (140). Henry additionally reinforces his *arete* or virtue by a biblical analogy comparing his three fallen lords to prelapsarian Adams (141–2). Akin to his other analogies, Henry's biblical analogy carries argumentative weight: it is an *enthymeme* proclaiming that the lords are fallen Adams because they were tempted and deceived by a 'cunning fiend' (111) to commit a crime. In attributing the cause of their treason to temptation rather than to any ill will on their part, Henry's analogy attenuates the severity of the lords' crime; his goodness appears to salvage the lords' reputable characters and, by implication, makes their treason appear even more diabolical. In stressing his Christian virtue and good will, Henry aspires to rouse the lords' shame and guilt as a way of eliciting their repentance.

In further reinforcing his virtue through the rhetorical figure of *enargia*, Henry condemns the lords' intention to deceive him even though it is he who, ironically, deceives them. The *enargia*, a vivid description of the hypothetical consequences of the lords' temptation, instantiates Henry's use of 'presence'. According to Perelman and Olbrechts-Tyteca, presence is a rhetorical strategy that 'make[s] present, by verbal magic ... , what is actually absent but what [one] considers important to [one's] argument'.[59] Henry succeeds in (re)creating the presence of the biblical Fall by alluding to Tartarus, by personifying treason and murder as 'two yoke-devils' (103), and by employing direct dialogue on behalf of the hypothetical devil tempter so as to affectively overpower his hearers as he hints at their probable damnation:

> Treason and murder ever kept together,
> As two yoke-devils sworn to either's purpose,
> Working so grossly in a natural cause
> That admiration did not whoop at them.
> But thou, 'gainst all proportion, didst bring in
> Wonder to wait on treason and on murder;
> And whatsoever cunning fiend it was
> That wrought upon thee so preposterously
> Hath got the voice in hell for excellence.
> And other devils that suggest by treasons
> Do botch and bungle up damnation
> With patches, colours and with forms being fetched
> From glistering semblances of piety;
> But he that tempered thee, bade thee stand up,
> Gave thee no instance why thou shouldst do treason
> Unless to dub thee with the name of traitor.
> If that same demon that hath gulled thee thus

Should with his lion-gait walk the whole world,
He might return to vasty Tartar back
And tell the legions, 'I can never win
A soul so easy as that Englishman's.'

(2.2.105–25)

Heralding the end of Henry's use of presence, the anaphoric 'Why, so didst thou' – which counterpoints Henry's initial anaphora of disbelief (96–8) – is accusatory for the anaphora is tailgated by *epiplexis,* or the enumeration of rhetorical questions that serve to condemn the extent of the lords' infamy.[60] Henry uses this anaphora to perform the illocutionary act of condemning the lords as he fashions himself as an authoritative judge carrying out the verdict of his men's guilt:

Show men dutiful?
Why, so didst thou. Seem they grave and learned?
Why, so didst thou. Come they of noble family?
Why, so didst thou. Seem they religious?
Why, so didst thou.

(2.2.127–31)

The persistent repetition of 'Why, so didst thou' registers the resoluteness and finality of Henry's condemnation. However, his image as a righteous and God-like ruler who doles out Christian justice that is evoked by the anaphora is ironic, since Henry is guilty of the same deceit of which he accuses his men. Not only does Henry denounce the lords for 'hiding behind "semblances of piety"' when he is guilty of the same in appealing to the covetous ecclesiastics for their political support (1.2), as Karl P. Wentersdorf has suggested, but he also deceives the lords prior to this confrontation when he dangles his pardon of a drunken man's raillery in front of them to make them condemn themselves (2.2.79–83).[61] Presenting his lords with a choice regarding whether he should mercifully pardon or punish the imaginary drunken man who rails against his person, Henry shows that this choice is predicated on damnation: the lords inadvertently condemn themselves in condemning the drunken man. In granting the lords the authority and the free will to indirectly accuse themselves by accusing the drunken man, Henry makes them responsible for their own fates, much in the same way that he grants Canterbury the authority to determine whether or not to wage war against France while holding him accountable for the course of action he counsels (1.2.21–3). Henry thus performs the role of devil tempter and undermines his rhetorical display of a virtuous, morally upright and honest Christian king as he entraps the lords with their own logic by offering them a choice predicated on damnation as they unwittingly condemn the king's pardon of the drunken man.

If Henry implicates himself as a traitor in the very crime he condemns, so does the Eastcheap scene which immediately succeeds Henry's confrontation with his lords. The tavern Hostess's remark that 'the King has killed [Falstaff's] heart' (2.1.88) and her report of the fat knight's death (2.3.9–25), along with Pistol's grief over the loss of Falstaff, elicit a pathos that juxtaposes against Henry's callous and rationally calculated rejection of his friend in *2 Henry IV*. The scene puts Henry's personal disloyalty to Falstaff on a par with the lords' political treason to suggest that Henry himself is not innocent: if the lords sever their allegiance to the king and sell themselves to France for personal profit, Henry also severs his loyalty to Falstaff to fulfil his obligations as king. Just as Henry betrays his betrayers, Falstaff's death exposes Henry as a betrayer. This scene in the subplot casts a shadow over Henry's ethos of moral righteousness to highlight the possibility of his self-serving strategies.

The logical fallacies following Henry's confrontation with his lords reveal a faulty logic that further destabilizes the God-like image he projects to his lords and feeds the speculation of his Machiavellianism. Once the three lords depart, Henry attributes his success in unearthing treason to God and reckons that this success heralds the success of the English in their war against France:

> We doubt not of a fair and lucky war,
> Since God so graciously hath brought to light
> This dangerous treason lurking in our way
> To hinder our beginnings. We doubt not now
> But every rub is smoothed on our way.
>
> (2.2.185–9)

This pronouncement instantiates Henry's first fallacy of *non causa pro causa* or causal fallacy: Henry identifies God as the cause of an event (God brings treason to light) without having previously demonstrated that God *is* the cause (God is never mentioned in his encounter with his lords) and merely appends Him at the end to justify his *arete*. Henry's untruthful declaration may be categorized as a post-hoc inference fallacy, which operates on the assumption that there is a direct, causal relationship between God (A) and the discovery of treason (C) simply because (A) occurs before (C).[62] In attributing the discovery of, and thus the responsibility for, treason to God's *a priori* existence and in removing himself as the efficient cause (B) or agent of God's will, Henry makes the success of his recent rhetorical performance contingent on divine intervention.[63] In doing so, Henry promulgates his Christian ethos by showing his auditors that his moral rectitude is premised on his obedience to God's authority and that his actions – as legitimate king and divinely appointed heir to the English throne – are divinely sanctioned. Henry's second fallacy is embedded in the claim that this recent discovery of treason guarantees a 'fair and lucky war' (185) for the English: because God has done X, he will also do Y. However, since the premise that God has exposed treason is not true, the conclusion – that the outcome of the war will be favourable for the English – is not necessarily true or certain. Both of Henry's fallacies constitute the larger logical fallacy of *argumentum ad consequentiam,* in which the belief in something (God) leads to positive consequences, even though these consequences do not necessarily prove that God has brought treason to light. Although Henry attempts to logically convince his auditors of the justness of his war against

France by appropriating God, his logical fallacies damage his ethos by undermining the moral authority with which Henry condemns and punishes his lords' treason.

Paralleling Henry's rhetorically persuasive encounter with his three lords is his exchange with the three soldiers, Williams, Court and Bates (4.1). This encounter, however, displays Henry's failure to persuade his soldiers of the justness of his war, for the logical fallacies that perforate Henry's speech compromise the wisdom, goodness and good will that uphold his ethos. Donning Sir Thomas Erpingham's cloak to disguise himself as a common soldier, Henry-as-soldier tries to indirectly buttress Henry-the-king's ethos by arguing in the king's name in order to persuade his three soldiers of the nobleness of the king's war and to secure their loyalty. Henry-as-soldier, in effect, embodies the perlocutionary uptake of Henry-the-king's speeches, which Henry intends all of his soldiers to have: the obedience and allegiance to the king exhibited by Henry-as-soldier ('Methinks I could not die anywhere so contented as in the King's company' [4.1.126–7]), along with his sympathetic understanding of the king ('I think the King is but a man, as I am' [4.1.102]), are intended to inspire Williams, Bates and Court of the same.[64] In order to fortify his soldiers' belief in the king's good will (*eunoia*) towards his men, Henry uses parallelism to persuade his hearers of the fundamentally shared humanness, via shared experiences, between soldier and monarch: 'the violet smells to him as it doth to me; the element shows to him as it doth to me' (4.1.103–4). Although Henry claims comradeship with his men based on shared passions – he asserts that the king's fears 'be of the same relish as ours are' (4.1.110) – he quickly turns this comradeship into a prohibitive warning that 'no man should possess [the king] with any appearance of fear, lest [the king], by showing it, should dishearten his army' (4.1.110–12). The warning, a speech act that counsels the three soldiers to abstain from showing fear, unsettles the king's ethos since it places responsibility for the king's own potential fearfulness onto his men. Formulated as an *enthymeme* or rhetorical syllogism, Henry-as-soldier's persuasive argumentation would read as follows: A) The king is a man like his soldiers; B) The king's fears are like those of his men; C) Therefore, no man should excite the king with fear.[65] However, the *enthymeme* embodies the fallacy of *ignoratio elenchi,* or the fallacy of ignoring the issue, for the conclusion (C), which logically digresses from the two premises (A and B), is irrelevant, given that it harps on the tangential issue of responsibility. Amending Henry's logic, Bates's retort produces a valid conclusion that logically follows from the premises: '[The king] may show what outward courage he will, but I believe, as cold a night as 'tis, he could wish himself in Thames up to the neck' (113–15). Bates's modified *enthymeme* states that if (A) the king is a man like his soldiers and (B) he shares their fear, then (C) the king would wish to be anywhere but on the battlefield. By turning Henry's fallacy into a logically valid *enthymeme*, Bates exposes Henry's sophistic logic, which undermines the brotherhood and solidarity he seeks to rhetorically establish with his men. Bates highlights a social hierarchy between the king and his soldiers who, as the king's subordinates, are to be used for the king's benefit by inspiring *him* with courage and boosting his morale rather than vice versa. Bates's revelation, along with the audience's awareness of Henry's disguise, renders Henry's initial claim that 'the King is but a man, as I am' (4.1.102) ironic for the speaker is clearly not the man he pretends to be: his disguise compromises his rhetorical ethos by erasing the authority vested in the king's visible presence.

The dramatic irony hinging on Henry's disguise is enhanced by the patriotic and propagandistic Chorus, whose attempt to uphold Henry's ethos as a virtuous Christian monarch is at odds with the self-oriented Henry presented on stage. The Chorus describes Henry as a vigilant, Christ-like monarch who moves among his 'ruined band' (4.0.29) of 'poor condemned English' (4.0.22) so as to boost their morale before the battle at Agincourt (4.0.40–7). The Chorus suggests that it is Henry's sense of Christian fellowship and his altruism that impel him to instil his band of crestfallen men with sun-like cheer and comforting optimism in order to alleviate or 'thaw' their 'cold fear' (4.0.45). Nevertheless, the Henry witnessed by the audience prior to his conversation with Bates appears discomfited. As Henry's comment to the elderly Erpingham seems to suggest, Henry may not be consoling his men but rather commiserating with them or even testing their loyalty: 'A good soft pillow for that good white head / Were better than a churlish turf of France' (4.1.14–15). Henry's disguise may serve to cathartically cleanse his mind of misgivings regarding either the justice of his war or the allegiance of his men, or it may serve to renew his faith in his cause and to boost his own morale. Rather than sublimate his personal cares to tend to others, Henry impersonates a soldier for seemingly self-serving rather than altruistic ends. Reminiscent of the scheming Hal of Falstaff's Eastcheap, the Henry enacted on stage destabilizes the Chorus's presentation of him and prompts the audience to question the motives underlying his impersonation.

Just as Bates pinpoints Henry's fallacious reasoning, the exchange between Williams and Henry-as-soldier magnifies how Henry's logical fallacies undercut his own credibility. Henry, claiming that the king's 'cause [is] just and his quarrel honourable' (4.1.127–8), subsequently fails to logically support his own argument or even address Williams's thesis. Although Williams and Bates sagaciously respond that it is impossible to know the king's motives and whether the war is just or not, and that it is futile to even seek this knowledge ('That's more than we know' and 'more than we should seek after' [4.1.129–30]), Williams tells Henry that the king, to whom his soldiers owe their allegiance and their duty, has a moral obligation to ensure that his soldiers 'die well' (144), otherwise it would be a 'black matter for the King, that led them to it' (144–5). Williams thus insinuates that the king, if he is a Christian monarch, is answerable to a higher moral authority to which he owes allegiance and that the king's will should work in accordance with the Divine Will to ensure his clear conscience. Williams further raises the possibility that the war is not 'just' since the means of war (the soldiers' inevitable deaths) cannot justify its ends (the hypothetically successful outcome of the war), and thus implicitly questions the very justness of a war that does not allow men to die virtuously 'when blood is their argument' (143; see 141–3). Rather than logically prove his claim that his war is indeed just, Henry's response to Williams instead registers the fallacy of *ignoratio elenchi* through his misuse of analogy. Henry compares the king and his men to a father and his merchant son (147–50) as well as to a master and his servant (150–4) to argue that his soldiers are obliged to perform their duties like the father's son and the master's servant. Nevertheless, the tenor and the vehicle in these twinned analogies fail to correspond: unlike the soldier, the son and the servant are not sent on errands where the chances of their deaths are highly probable. What is more, the king's relationship to his soldiers, unlike that between a father and his son, is not based on a blood bond. In comparing the king to both a father and a master, which strongly evokes the distinction Erasmus makes between a Christian prince (a 'conscientious father') and a tyrant (a 'cruel master'), Henry puts the father's Christian self-sacrifice on a par with the master's politic selfishness in a manner that intimates his Machiavellianism.[66] Not only does Henry's incongruous comparison between a soldier and a son/servant make death in war seem accidental instead of highly probable, but it also underscores that soldiers have free will and that they, rather than the king, are responsible for their sinful or sinless actions: 'The King is not bound to answer the particular endings of his soldiers, the father of his son, nor the master of his servant; for they purpose not their death when they purpose their services' (155–8). The tenuous comparisons drawn by Henry's analogy serve to minimize his responsibility for the war by accentuating his soldiers' responsibility for their own souls. In doing so, they manifest a self-interested Machiavellian attitude that detracts from the selflessness that Henry projects. Henry's illogical analogy thus sidesteps the critical question of the justness of his war to deliver an argument for personal responsibility. Henry's reasoning can be expressed as a logically valid but unsound syllogism: since the king (A) is a man (B), and all men (B) are responsible for their own souls (C), then the king (A) is responsible only for his own soul (C). Because Henry applies the premise that all men are responsible for their own souls to himself in particular – without considering the difference in social roles between king and commoner – he is guilty of the *dicto simpliciter* fallacy, or the fallacy of sweeping generalization. A bidirectional responsibility defines the relationship between monarch and subject: if a king requires his subjects to remain loyal to him, then the king is obliged to protect his subjects and consider their welfare.[67] Downplaying the mutual obligation between a monarch and his subjects, Henry's fallacy exposes his attempt to absolve himself from moral responsibility as he highlights his soldiers' personal duty towards their own souls (175–7) while it is public duty, as Williams rightly observes, that is at issue in the debate. Henry purposefully changes the subject through substitution.

Since Henry's *ignoratio elenchi* fallacy prevents him from either refuting Williams's point or proving his own thesis that the king's cause is 'just and his quarrel honourable' (128), he proceeds to prove that war itself is just. Henry argues that war is just since it provides punishment, in the form of death, for criminals who have 'defeated the law and outrun native punishment' (166–7). Should the criminals survive, however, Henry avers that war would still be just for it would allow them to recognize the divine workings of God, to redeem themselves and to help others 'prepare' for their deaths (4.1.180–4). In proclaiming that war is God's 'beadle' (168) or means of punishment, Henry, in a characteristic move, lays responsibility on God and His laws to prove that God's vengeance is divinely sanctioned. By making war an agent of God's retributive justice and effectively ignoring his own agency, Henry expounds to Williams, Bates and Court the morality of war in order to justify his decision to wage it. Appropriating morality as an afterthought rather than showing it to be the leading cause of his actions as he did in his encounter with Scroop, Cambridge and Grey, Henry is once again guilty of committing the *argumentum ad consequentiam* fallacy: he establishes a causal connection between war and virtue – where otherwise there is none – in suggesting that the end result of war (death) deductively proves that war is just or a means of good. In thus making war a standard-bearer for justice, Henry dodges the claim that death in war is unjust by substituting in its place the question of his soldiers' personal virtue. Henry's logical fallacies, which frustrate his attempt to persuade his three soldiers that his war is just or to disprove Williams's claim that the king is morally responsible for his men's lives, demolish his prudence (*phronesis*) and tarnish the credibility needed to sustain his ethos as a just, kind-hearted and devout Christian ruler.

'Plain' and honest speaking: Henry's ethos as soldier

Aside from performing his ethos as a pious Christian monarch to persuade his interlocutors of the justness of his war and legitimate his claim to the throne, Henry also performs the ethos of an honest-speaking and plain soldier in order to gain favour in ascending the French throne. In his wooing of Katherine (5.2), Henry strives to persuade the French princess of his love for her in order to secure her hand in marriage. However, the persuasiveness of the rhetoric which builds his ethos as a soldier is undermined by its argumentative logic, which exposes Henry's ultimate motive to consolidate his political domination of France through Katherine herself. The peace negotiation between Henry and the French nobles which precedes the wooing scene reveals that Katherine is not, as Henry proclaims, an object of his love but rather a bargaining chip between England and France. Henry has already made Katherine his legal 'capital demand, comprised / Within the fore-rank of our articles' (5.2.96–7) and promises peace to King Charles in exchange for her hand in marriage. In spite of the transactional nature of this peace accord, Henry's wooing of the princess is still necessary for Henry's ability to successfully persuade Katherine of his love would entail her consent to marry him and thus signal her good will and favour towards Henry, which would in turn prove instrumental in allowing Henry to effectively enforce his power over both her and France. Framed in these contractual terms, the wooing scene reinforces Henry's Machiavellian expediency by exposing his affection for the princess as a means to his ultimate end of augmenting and consolidating his power as a monarch of both England and France.

Henry presents himself to Katherine as a humble and simple soldier or a 'fellow of plain and uncoined constancy' (5.2.153–4) who is unversed in the art of wooing. Nevertheless, his rhetorical use of language ironically undercuts his ethos as an honest and plain-speaking soldier by exposing his artfulness and duplicity. Henry strives to convince Katherine that his speech is free of deception and devoid of hidden intentions; its plainness, he suggests, betokens his honesty and humility, which he shares with the working classes: 'My wooing is fit for thy understanding. I am glad thou canst speak no better English, for if thou couldst thou wouldst find me such a plain king that thou wouldst think I had sold my farm to buy my crown' (5.2.123–7). Henry foregrounds his humility and modesty in beseeching Katherine to 'teach' him how to woo her:

> Fair Katherine, and most fair,
> Will you vouchsafe to teach a soldier terms
> Such as will enter at a lady's ear
> And plead his love-suit to her gentle heart?
>
> (5.2.98–101)

Henry's request, however, works against the plainness he aspires to convey by highlighting his rhetorical flattery of the princess. Rather than attest to Henry's naïveté as a plain soldier, the diction in his request reveals that Henry is capable of wooing Katherine and knows how to carefully select his words to ingratiate himself with a 'gentle' 'lady' in order to win her over. Henry plays on the word 'fair', which signifies both physical beauty and moral goodness, to urge Katherine to give in to his request by calling upon her to suit her moral nature to the beauty of her appearance. In appealing to her 'fairness' while also implying that he is a lover of virtue to strengthen his ethos, Henry flatters Katherine not once but twice: 'Speak, my fair, and fairly, I pray thee' (167–8). In a similar manner, Henry's pun on 'like' further undermines his assertion of modest plain-speaking. In explicitly asking Katherine 'Do you like me, Kate?' (5.2.106–7), Henry enjoins her to express either her affection or her dislike of him in imperfect English. Upon learning of her incomprehension ('I cannot tell vat is "like" me' [108–9]), however, Henry quickly changes the meaning of 'like' from affection to resemblance to flatter her further: 'An angel is like you, Kate, and you are like an angel' (5.2.110–11). This deft rhetorical manoeuvring showcases Henry's skill in courting Katherine as he tries to endear himself towards her. In urging her to speak her mind and confess her feelings, Henry grants Katherine the illusion of exercising choice and controlling her own fate – much in the same way as he had done with the three lords – even though her fate is already decided for her as he attempts to maximize her sympathy towards him. While Henry realizes that his compliment may be interpreted as untruthful and hints at his embarrassment as a way of reminding the princess of the modesty and innocence he professes to have ('I said so, dear Katherine, and I must not blush to affirm it' [113–14]), the audience has nevertheless just witnessed Henry's performance as a well-versed courtier. Although Henry distances himself from the hyperbolic conventions used by Petrarchan lovers to express the extremity of their love ('to say to thee that I shall die is true; but for thy love, by the Lord, no; yet I love thee too' [5.2.151–3]), his words are just as misleading for his language exudes a rhetorical sophistication that betrays his political intentions. Henry's wordplay, or what he 'does' with rhetoric, effectively undercuts his constative use of language or his claim to be a plain-speaking soldier and lends an irony to his rhetorical posturing.

Henry's protracted speech to Katherine (5.2.133–68), moreover, serves to bolster his ethos of humility and modesty through self-negation but instead brings to the fore the self-praise that destabilizes his ethos. Claiming that he has no ability to impress women either with his talents or with his eloquence, Henry asserts that he does have a good heart which, like the sun, 'shines bright and never changes, but keeps his course truly' (5.2.164–5). Although Henry makes a case for his constancy in virtue, his changeability is evidenced in the rhetorical figures he uses, which veer away from his 'true' course of persuasion to convey a boastful complacency that is anything but virtuous or modest. Through a triple pun on 'measure', Henry professes to lack the ability to recite poetry in metre ('measure') and the talent ('measure') for dancing but claims to possess a fair degree ('measure') of physical strength: 'For the one I have neither words nor measure, and for the other I have no strength in measure, yet a reasonable measure in strength' (5.2.134–7). The antimetabole places Henry's physical fortitude and military puissance on an equilibrium with the skill in dancing he claims to lack. It exhibits, in effect, the skilful linguistic 'dance' that Henry performs with his rhetoric, which forebodingly hints at his Machiavellian campaign to domesticate and lord over Katherine through force. As Henry enumerates the eventual demise of those physical attributes he claims to lack ('A good leg will fall, a straight back will stoop, a black beard will turn white, a curled pate will grow bald, a fair face will wither, a full eye will wax hollow' [5.2.159–62]), he immodestly foregrounds the longevity of his good-heartedness by comparing it to the sun's constancy. Henry's comparison indicates that his bright and persistent virtue is not subject to the natural laws of the universe but rather rules over the natural universe. It is this virtuous rule of his heart and, by extension, his proclaimed good intentions that the offstage audience is driven to question. The anadiplosis or repetition of words in successive clauses that constitutes Henry's concluding remark signals a steady escalation from speaker ('me'), to soldier, to king to highlight his ascendant superiority as a monarch: 'If thou would have such a one, take me; and take me, take a soldier; take a soldier, take a king' (5.2.165–6). Ending on the climactic 'king' whose virtue, like the sun, shines upon but also outshines the natural realm, Henry's anadiplosis suggests a self-complacency that attends his authority as a monarch and effectively cancels his self-proclaimed humility.

Determined to win Katherine's consent through his display of good-heartedness and virtue, Henry proceeds to assure Katherine of their equality as husband and wife. Nevertheless, the equality that Henry proposes gives way to a fallacy that exposes their inequality and Henry's superiority. Henry expresses his wish to Katherine that their unborn male child, who would instantiate the equality between them in being 'half French, half English' (205), unite the English and French nations in war against the Ottoman Turks (5.2.206–7). He promulgates this equality between their two nations by levelling the differences between the French and English tongues. Henry declares that 'thy speaking of my tongue, and I thine, most truly-falsely, must needs be granted to be much at one' (5.2.189–91). While Henry posits that their imperfect speaking of each other's language is equivalent or 'at one', the ambiguity of the adverbs 'truly-falsely' produces an equivocation or material fallacy that implies a hierarchy and moral inequality between the two languages. On the one hand, Henry is explicitly stating that he and the princess speak each other's language truthfully – their words faithfully ('truly') express their intentions – albeit imperfectly, since they are not fluent in the other's tongue ('falsely'). On the other hand, Henry is claiming that he speaks French 'truly' or authentically as a native speaker but in a dishonest or devious way ('falsely') to achieve his goal of persuasion. This second meaning points back to Hal's boast in *1 Henry IV* that he can 'drink with a tinker in his own language' (2.4.19); Henry, as the audience would know, is 'proficient' in many languages and dialects, which renders the reiterated excuses of his poor French ironic and a part of the modesty topos of his ethos. The ambiguity of the adverbs gives rise to a Machiavellian reading of Henry's language ability used to uphold his modesty topos.

If Henry discloses his attempt to deceive Katherine by pretending he does not speak French perfectly, he also implies that Katherine feigns incomprehension and tries to deceive *him* since her English, in spite of it being 'broken' or grammatically incorrect ('false'), is far superior to what she claims and approximates that of a native speaker. Responding to Katherine's statement that 'the tongues of men are full of deceits' (118–19), Henry ironically asserts that 'the Princess is the better Englishwoman' (122) since she is capable of understanding the truthful intentions behind his words – she speaks his language 'truly' – and is hence able to detect dishonest or 'false' speech. In thus discreetly praising Katherine, Henry implies that English, his native tongue, is the superior language since it is more substantial. English contains or is able to express the truth: 'By mine honour, in true English, I love thee, Kate' (5.2.218–19). By contrast, French is labelled as deceptive and superficial. Henry denigrates the French language by effeminizing it: he claims it hangs 'upon [his] tongue like a new-married wife about her husband's neck, hardly to be shook off' (5.2.179–80). French is a purely ornamental and passive language that constrains self-expression, while English is a functional and active language that performs deeds.[68] Underwritten by this gendered moral hierarchy that Henry maps onto the two languages, Henry's declaration of the equality between them takes on a third meaning: the equivocation on 'truly-falsely' signifies that he speaks French deviously ('falsely') but nevertheless 'truly', or in a way that is 'true' or consonant with the deception inherent to the French language. Henry characteristically disowns responsibility for what he says by making the French language, rather than himself as its speaker, an agent of deception. Nevertheless, Henry's contractual arrangement with the French king as well as his ornamental use of rhetoric ironically reveal his deceptive use of English. Although Henry asserts an equality between French and English in proclaiming them to be 'much at one' (91), his equivocation reveals his belief in their essential moral difference even as his persuasive manoeuvring ironically suggests that a pure, sincere and plain English language is commensurate with a false and deceitful French tongue. It is this ascription of difference to the two languages that informs Henry's intention to subdue and dominate France through a show of his superior force.

The equality that Henry preaches is further rendered dubious by the invalid logic underwriting his use of antimetabole. To convince Katherine of his good will or *eunoia*, Henry tries to accommodate himself to her by showing that he shares her values – specifically, her love of her country: 'I love France so well that I will not part with a village of it; I will have it all mine' (173–5). This ethos-building proclamation serves as a prelude to Henry's declaration to Katherine that 'when France is mine, and I am yours, then yours is France, and you are mine' (175–6). The declarative statement, which takes the form of an antimetabole (a successive repetition of a clause or phrase in reverse order) displays the equality or commensurateness between husband and wife. Henry's use of this antimetabole in a rhetorically argumentative fashion, however, discloses to the audience his Machiavellian intention to dominate France. The antimetabole is premised on logical equivalence, or the idea in logic that if A = B (premise 1), and B = C (premise 2), then A = C (conclusion). The conclusion can only be valid if both premises are true. Henry's antimetabole, however, underlines the logical invalidity of his statement and hints at the unequal power between husband and wife as Henry intends to dominate Katherine just as he dominates France. Henry claims that when France is his (A = B) and when he belongs to Katherine (B = C), then Katherine will have possession of France (C = A). However, the conclusion ('then yours is France') is invalid since it does not logically follow from Henry's first premise ('when France is mine'). Henry suggests that Katherine's possession of France is conditional on his success in gaining the French throne, but this is clearly untrue since Katherine, as her father's heir, already possesses France. Although the antimetabole suggests that husband and wife would have equal share in their possession of and rule over France by virtue of their marriage, which would only consolidate their power, its illogical use creates a hierarchy that renders both his and her possession conditional on Henry's authoritarian rule: it suggests that Katherine's rule over France would only be possible – and permissible – through Henry's supreme reign over both France and Katherine. Henry's conquest of France is a synecdoche for his domestication of Katherine; his use of military force prefigures his forceful rhetorical persuasion in a way that eerily evokes his promise that he will either 'bend [France] to our awe / Or break it all to pieces' (1.2.225–6). In just such a way, Henry's reassuring promise to Katherine that their marriage 'will please [her father] well' (5.2.245) uneasily merges into a foreboding command ('it shall please him, Kate' [245–6]) insinuating the aggression expressed in Henry's threats to the Dauphin. Henry's forceful act of kissing Katherine, with which he teaches her to 'patiently, and yielding' (272) give way to him, is his way of showing her that the English tongue holds superior sway. Although Henry tries to win Katherine's favour by persuading her of his ethos as an honest, virtuous and good-hearted soldier who loves her, his ethos loses force due to his use of fanciful rhetoric and the logic underlying it, which contradict his statements and effectively 'reason' him out of persuasion by glancing at the Machiavellian coercion that drives his speech.

While Henry certainly is the 'mirror of all Christian kings' (2.0.6), as the Chorus emphatically claims, he is not the paragon of a Christian sovereign but merely the imitative copy of one as he strives to achieve the spiritual values of a divinely anointed monarch through political expediency and rhetorical persuasion. As a descendent of the usurping Bolingbroke, Henry V has no *a priori* claim to sovereignty through a divinely sanctioned right to rule and must therefore 'plod' 'like a man for working-days' (1.2.278) to win his right.

Henry's rhetorical performances, constantly gesturing towards a legitimacy he does not yet possess, achieve their authority through their ability to persuade his audience of his ethos as a meek and merciful Christian king and as a humble and plain-speaking soldier. However, the imperfect argumentative logic of his rhetoric undermines this ethos by betraying the instrumentality of his words, which convey his intention to invade France in order to legitimate his right. Henry's speech in his exchanges with his ecclesiastics, lords, soldiers and the French princess inadvertently exposes his illegitimacy even as he proclaims his legitimacy. Even so, Henry is not a Machiavel with hidden motives. While he may be a political opportunist who abides by Machiavelli's utilitarian ethics, Henry is not a scheming hypocrite in essence but only in rhetorical practice: it is Henry's rhetorical performances that create the impression of his Machiavellianism. The friction between Henry's logos, which argumentatively conveys his political expediency – evidenced in his use of modal verbs, faulty analogies and fallacies – and his constative utterances, which serve to carve out the *arete, eunoia* and *phronesis* of his ethos, throws into relief a Machiavellian wiliness that discredits Henry's Christian self-presentation and renders him morally dubious. The audience's impression of Henry's Machiavellianism is strengthened by the dramatic irony arising from the juxtaposition of scenes, as well as from Henry's conflicting self-presentation within scenes, which Shakespeare puts into motion to make us question Henry's rhetorically crafted ethos as a soldier and a king. Henry's moral ambiguity is thus not intrinsic to his character but is instead a linguistic effect created by the failure of his logos to coalesce with his ethos in persuasive argumentation. As a result, Henry is neither a Machiavellian politician nor a Christian king but, first and foremost, a formidable orator whose 'sweet and honeyed sentences' (1.1.50) serve 'his discourse of war' to achieve legitimate kingship. Shakespeare shows us that the 'rabbit' and the 'duck' are both endemic to Henry as an orator and that the Machiavel is an integral part of Christian kingship.

4

Kate's Defiant Obedience in *The Taming of the Shrew*

In the first of the two Inductions that frame the taming plot of *The Taming of the Shrew*, the Lord instructs his huntsmen on how to stage a play that would persuade the drunken tinker Christopher Sly into thinking that he is a true lord. The success of the performance to produce a realistic effect lies in the huntsmen's 'true diligence' in personating Sly's servants and according their speech with the requisite music, gestures, props and costumes of dramatic illusion, as the First Huntsman's promise to the Lord reveals: 'My lord, I warrant you we will play our part / As he shall think by our true diligence / He is no less than what we say he is' (1.68–70).[1] What the offstage audience witnesses is both the intended perlocutionary effect of the Lord's play – Sly is convinced that he is an aristocrat – and what the huntsmen 'do' to pull off the dramatic illusion; the audience has a dual awareness of the play's theatrical artifice and the realistic effect it produces as they watch Sly watching the play. The absence of the Sly frame at the end of the Folio, however, forces the offstage audience to relinquish its omniscience as it witnesses another performance: that of Kate's obedience. Thrust into Sly's vulnerable position, the audience is left to question the sincerity of Kate's speech: has Kate, directed by her 'lord' Petruccio, truly surrendered to her husband – has she persuaded us that she is 'no less than what [she] say[s] she is'? Or is her submission a theatrical illusion? The answer is both.

The critical response to Kate's sole monologue or her so-called 'obedience' speech has been bifurcated for the better part of the twentieth century. Critics have either subscribed to the patriarchal ideology shaping the marriage plot in the play to read Kate's speech as a sign of her unquestioning acceptance of and submission to Petruccio's dominance or, inspired by a wave of feminist readings, have discerned notes of subversive defiance in her speech that point to an indomitable Kate who undermines Petruccio's taming enterprise under the guise of her submission.[2] Other critics, endorsing neither Kate's acceptance nor her rejection of submission, offer a more balanced interpretation that transcends these binary views in claiming that Kate's subordination is a public façade that masks her complicity with Petruccio.[3] Driving these variegated interpretations are the polarized assumptions that Kate is either a stock character of farce or a real person. Whereas critics aligned with the play's patriarchal or misogynistic treatment of Kate read her as a one-dimensional character of farce who lacks depth, personal motives and individualized character traits, critics of the feminist-inspired and conciliatory camps tend to humanize Kate as a 'real' person with a secret inner life.[4] Wayne Rebhorn and Coppélia Kahn, for instance, who claim that Kate's rhetoric allows her to subvert and resist male authority through performance, deem that she is 'able to maintain her interior distance' from Petruccio (Rebhorn) by being 'outwardly compliant but inwardly independent' (Kahn), while Jay Halio, arguing for Kate's covert compliance with Petruccio, declares that a loving and helpful Petruccio 'gets Kate to reveal her true self'.[5]

To posit that Kate is a stock character, however, is to deny her agency and to overlook the ostentatious meta-theatricality of her monologue. To posit her reality as a person similarly involves neglecting the meta-theatrical dimension of her speech – which hinges on the boy actor personating her – in an attempt to grant her autonomous agency. While the play, as John C. Bean notes, progressively marks the 'emergence of a humanized heroine against the background of depersonalizing farce unassimilated from the play's fabliau sources', this 'humanization' or idiosyncratic three-dimensionality which feminist-inspired and conciliatory critics attribute to Kate in her monologue does not arise from an inaccessible inwardness.[6] Rather, the rhetorical skilfulness of her speech demands that we more carefully evaluate Kate as a linguistically conscious speaker with particular communicative goals. Instead of arguing either for or against Kate's obedience, which would neither resolve the impasse that has beleaguered critical analysis of her character nor generate any novel insight into Kate as a character, I explore how Kate's anamorphic ambiguity is produced through her use of language. Like Henry V, Kate is both a 'rabbit' and a 'duck': she shuttles between a shrew and an obedient wife in her final speech to illustrate that, as Barbara Hodgdon aptly puts it, 'both are inescapably *there*: a viewer searches for the one in the other, wonders (like Lucentio) whether they do represent the same person, and attempts to merge the two images into a single, recognizably discrete entity'.[7] The offstage audience's impression that there is a defiant 'duck' peering behind the harmless 'rabbit' arises from Kate's pragmatic use of language in her rhetorical speech and grants her palpable presence.

Foregrounding Petruccio as the play's rhetorically astute user of language, critics in the 1980s and '90s minimized Kate's linguistic power by deeming her language to be reflective of her subservience in the play. Although they noted the punning, wordplay and irony in Kate's speech, these critics limited its power to Kate's subversion of Petruccio's patriarchal dominance. Tita French Baumlin and Karen Newman reckoned that Kate's language is purely mimetic or imitative, whereas Petruccio's language, according to Baumlin, is supremely '*epistemic*' or 'generative', able to re-create reality.[8] Kate's subordinate status in the play enables her to use puns and wordplay only as 'strategies of italics, mimetic strategies' to 'deform language by sub-verting it', as Newman noted.[9] Although Wayne Rebhorn was among the first to recognize that Kate's adoption of male rhetorical strategies renders her as much a *rhetor* as Petruccio is, he nevertheless claimed that Kate is 'empowered' by Petruccio and that her subversion of the social order through the use of antithesis and irony is nevertheless contained by the 'male authorities ... whose commands she otherwise has no choice but to obey'.[10] Despite his historicist reading, Rebhorn nevertheless maintains that Kate's resistance to patriarchal structures intimates her 'interior distance' from Petruccio.[11] Even though they recognize Kate as an adept user of language, New Historicist critics deny Kate the performative power to linguistically (re)fashion herself.

Although recent accounts of Kate's language have counteracted this imbalance by granting her the performative power to negotiate her place within patriarchal discourse, they tend to focus on Kate's rhetorical persuasion to the exclusion of her communicative intentions. Contextualizing Kate's rhetoric within humanist education practices, Megan D. Little and Elizabeth Ann Mackay have designated Kate, rather than Petruccio, as the play's foremost rhetorician.[12] Both Little and Mackay demonstrate that Kate does not simply subvert or reject Petruccio's domination but rather reshapes gender and social hierarchies to create a more equal or companionate marriage. Mackay claims that Kate, schooled by Petruccio, exploits and turns 'grammatical devices to her own argumentative purposes': she uses nouns, V and T pronouns, and the trope of *hysteron proteron* to 'reverse[] Petruchio's possession of her' and to highlight her ability to take control as she harnesses the roles of 'good' wife, 'good' student of vernacular grammar and shrew to her advantage.[13] Megan D. Little similarly demonstrates that Kate does not merely mimic Petruccio's rhetoric 'but expand[s] upon the [rhetorical] conventions she learned' from him; she comes to possess 'the linguistic mobility to shift in and out of rhetorical modes with ease'.[14] Little notes that while Kate's final speech focuses on praising men and dispraising women, it is her use of antiphrasis and the paradoxical encomium – taught to her by Petruccio – that highlights her reversal of this praise and dispraise. Her 'rhetorical training enables her to reassure those in power while harnessing the linguistic mobility enjoyed by those who maintain power'.[15] Although Little recognizes that Kate's speech generates uncertainty as to whether she is a *rhetor* who doles out empty praise or a truthfully good woman, she reads Kate not as an idiosyncratic character with linguistic agency but as a representation that, like Isabella in *Measure for Measure*, serves as a 'prime figuration[] of ambivalence toward rhetoric in the early modern era'.[16]

Like these accounts of Kate's rhetorical self-fashioning, Marilyn Cooper's pragmatic study of the play has also failed to consider Kate's distinct communicative goals as a speaker. In the only pragmatic study of the play, dating from 1981, Cooper applies Grice's theory of conversational implicature to the courtship scene between Kate and Petruccio to explain how critics arrive at their disparate views of Katherine.[17] Counterpointing Coppélia Kahn's reading of Kate as a defensive woman to Robert Heilman's misogynistic reading of Kate as the provocative shrew of farce, Cooper argues that Kate's ambiguity cannot be ascertained merely by a pragmatic application of Grice's theory to her speech, since the linguistic inferences drawn by an audience are contained within and shaped by the generic and cultural conventions of the play. These conventions, deems Cooper, ultimately determine the meanings produced by Kate's conversational implicatures. Although Cooper rightly illuminates the importance of attending to dramatic conventions and contexts in assessing speaker meaning, she does not recognize that a character's speech has the linguistic power to challenge, play with and re-shape contexts and conventions rather than merely reflect or instantiate them.

I examine Kate both as a rhetorician who seeks to persuade her audience of her obedience and as a pragmatic speaker with a distinct intention to communicate a message to her audience. Since Kate is commonly perceived as a rhetorician, the intended and unintended perlocutionary effects produced by her speech – i.e. her success and her failure to persuade her audience of her sincerity – give rise to, and become the measure of, her ambiguity as a character. However, Kate's rhetorical intentions are also compounded by the pragmatic intentions of a speaker who seeks to address a group of disparate hearers; thus, the failure of Kate's rhetoric to persuade her audience that she is mild, meek and submissive also registers her *success* in pragmatically conveying a message of defiance to her female audience. Kate does not relinquish her scripted role as shrew by the end of the play but instead makes prudent use of it to present herself as a submissive wife even as she mocks this enforced submission. I contend that Kate's argumentative use of comparisons in her final speech serves to uphold her ethos as an obedient wife and displays her obedience to her male audience while the presence of echoic utterances, puns and semantic ambiguity give rise to conversational implicatures that destabilize this ethos by registering her insubordination and conveying her critique of wifely obedience to her female audience. The hint of a defiant Kate in the implicatures she produces is reinforced by the boy actor's meta-theatrical defiance of the adult actor to whom he is apprenticed. This interplay between the boy's voice and Kate's voice, as well as the divergent reactions of her onstage audience, underscores Kate's ambiguity and produces her anteriority as a character.

Before turning to Kate's monologue, I first examine the rhetorical and pragmatic strategies that define her verbal interactions with Petruccio in the courtship scene (2.1) and in the sun/moon scene (4.5) to demonstrate how Kate's linguistic manoeuvring allows her to hold in equilibrium her subordination with her defiance. Kate's complicity and her defiant non-complicity with Petruccio, which are evidenced in these early scenes of the play, structure her communicative and persuasive intentions in the monologue. That the verbal behaviour of Shakespeare's Kate is markedly distinct from that of other 'household Kates' (2.1.280) found in his historical sources pinpoints Shakespeare's attempt to individualize and differentiate his 'shrew' from the shrew of farce.

Shakespeare's shrewd shrew

Although Kate seems to transcend her scripted role as a shrew by the time she delivers her obedience speech, her wagging and aggressive tongue as well as her unruly behaviour in the early scenes of the play render her heir to the early modern shrew. Depicted as a garrulous, scolding and threatening woman who engages in vehement arguments with the opposite sex, the shrew was the subject of male derision and condemnation in early modern popular literature from ballads and pamphlets to advice manuals, as well as in folktales, riddles, jokes and proverbs.[18] In the opening scenes of *The Taming of the Shrew*, Kate is introduced to the audience as a stereotypical shrew: she is condemned by her male suitors for being a devil (1.1.66) or a 'fiend of hell' (1.1.89) and a 'shrewd and froward' (1.2.89) woman who is 'renowned in Padua for her scolding tongue' (1.2.99). She is, as Grumio warns Petruccio in his rhyming couplet, '"Katherine the Curst" – / A title for a maid of all titles the worst' (1.2.127–8). Kate's verbal aggression, manifested in her threats to Hortensio ('To comb your noodle with a three-legged stool / And paint your face and use you like a fool' [1.1.64–5]) and in her commands to Bianca ('I charge thee tell / Whom thou lov'st best' [2.1.8–9]), is accompanied by physical violence: Kate breaks a lute over her music tutor's head (2.1.147–58) and not only binds Bianca's hands but also strikes her (2.1.22).

Kate's linguistic and physical aggression, and overall her obdurate resistance to male authority, find their parallels in the shrew of the anonymous English folk ballad *A Merry Jest of a Shrewd and Curst Wife Lapped in Morell's Skin for Her Good Behaviour* (*c.* 1550), which serves as one of the sources for Shakespeare's play. The shrewish wife of the ballad possesses a 'proude harte' and 'lewde tongue' that make her, according to the men around her, a 'deuillishe fende of hell': refusing to let her husband domineer over her, she usurps her husband's role and plays the 'maister' to make him bow down to her.[19] The shrew's hostile speech, rife with expletives and oaths, curses, threats and commands, is mirrored in her exhibition of physical violence. Even so, her unruliness is quelled by her husband, who punishes her by beating her and wrapping her in the salted skin of his dead horse. The contours of this belligerent shrew are clearly present in Kate's spewing of threats, commands and insults in the early scenes of the play but they are also visible in Petruccio's speech, which is characterized by extensive curses and oaths. Like the garrulous shrew of the ballad, Petruccio out-speaks his spouse and is responsible for withholding food and drink from Kate; he is, as his servant Curtis ironically observes, 'more shrew than she' (4.1.76). Nevertheless, while the ballad shrew's volubility and hostility are hereditary – she is simply 'curste as her mother in word and deede' – Kate's linguistic aggression is reactionary and fuelled by her desire to redress her unjust treatment. Even though Kate has a motive that justifies her shrewish behaviour in the play, she is still a stock character at this early stage rather than the three-dimensional Kate of the monologue who later emerges.

Kate's shrewish threats, commands and insults can also be traced to the titular shrew of the anonymous play *The Taming of a Shrew* (1594), who not only serves as a model of shrewishness but also exemplifies wifely obedience towards the end of the play. While the play closely resembles Shakespeare's, the provenance of *A Shrew* and its relationship to *The Shrew* remain critically vexed questions. Editors have variously hypothesized that it may be a derivative text of *The Shrew*, an early draft, a 'bad' quarto or a source text. Whatever the connection between the two plays may be, *A Shrew* is undeniably embedded in the same misogynistic discourse that gives shape to Shakespeare's play and should be treated as a valuable intertext to *The Shrew*.[20] In *A Shrew*,

Kate's early speech is similarly constituted by threats and commands as she, like Shakespeare's Kate, rejects her suitor Ferando's advances (3.142–59).[21] Her speech in the courtship scene is that of an unruly scold but it is not motivated by any criticism of Ferando's patriarchal stance. Both in the sun/moon scene and in her obedience speech, *A Shrew*'s Kate is presented as the ideal submissive wife who merely voices the speech pertaining to the character type she embodies. In the sun/moon scene, her speech perfectly matches Ferando's and marks her complete submission to him (12.11–12). In her monologue, where she ventriloquizes patristic discourse and alludes to the biblical account of creation to argue for female weakness and subjection (14.114–42), Kate's speech similarly signals her unquestioning submission to her husband and is wholly devoid of the reactionary aspect of Kate's monologue in *The Shrew* that individualizes her as a character. *A Shrew*'s Kate is a character type: she is the shrew of farce as well as the obedient wife of male fantasy.

The Shrew's Kate, however, is more than a type and more than just her scripted roles. By the end of Shakespeare's play, Kate does not relinquish her shrewish obstinance to fit into her new role as obedient wife; instead, she continues to defiantly question and respond to this new role and the patriarchy that creates it even as she voices the role of obedient wife. Her speech is marked by a performative use of language – she 'does' things with her words. Both in her exchanges with Petruccio and in her final speech, Kate picks up on, re-uses and echoes Petruccio's words in an attempt to carve out an identity for herself that is distinct from the ones assigned to her by patriarchal ideology. Lacking the linguistic inertia of *A Shrew*'s Kate, Shakespeare's Kate is neither an unruly scold nor a submissive wife but uses the linguistic habits of both to transcend her male-scripted roles. Shakespeare makes Kate a more vocally layered character whose defiant tongue mingles with her professed meekness in the monologue to both appease her husband and challenge her place in a marital union. Shakespeare's Kate is linguistically resourceful or, to borrow the terms ascribed by Pamela Allen Brown to the shrews of household manuals, a 'shrewd' or 'savvy' shrew.[22]

Puns, wordplay and Kate's conversational implicatures: A scorn of patriarchy

The feistiness and the aggressive insults that mark Kate as a shrew are immediately apparent in the courtship scene that transpires between her and Petruccio (2.1). Riddled with puns and wordplay, their exchange is structured on conversational implicatures that succeed each other with a stichomythic rapidity indicative of the struggle for domination between two equally matched opponents. Petruccio makes it no secret that his intention to wed and bed Katherine is motivated by the prospect of financial gain, as he admits to Hortensio: 'I come to wive it wealthily in Padua; / If wealthily, then happily in Padua' (1.2.74–5). The promise of his aristocratic wife's inheritance is only fuelled by the further prospect of the monetary reward promised him by Hortensio and Tranio, should he succeed in 'freeing' Bianca by winning her older sister's hand in marriage (1.2.264–73). Petruccio hopes to win Kate's assent by moving her to admire his rhetorical skill. Kate, however, resists Petruccio not because she is an innate shrew but because she retaliates against her father's unjust treatment of her. Kate disproves of her father's preferential treatment of Bianca, for this treatment makes her a mere decoy that is purely instrumental to Bianca's marriage: 'I pray you, sir, is it your will / To make a stale of me amongst these mates?' (1.1.57–8). Wary that her sentiments and inclinations are not solicited concerning the matter of marriage, Kate perceives that she is treated as a good to be passed along to the highest-bidding suitor. While she makes it sufficiently clear in her lamentation to her father that she does hope to have a husband (2.1.31–6), Kate rejects Petruccio's advances because she knows his wooing enterprise is motivated by her father's promise of profit and she refuses to be treated as an object of male possession. Kate's defiance, in other words, is impelled by her resentment of marriage as a business transaction in which she has no voice, agency or free will and is subordinated to patriarchal rule. Her shrewishness is motivated by a just grievance.

Kate's shrewish defiance of Petruccio and her resistance to his wooing are signalled by her conversational implicatures, which serve to attack Petruccio's face as wooer and critique his profit-driven and patriarchally inflected wooing enterprise. While her implicatures may suggest her willingness to cooperate with Petruccio by playing his game, they reveal that she does so in order to assert her own superiority and power. Petruccio initiates their conversation with an implicature in his opening greeting to Katherine: 'Good morrow, Kate, for that's your name, I hear' (2.1.181). His greeting violates the Gricean maxim of quantity ('make your contribution as informative as is required') by providing more information than is necessary ('for that's your name, I hear').[23] Not only does Petruccio attempt to establish familiarity with Kate by using the diminutive 'Kate', but his implicature also conveys to her his awareness of the rumours surrounding Kate's cursed tongue. The implicature invites or challenges Kate to confirm her name and her rumoured association with shrewishness. Kate agrees to take her turn in the exchange by responding to Petruccio, but she only does so to insult him: 'Well have you heard, but something hard of hearing: / They call me Katherine that do talk of me' (2.1.182–3). Kate's wordplay on Petruccio's 'I hear' with 'heard' and 'hearing' marks her violation of the Gricean maxim of manner ('be brief', 'be orderly', 'avoid ambiguity')[24] as she scornfully disparages Petruccio's face as wooer and emphasizes the distance between them. Kate's corrective assertion ('They call me Katherine that do talk of me') underscores her aristocratic status as she attempts to redress her negative face – or her desire to be unimpeded by others – by asserting her social superiority. In doing so, she implicitly highlights the social distance and hence incompatibility between them. Refusing to let Kate have the upper hand, Petruccio accuses Kate of lying and proceeds to redress his image as a wooer by impressing her with his rhetorical flattery. He calls her pretty (186), 'bonny' (185) and 'super-dainty' (187), and conventionally albeit ironically praises Kate as the chaste, mild and beautiful beloved that they both know she is not:

> Hearing thy mildness praised in every town,
> Thy virtues spoke of and thy beauty sounded –
> Yet not so deeply as to thee belongs –
> Myself am moved to woo thee for my wife
>
> (2.1.190–3)

Kate, however, is able to see through Petruccio's guise of love to his profit-driven intention to wed. Her wordplay on Petruccio's 'moved', which urges him to depart, again flouts Grice's maxim of manner to produce an implicature with which she insults him: '"Moved". In good time, let him that moved you hither / Re-move you hence. I knew you at the first / You were a movable' (194–6). Punning on 'movable', Kate accuses Petruccio of being fickle or mercurial ('movable'): she detects a discrepancy between his knowledge of her shrewish reputation and his attempt to woo a curst-tongued woman he ought to scorn rather than flatter. She may also be insinuating that she is wary of his plan to 'woo her with some spirit' (2.1.168), as he confesses in his soliloquy (2.1.167–79), by contrarily praising her for being what she is not. In showing him to be mercurial, Kate indirectly censures Petruccio for being a social climber (a 'movable') whose goal is to 'wive it wealthily in Padua' (1.2.74). Kate's additional punning on 'movable' to mean 'a joint-stool' (198) amplifies her attack on her wooer's face by demeaning his social status in calling him a lowly and common piece of household furniture. However, this insult is also Kate's way of telling Petruccio that she knows he is being used, as a joint-stool, by others who yearn to reach

Bianca. If Petruccio hopes to fool Kate by professing that his love for her 'moves' him to woo her, Kate shows Petruccio that she cannot be so easily fooled, knowing as she does that he is 'moved' or put into action by someone else (a vague 'he') to bait her into marriage so as to smooth the way to Bianca's betrothal. Kate's implicatures insult Petruccio and criticize the insincerity of his love suit.

Alongside insulting Petruccio and undercutting his attempt to woo her, Kate's implicatures also serve to reinstate her superiority in response to Petruccio's attempt to render her inferior and subject to his control. Responding to Kate's insult 'Asses are made to bear, and so are you' (2.1.200), Petruccio puns on 'bear' to denigrate Kate by pointing out that she belongs to the weaker sex who are vessels created to bear the weight of men as well as to bear children: 'Women are made to bear, and so are you' (201). Pretending to renounce his wooing enterprise, Petruccio further disparages Kate through his pun on 'light': he claims that he will not 'burden' Kate in bed since she is 'but young and light' (203–4). While Petruccio seems to be claiming that Kate is too fragile or weak ('light') to bear a man in bed, the implicature created by his pun additionally suggests that he is renouncing her for being wanton ('light'). Implying Kate's sexual promiscuity, Petruccio's insult jars with his idealized image of Kate as the mild and beauteous woman of high reputation he praised in his opening lines. He not only betrays that he is, in fact, fickle or 'movable' in exposing his manipulative tactics of seduction, but also voices the egoistic male desire for a chaste woman whom he can possess and who will serve his, and only his, turn. Kate, claims Petruccio, is too inferior to be his wife. Punning on Petruccio's use of 'light', Kate's retort denies his implicit charge of wantonness and valorizes her superiority: 'Too light for such a swain as you to catch, / And yet as heavy as my weight should be' (205–6). Kate suggests that it is her quick-wittedness or lightness that renders her superior to Petruccio and his feeble-wittedness and makes it impossible for him to seize her; if Petruccio's domination rests on his control of her body,

Kate avows that he will not be able to either grasp or control her mind or her linguistic skill. She shows that she is able to outwit him. Reminding Petruccio of her 'weight' or social prominence, Kate underlines her superiority to Petruccio, whom she labels a property-less 'swain', to imply that she is out of his social league. Kate thus uses puns and wordplay to create implicatures that bespeak her defiance of Petruccio's wooing and demonstrate her insubordination to his verbal and sexual dominance. Her offensive attacks on Petruccio and the patriarchy he endorses also serve as defensive measures to safeguard her negative face from being impeded by others. Although Petruccio instigates, controls and ends their conversation, Katherine demonstrates her adroitness in playing Petruccio's language games to spurn an arranged marriage where profit trumps love.

Epideictic rhetoric and Kate's echoic utterances

As in the courtship scene, Kate's exchange with Petruccio in the sun/moon scene demonstrates that she is a willing participant in his linguistic taming game but only so that she can censure his role as a dominant and domineering husband whose endorsement of patriarchy mandates her subjugation. Although the scene briefly opens with the stichomythic dialogue reminiscent of Kate and Petruccio's verbal sparring in the courtship scene, the audience witnesses Kate quickly relinquish her verbal aggression to cooperate with Petruccio. Instead of contradicting Petruccio's ludicrous claim that the sun is the moon (4.5.3), Kate agrees to the truth of what Petruccio professes out of fear that he may forestall their progress to Bianca's nuptials. Kate's vow betokens her compliance to Petruccio's demands and thus, for some critics, marks the point at which she sincerely submits to Petruccio: 'And be it moon or sun or what you please, / And if you please to call it a rush-candle, / Henceforth I vow it shall be so for me' (4.5.13–15). Kate's vow is quickly reinforced by an oath to reassure Petruccio that she will abide by his words: 'What you will have it named, even that it is, / And so it shall be so for Katherine' (4.5.22–3). But while her oath certainly marks her resignation to her husband's demands, it also registers her silent rebellion against him. In ironically referring to herself in the third person in this second promise, Kate intimates her distance from the obedience she will assume as 'Katherine' to imply that this promised obedience may very well be feigned. The ironic use of 'Katherine' also registers the mocking voice of the boy actor who, speaking as Kate, may be similarly asserting that he will persist in his defiance despite the submission he promises to enact.[25] The dramatic and verbal irony attending Kate's vow foreshadow how she indirectly critiques Petruccio using the epideictic rhetoric she addresses to old Vincentio.

While Kate's rhetorical praise of old Vincentio marks her compliance to Petruccio's behest, it also marks her pragmatic use of irony to scathingly mock Petruccio's patriarchal stance which requires women to be meek, submissive and passive objects of male possession. Kate intends her epideictic rhetoric to persuade Petruccio of her obedience while also using it to subtly and pragmatically convey her ridicule of Petruccio to him. Comically accosting the old and unsuspecting Vincentio as a 'fair lovely maid' (34), Petruccio models to Kate how she should praise the old man:

Good morrow, gentle mistress, where away?
– Tell me, sweet Kate, and tell me truly too,
Hast thou beheld a fresher gentlewoman,
Such war of white and red within her cheeks?
What stars do spangle heaven with such beauty
As those two eyes become that heavenly face?
– Fair lovely maid, once more good day to thee.
– Sweet Kate, embrace her for her beauty's sake.

(4.5.28–35)

Replete with flattery, Petruccio's speech serves to instruct Kate how to flatter the old man as he urges her to imitate his rhetoric. Petruccio uses Petrarchan convention to emblazon Vincentio; in noting the 'white and red' (31) in Vincentio's cheeks and in comparing his eyes to 'stars' that 'spangle' (32) his 'heavenly face' (33), he casts the old man as the ideal and inaccessible beloved of the Petrarchan sonnet tradition as he performs the role of lover.[26] Heeding Petruccio's cue, Kate adopts the voice of Petrarchan wooer to praise Vincentio after Petruccio's manner but also turns this praise of Vincentio into a dispraise of Petruccio and the patriarchal norms undergirding courtship and marriage through her pragmatic use of irony. In their pragmatic account of verbal irony, Dan Sperber and Deirdre Wilson define irony as 'implicit echoic mention': for an utterance to be ironic, it must refer to or 'echo' a prior proposition, utterance, or the thoughts and opinions held by someone in a previous conversation or situation.[27] Ironic utterances can just as well echo an unstated premise, assumption or cultural conventions, norms and ideas that may not have been made explicit; Sperber and Wilson note that the source may be indirect or have 'a vaguer origin'.[28] An echoic utterance evokes propositions that 'have been, or might have been, actually entertained by someone' but not verbatim, since the point is not to convey the content of the utterance but to indicate that the 'preceding utterance has been heard and understood' by the speaker, who conveys his or her reaction or attitude towards this utterance in echoing it.[29] The speaker's choice of words, tone and the immediate speech context of the utterance signal his or her attitude towards the utterance echoed in his or her speech. Verbal irony, as Sperber and Wilson demonstrate, is not simply a matter of implying the opposite of what is explicitly stated by way of an implicature that violates the maxim of quality (specifically, 'do not say what you believe to be false'), as Grice holds.[30] It is, instead, an echoic utterance that expresses the speaker's critical or scornful attitude towards, as well as his or her disassociation from, the words or thoughts originally pronounced or entertained by others.[31]

Greeting Vincentio as a 'young budding virgin, fair, and fresh, and sweet' (38), Kate exemplifies the use of echoic mention: her utterance echoes, while also expanding on, Petruccio's use of Petrarchan tropes in depicting Vincentio as a delicate and innocent flower. The succeeding lines of her speech more visibly register her mockery and disapproval of Petruccio as she makes the virginal maiden Vincentio into the object of male desire:

> Young budding virgin, fair, and fresh, and sweet,
> Whither away, or where is thy abode?
> Happy the parents of so fair a child;
> Happier the man whom favourable stars
> Allots thee for his lovely bedfellow.
>
> (38–42)

While Kate's interrogative 'Whither away, or where is thy abode?' (39) clearly echoes Petruccio's opening question ('Good morrow, gentle mistress, where away?' [28]), her addition of the words 'where is thy abode?' inscribes her disapproving attitude towards Petruccio as lover as she implies that the Petrarchan lover's rhetorical flattery is underwritten by a fervent desire to pursue and sexually possess his beloved. Kate ironically voices not the words explicitly uttered by Petruccio but rather the unavowed intention underlying his praise so as to expose a man's hypocrisy in making women believe that they are anything more than objects of male possession. In praising Vincentio's virginal beauty ('so fair a child'), Kate-as-wooer insinuates that a physically attractive young woman not only brings her parents happiness – with the unstated assumption that her attractiveness would make her more marriageable – but also brings her future husband even greater happiness in being a 'lovely bedfellow' who can fulfil his sexual needs: 'Happy the parents of so fair a child; / Happier the man whom favourable stars / Allots thee for his lovely bedfellow' (40–2). Kate's praise thus underscores her scorn of patriarchal marriage in which women are 'allotted' or assigned by 'fate' to their husband-owners without exercising their right of choice; she is also lamenting her own situation as a woman who has been indirectly 'allotted' to her husband by her father. Her echoic utterance is, in large part, also a reaction against Petruccio's declaration that he will be 'master' of his Kate: 'She is my goods, my chattels; she is my house, / My household-stuff, my field, my barn, / My horse, my ox, my ass, my anything' (3.2.231–3). In thus directly praising Vincentio-as-fair-maid in her role as male wooer to persuade her husband of her obedience, Kate uses irony to indirectly critique the male domination of women in a state of matrimony and Petruccio, in particular, who subscribes to patriarchal values that demand her submission to him. Kate's echoic utterances attest to a shrewish defiance that she does not altogether stifle or banish but instead attenuates by channelling it through her rhetoric in order to both propitiate her husband and to get what she ultimately wants: to see her family again.

Kate's apology to old Vincentio further instantiates her use of echoic mention to covertly deliver her critique of Petruccio. Heeding Petruccio's prompt to apologize to Vincentio for mistaking the 'old, wrinkled, faded, withered' man (44) as a young and fair maiden, Kate blames her 'mad mistaking' on the blinding sun: 'Pardon, old father, my mistaking eyes / That have been so bedazzled with the sun / That everything I look on seemeth green' (46–8). Kate's reference to the sun is an ironic echo of the stichomythic dispute between her and Petruccio that opens the scene (4.5.1–5). In calling the sun the 'moon', a cross Petruccio vows that 'Now by my mother's son – and that's myself – / It shall be moon or star or what I list' (6–7). In punning on 'sun' to signify son (Petruccio), Kate ironically echoes Petruccio's authoritarianism to deride her husband as she accuses him of blinding her with the deceptive brilliance of his performative reversals. The evident obsequiousness of her apology to Vincentio is intended to persuade Petruccio of her utmost obedience to him so as to clear herself of blame, even as it works to implicitly show that it is Petruccio who is at fault for stringently enforcing this obedience. Kate here adopts the role of obedient wife to mock her husband's domination over her even as she displays her praiseworthy constancy to the sun/son. In doing so, she highlights Petruccio's mercurialness as a man whose words are dictated by the inconstant moon. Kate thus shrewdly eclipses Petruccio by conveying her superiority to him through echoic mention while rhetorically displaying her inferiority as a meek wife.

The belief and suspicion entertained by Kate's onstage audience concerning her rhetorical performance further underscore the counterpointing of obedience with shrewish defiance in her speech that marks her ambiguity as a character. That Kate has persuaded both Hortensio and Petruccio of her submission to Petruccio is evident in their commentary following her vow: both men agree that, as Hortensio states, 'the field is won' (24) as Petruccio compares his mastery of Kate to the game of bowls, in which he boastfully claims to have coerced Kate (the 'bowl') to yield to him in accordance with her submissive nature: 'thus the bowl should run, / And not unluckily against the bias' (25–6). While Petruccio's failure to acknowledge or respond to the echoic utterances in Kate's epideictic speech may convey his belief in her veritable submission, it may also betoken that he is complicit in her feigning but desires to persuade his audience (here, Hortensio) that he is a successful tamer of a shrewish wife. Nevertheless, it is Hortensio's aside at the end of the scene that highlights for the offstage audience that one auditor, at least, is persuaded by Kate's compliance and the efficacy of Petruccio's taming methods: 'Well, Petruccio, this has put me in heart. / Have to my widow, and if she be forward, / Then hast thou taught Hortensio to be untoward' (78–80). Believing what he has witnessed to be sincere, Hortensio has not understood or picked up on Kate's pragmatic use of language. Old Vincentio's doubt, by contrast, signals to the offstage audience that Kate's rhetoric fails as much as it succeeds. Confessing to be 'amazed' by the 'strange encounter' (55) or praise that Kate has showered upon him, Vincentio additionally questions the truthfulness of Petruccio's claim that Vincentio is his 'loving father' (62): 'is this true, or is it else your pleasure, / Like pleasant travellers, to break a jest / Upon the company you overtake?' (4.5.72–4). Both unpersuaded by Kate's speech and by Petruccio's words, the sceptical Vincentio reinforces the offstage audience's suspicion that Katherine's rhetoric of obedience is feigned by an actor who intends to deceive her male audience (Petruccio and Hortensio). His suspicion of the theatrical illusion attunes the offstage audience to be more attentive not only to what Kate rhetorically says but also to what she pragmatically does or communicates through her rhetoric – in other words, to attend to the possibility of being duped by Kate the actor.

Exposing the meta-theatricality of the sun/moon scene, Vincentio's reaction of suspicion serves to highlight the dramatic irony framing Kate's verbal irony that contributes to her anteriority as a character. Vincentio seems to usurp the function of the Induction by making the offstage audience conscious of watching a play-within-a-play. In suggesting that Kate may be an actor who merely performs her obedience, Vincentio gestures towards the boy actor who personates Kate performing the role of an obedient wife, in other words the boy actor playing the character playing an actor. As Richard Madelaine and Juliet Dusinberre have demonstrated, Petruccio's taming of Katherine parallels and is overlaid by the meta-theatrical 'taming' plot of the adult actor training his boy apprentice.[32] Just as Kate shrewishly resists Petruccio's sexual domination, which calls for her adherence to her patriarchally-scripted role as obedient wife, the apprentice actor shrewishly resists his subservience to his master in the social hierarchy of the theatre which requires that he perform 'a stereotypical "feminine" role at this stage of his training' rather than a male role that would grant him equal status to an adult actor.[33] Both Kate and the boy actor personating her strive to transcend their scripted roles as obedient wife and disobedient shrew to defiantly challenge or criticize authority. Kate's implicit critique of Petruccio and patriarchy through her echoic utterances is also indicative of the boy actor's scornful mockery of the rhetoric of a male wooer that he stages even as he performs this role. Through his mockery, the boy actor underscores for his audience his superior acting skills, which allow him to both produce and puncture the lifelike image of female obedience he enacts. If the adult actor, like Petruccio, impersonates female fickleness in the sun/moon scene in order to teach his apprentice how not to act, it is the boy apprentice, as Kate, who ironically teaches his master that he is the more skilful actor by emphasizing his equally masterful use of presentational and representational acting to produce a realistic illusion that has the potential to dazzle his audience. The incongruence between what Kate rhetorically says in her speech and what she pragmatically does with it is refracted by the boy actor impersonating her, who lends credence to the defiance mobilizing her pragmatic use of irony and thus marks her anteriority. Through the divergent responses of Hortensio and Vincentio, Shakespeare instils in his offstage audience a dual awareness of Kate as both an obedient wife and a shrew – as well as a boy actor and the character he portrays – and thereby orchestrates our impression of Kate's ambiguity that comes to define her anteriority as a character. What Kate does with her language in the sun/moon scene serves a dress rehearsal for her final speech.

Offering war and kneeling for peace: Kate's monologue

Upon winning a wager with Lucentio and Hortensio that Kate is the most obedient of their three wives, Petruccio commands Kate to 'tell these headstrong women / What duty they do owe their lords and husbands' (5.2.136–7) to showcase Kate's 'new-built virtue and obedience' (124). His goal is to win the praise and admiration of the other husbands by displaying his successfully tamed wife. Kate's aim, however, is more diverse. As in the sun/moon scene where she made skilful use of epideictic rhetoric to praise Vincentio in order to propitiate her husband, she similarly, yet more masterfully, uses deliberative rhetoric in her monologue to exhort her female audience to obey their husbands in order to display her obedience and thereby please her husband. Nevertheless, even though Kate acquiesces to Petruccio's command, she does not fail to signal her defiant criticism of the obedience she is forced to adopt. Kate's monologue is essentially addressed to two different audiences. In adopting the ethos of an obedient wife to urge other wives to submit to their husbands, Kate addresses her male audience (including Petruccio) in order to persuade them of her virtuous submission. However, Kate also disrupts her rhetorical ethos through her pragmatic use of language, which serves to criticize the patriarchal structure of marriage that denies women freedom, to covertly address Bianca and the Widow but also the offstage female audience in order to counsel them against adopting the very submission she preaches. More specifically, the comparisons in Kate's speech serve to argumentatively uphold her ethos as an obedient wife by displaying her endorsement of female subordination while the echoic utterances, puns and semantic ambiguity in her speech create implicatures that destabilize her argumentation and imply her criticism of the obedience she voices.

The first part of Kate's lengthy speech (5.2.142–66) exhibits her use of persuasive argumentation to convey to her male and female audiences her endorsement of female subordination. Kate employs a series of comparisons which serve as logical appeals to highlight the duties that women should owe their husbands.[34] Nevertheless, the echoic utterances saturating these comparisons undercut her argumentation by revealing her mockery of the patriarchal image of women she presents. Rebuking Bianca and the Widow for their recalcitrance and ordering them to 'uknit' their 'threatening unkind brow[s]' and to 'dart not scornful glances' from their eyes (142–3), Kate juxtaposes their scornful expressions against her idealized depiction of the dainty and beauteous women they should be. Kate invokes the image of a stereotypical woman through a series of comparisons that imply a woman's duty. She urges the two wives to discard their scornful expression for

> It blots thy beauty as frosts do bite the meads,
> Confounds thy fame as whirlwinds shake fair buds
> And in no sense is meet or amiable.
> A woman moved is like a fountain troubled,
> Muddy, ill-seeming, thick, bereft of beauty
> And while it is so, none so dry or thirsty
> Will deign to sip or touch one drop of it
>
> (5.2.145–51)

Comparing a woman's physical beauty to 'meads' (145) and her reputation to 'fair buds' (146), whose youthful and spring-like vitality are threatened by wintery scorn, Kate employs two similes to depict women as fair, fragile and meek elements of nature. In doing so, she implies that a woman's duty is to mind her nature and to be 'meet or amiable' (147) or pleasing to her husband, both in her appearance and in her behaviour, for she exists to adorn and satisfy him. Kate's third simile compares an angry woman to a 'fountain troubled, / Muddy, ill-seeming, thick, bereft of beauty' (148–9) and serves as a warning to her female auditors that 'dry' or 'thirsty' men '[w]ill [not] deign to sip or touch one drop' (150–1) of them if they persist in the repulsive defiance that physically disfigures them. Her warning underscores that a woman's duty is to be serviceable to her husband and to fulfil his needs as his life source. After informing Bianca and the Widow of their wifely duties, Kate uses an analogy to explain to them why women should obey their husbands. She tells them that a husband is:

> Thy head, thy sovereign: one that cares for thee
> And for thy maintenance; commits his body
> To painful labour both by sea and land,
> To watch the night in storms, the day in cold,
> Whilst thou liest warm at home, secure and safe,
> And craves no other tribute at thy hands
> But love, fair looks and true obedience –
> Too little payment for so great a debt.
>
> (5.2.153–60)

Kate compares a husband to a merchant who undertakes a long and arduous journey 'by sea and land' to ensure the comfort and peace enjoyed by his wife at home. Juxtaposing a husband's distressful worldly activity to a wife's peaceful domestic complacency to portray the desirability of the latter, Kate claims that a wife is obligated to bestow on her husband 'love, fair looks and true obedience' (159) as a sign of her gratitude for having her basic needs met. Complementing her similes, Kate's analogy propagates female passivity but it also signals her covert critique of women's marital role by way of the echoic mention permeating it. The love and obedience that a woman owes her husband are glossed in economic terms: they are the 'little payment' with which a wife reimburses her husband for the expense he incurs in ensuring her material well-being – she is, in other words, indebted to her creditor for his care. In thus making wifely obedience the currency of the exchange, Kate's utterance 'Too little payment for so great a debt' (160) ironically echoes the notion of marriage as a business transaction which pervades the play. Her analogy invokes her father's pronouncement that he plays 'a merchant's part / And venture[s] madly on a desperate mart' (2.1.330–1) in giving his daughter to Petruccio in marriage. Tranio, responding to Baptista, concurs that the unmarried Katherine is 'a commodity lay fretting by you; / 'Twill bring you gain, or perish on the seas' (332–3). Kate's echoic mention allows her to ridicule this exchange, which makes a woman a valuable good to be owned and traded among men in the hope of a profitable return. In expressing his desire for a wife, then, a suitor is a merchant who yearns to take possession of a valuable commodity, as Hortensio's confession of his love for Bianca reveals: 'For in Baptista's keep my treasure is. / He hath the jewel of my life in hold' (1.2.116–17). Within this marital economy, a woman's love is a prize that can be bought and sold to the highest bidder, as Baptista informs Bianca's suitors: ''Tis deeds must win the prize, and he of both / That can assure my daughter greatest dower / Shall have my Bianca's love' (2.1.346–8). Kate's echoic mention registers her revulsion at the oppressive patriarchal treatment of women and allows her to scornfully mock the transactional nature of marriage voiced by her father and the suitors in the play, which makes women lifeless commodities owned by men. Her pragmatic use of irony indirectly yet nonetheless defiantly condones the dutiful obedience she preaches to her female audience by showing them the reality of repressive mastery and imprisonment that bely the promise of comfortable domesticity. The offstage audience's awareness of the domestic abuse suffered by Kate at Petruccio's hands, which makes her marital 'home' anything but a sanctuary of warmth and security, renders her verbal irony doubly ironic.

Kate's pragmatic use of irony also affects her second analogy and further destabilizes her persuasive argumentation by revealing her endorsement of female insubordination. To buttress her argument for wifely servility, Kate compares a wife's dutiful obedience to her husband to a political subject's allegiance to his or her monarch: 'Such duty as the subject owes the prince, / Even such a woman oweth her husband' (161–2). Nevertheless, Kate's analogy remains suspiciously underdeveloped as it quickly dovetails into a rhetorical question that serves to depict political rebellion rather than the loyalty she asks her female audience to cultivate:

> And when she is froward, peevish, sullen, sour
> And not obedient to his honest will,
> What is she but a foul contending rebel
> And graceless traitor to her loving lord?
>
> (163–6)

As a woman subordinated to her husband, Kate echoically voices received patriarchal values that require women-subjects to remain in their ascribed places within the social and political hierarchy governed by the man-monarch. However, her analogy nevertheless challenges and mocks the moral justness of a husband's reign by ironically implying his forceful domination and tyrannical rule over his wife in referencing Bianca's and the Wife's rebellion. Kate castigates the women as political rebels and traitors who 'offer war where they should kneel for peace' (168) to showcase her condemnation of their insolence towards their husbands to them. However, in doing so, she also coveys to the women that they have the power to reject their subjection and harm their husbands through their behaviour and facial expressions – specifically, by means of their 'threatening' brow (142) and eyes that 'dart' with scorn (143), with which Kate's oration opens. Although women are 'bound to serve, love and obey' (170), Kate suggests that they have the power to rebel by transforming their amicable demeanours into defiant demeanours. If marriage, as Kate has suggested, is an arrangement driven by profit rather than love, then rebellion may very well be justified, especially if submission is tyrannically enforced. Kate's rhetorical performance appeases her male audience for it allows her to berate the unruly wives for offering 'war' (168); at the same time, she uses this performance to counsel her female audience to resist the obedience she preaches as she encourages them to harness, rather than renounce, their power.

Along with the verbal irony infusing her comparisons, Kate's use of puns and semantic ambiguity in the second half of her monologue create implicatures that convey her defiance and her message of disobedience to her female audience. Kate extends her argument for women's servile obedience by using erotema or a rhetorical question that echoes the patristic account of female weakness:

> Why are our bodies soft, and weak, and smooth,
> Unapt to toil and trouble in the world,
> But that our soft conditions and our hearts
> Should well agree with our external parts?
>
> (5.2.171–4)

Conveying her affirmation of female inferiority, the erotema firmly aligns Kate with the misogynistic and patriarchal values held by her male audience. In voicing patristic accounts which hold that a woman's 'soft condition' or her inner constitution is determined by her soft body, Kate urges her female audience to embrace their gentle conditions and make their emotions, behaviour and attitudes harmoniously accord with the softness of their bodies. However, Kate's double pun on 'parts' undermines her endorsement of female submission by inscribing a secondary meaning onto her utterance. Violating the Gricean maxim of manner, Kate's pun enables her to advise Bianca and the Widow, as well as women offstage, to abide by their theatrical 'parts' or part-scripts and to fulfil their social roles as obedient wives that are scripted for them by men. The pun reveals that Kate covertly instructs her female audience to publicly perform their obedience in a realistic or representational manner rather than to sincerely submit to their husbands' control. Kate thus intimates her own performative 'doing' as she propagates the creation of a theatrical illusion. In a similar manner, the offstage audience hears the voice of the boy actor who draws attention to his own skilful performance as he urges his fellow actors playing the roles of Bianca and the Widow to naturalistically perform their obedience so as to placate their adult masters. In doing so, the boy-as-Kate usurps the role of the Lord in the Induction who instructs his huntsmen how to put on a show of submission; the boy actor playing Kate may even possibly be the same actor playing the Lord's page/Sly's wife in the Induction, who passes along his received knowledge about how to impersonate the gestures, actions and speech of a gentle 'lady' (105–22) to his fellow actors. The boy-as-Kate thus models to his fellow actors-as-wives how to imitate and emulate his performance. The secondary pun on 'external parts', signifying genitalia, is produced by the boy actor himself to register his defiance of his scripted role as he undermines the softness he urges his female auditors to display. Pointing towards the sexual female 'parts' he clearly does not possess, the boy draws his fellow actors' attention to his cross-dressed body in a way that indirectly challenges the inferiority he preaches. Showing that a 'soft' condition cannot agree with a boy's external 'parts', the boy uses his pun to pragmatically convey to his fellow actors the necessity of retaliating against their unsuitable roles, which do not accommodate their nature as male actors. In advocating for the harmony between inner nature and outer expression as an obedient wife, the boy metadramatically reveals the unnatural correspondence between his masculinity and his feminized body even as he illuminates his superior acting skills which enable him to personate that which he naturally is not. In doing so, the boy underscores his performative power which mobilizes his defiance. Kate's pun, buttressed by the boy actor's use of the same, destabilizes the argumentative use of rhetoric that serves to persuade her male audience of her obedience by creating an implicature which conveys to her female audience her ridicule and dissent of the male-scripted role she is required to perform even as she performs it. The boy, like Kate, reacts against his perceived marginalization.

Complementing Kate's pun is the semantic ambiguity attending her pronouncement of female weakness. While Kate strives to dissuade her female audience from waging an aggressive 'war' against their husbands by telling them that women have no physical strength, the ambiguity of her words indicates her defiant endorsement of revolt as she asserts women's power: 'But now I see our lances are but straws, / Our strength as weak, our weakness past compare, / That seeming to be most which we indeed least are' (179–81). By comparing women's destructive weapons ('lances') to metaphorical straws, Kate underlines the futility of their aggressive attack by showing them that female weakness is incomparable to and incompatible with male strength; women, she claims, do not have the power to 'bandy word for word and frown for frown' (178). Nevertheless, the ambiguity of her last line ('That seeming to be most which we indeed least are') violates the Gricean maxim of manner ('be perspicuous') to produce an implicature that discreetly valorizes the meaning of 'weak'.[35] Although Kate is professing that women seem to be most strong when in reality they are least strong (or weak), she is also implying that women *seem* to be most weak when in fact they are least weak (i.e. strong); their 'weakness' poses a challenge to male strength. The semantic ambiguity of the line, caused in part by the deliberate absence of an adjective after 'most', allows Kate to forcefully assert herself as well as the power that she and the other wives possess through the very submission that denies her self-assertion. The ambiguity of Kate's utterance also invites meta-dramatic irony as the audience hears the boy actor announce that he stands in firm league with his fellow boy actors against their adult masters: he proclaims that they ('we') seem to be most female when 'indeed', or in the actions they perform on stage (in *deed*), they are least female. The boy thus valorizes the performative power of his masculinity – which his rhetorical performance of Petruccio's obedient wife denies – and encourages the other boy actors to assert their strength, to abstain from relinquishing their agency and to challenge authority by rupturing the illusion they create. The boy-as-Kate shows that he is capable of impersonating an obedient wife while at the same time displaying that he is a superb actor who is able to transcend this scripted role by injecting it with his trademark defiance. Kate-as-boy thus not only reacts against Petruccio-as-master by criticizing him but also champions her/his theatrical skill to create a mimetically real performance that succeeds in both persuading and pragmatically communicating different messages to his or her heterogeneous audience.

The ambivalent responses of Kate's onstage male audience to her deliberative rhetoric only fortify the ambiguity that the offstage audience detects in her monologue. Hortensio's claim that Petruccio 'hast tamed a curst shrew' (5.2.194) marks the efficacy of Kate's rhetoric to persuade her male audience of the sincerity of her submission, while Lucentio's exclamation that ''Tis a wonder, by your leave, she will be tamed so' (5.2.195), which mirrors old Vincentio's bewilderment, registers Lucentio's suspicion of an obedience brought about by Petruccio's domination. Lucentio's response, however, does not attest to Kate's failure to persuade part of her male audience of her obedience. Instead, his doubt sheds light on the aperture in her rhetoric created by her pragmatic intent to critique the unjust domination of women and to inspire her female auditors not to accept the subordination she seems to endorse. Kate's final gesture of placing her hand beneath her husband's foot, for certain members of her audience, visually parallels the subordination she voices in her speech while her offstage auditors – as well as a number of her onstage auditors – perceive the subversive potential of the gesture as she shrewishly displays her own power and readiness to knock her husband down.

Kate's monologue imparts to us the anamorphic image of an indomitable shrew existing alongside a conformable wife. It is this anamorphism, perceived by the offstage audience, that brings Katherine to life as a three-dimensional character who seems to transcend her male-scripted and stereotypically female roles as she attempts to individualize herself within patriarchal discourse. The absence of the Sly plot at the end of the play puts Kate's monologue squarely into the spotlight, as her rhetorical performance becomes the theatrical production that provides the offstage audience with both a behind-the-scenes look at how illusions are produced and at the various effects these illusions can have on an audience. Kate, usurping the role of the Lord in the Induction, reveals her intention to dupe her male audience while showing her female audience that these men are being duped. Our impression of Kate's ambiguity arises from the divergence between the persuasive and pragmatic intentions in her monologue: she aspires to rhetorically persuade Petruccio and her male audience of her ethos as an obedient wife at the same time as she strives to pragmatically convey to her female audience her critique of the patriarchy espoused by Petruccio. The echoic utterances, puns and semantic ambiguity in Kate's monologue give rise to conversational implicatures that display her defiance of the very submission she coaxes her female auditors into accepting and indirectly conveys her critique of a patriarchal marriage that enforces female subordination. Kate's implied meanings unsettle the rhetorical ethos of the obedient wife she projects through the argumentative use of comparisons in her monologue, which voice her endorsement of female submission and serve to persuade her male audience of her reformation. The incongruence between her pragmatic and persuasive intentions, along with the meta-theatricality of the boy actor playing her and the ambivalent reactions of her onstage auditors, produce the offstage audience's impression of her ambiguity as a character and lend her an anteriority that gives her extra-theatrical presence. Kate 'tell[s] the anger of [her] heart' (4.3.79) but in subdued terms as she learns to transmute her direct attacks on Petruccio into a discreet condemnation of patriarchy by the end of the play; she teaches wives disobedience by commanding their obedience. Kate strives to at least partially become the subject of her own script even though she is, ironically and inevitably, already scripted by the Shakespeare-like Petruccio who sanctions her linguistic performances. In a play that ostentatiously and unapologetically comments on its own theatricality, perhaps the greatest meta-theatrical irony of all is that Shakespeare's shrewd shrew serves as an allegory for his creation of character effects in the theatre.

Coda

Questioning Anteriority: Hamlet's Undecidability and Pragmatic Failure

With his dying words, Hamlet, knowing that he will not live long enough to 'hear the news from England' (5.2.338) regarding Denmark's election, instructs Horatio to tell Fortinbras that '[Fortinbras] has my dying voice' (5.2.340).[1] While editorial glosses note that in giving his 'voice' Hamlet is using his last breath to cast his vote for Fortinbras as his successor, Hamlet's final utterance also carries a second and hauntingly literal meaning that plays into the trope of doubling undergirding the play. In giving Fortinbras his voice, Hamlet is gifting, entrusting or delegating his voice to Fortinbras, who epitomizes the vengeful soldier and martial leader that Hamlet could never be. It is Fort(in)bras, a hero etymologically 'strong-in-arms', who puts into action on Hamlet's behalf what Hamlet could not perform himself. Fortinbras, ordering four captains to 'Bear Hamlet like a soldier to the stage, / For he was likely, had he been put on, / To have proved most royally' (380–2), scripts the deceased Hamlet as the honourable and princely avenger demanded by the ghost of old Hamlet, and stages a theatrical performance replete with music and rites of war which 'speak loudly' (384) for Hamlet's would-be heroic deed. It is Fortinbras's 'act' – his ability to theatrically direct Hamlet's performance – which complements the actions he performs as martial soldier that fulfils old Hamlet's command for vengeance.

Hamlet is a play not so much about the disjunction between the titular protagonist's words and deeds as much as it is about words-as-deeds and what these performative utterances both do and fail to do to other characters and to the theatre audience.[2] Hamlet's delay in taking revenge on Claudius is commonly attributed to his obsession with words, which characterize the extensive deliberation that ultimately thwarts him from taking vengeful action. I suggest, instead, that Hamlet delays not because his words impede his actions but because they perform actions that deviate from and conflict with the required scripted action of revenge. It is Hamlet's failure to enact his scripted role as an avenger that sets him apart from Shakespeare's other pragmatists. Falstaff, Cleopatra, Henry V and *The Shrew*'s Katherine all impeccably perform their scripted roles even as they pragmatically re-script them within their own speaking contexts; their linguistic performances reveal their anteriority, which produces the offstage audience's impression that these self-conscious characters are controlling agents of pre-existent discourses. Hamlet, however, distances himself from the avenger role that his deceased father scripts for him and opts instead to enact the 'antic disposition' (1.5.70) of a melancholic madman. Nevertheless, Hamlet's pragmatic use of this 'antic disposition' is imperfect: it so often melds with his irate misogyny that he seems to oscillate between possessing, and lacking, anteriority.

Hamlet's adoption of an antic disposition finds its parallel in one of Shakespeare's sources for his play, Saxo Grammaticus's *Vita Amlethi* in his *Gesta Danorum*. Unlike Hamlet, however, Saxo's heroic avenger Amleth effectively uses his antic disposition to carry out his revenge on Fengo (Claudius).

Saxo presents Amleth as a martial prince who uses madness as a disguise to conceal his intelligence regarding his father's murder and to ensure his safety in the king's court. Saxo notes that Amleth's words perfectly reflect his disguise: 'All he said was of a piece with [his] follies'.[3] Amleth is adept at mingling 'craft and candour in such wise that, though his words did lack truth, yet there was nothing to betoken the truth and betray how far his keenness went'.[4] He masks his knowledge of his father's murder so perfectly that '[n]one could open the secret lock of the young man's wisdom'.[5] Not only does Amleth's madness linguistically conceal him, as Saxo reveals, but it is also a weapon that renders his deeds 'valiant' for he is 'shrewdly armed with a feint of folly'.[6] Amleth's words exist in service to his noble deeds; his linguistic performance is so effective and instrumental to his revenge that Saxo puts it on a par with his courage: 'By this skilful defence of himself, and strenuous revenge for his parent, he has left it doubtful whether we are to think more of his wit or his bravery.'[7] Shakespeare severs the consonance that Saxo notes between the avenger's linguistic performance (his words) and his action (his vengeful deed) to highlight the deviant performativity of Hamlet's words. Unlike Amleth, Shakespeare's dramatic character betrays his knowledge, or at least his suspicion, of his father's murder to his onstage and offstage interlocutors through his pragmatic use of language; his language both conceals and reveals Hamlet in a way that makes him ultimately inscrutable as a character.

The critical attention afforded to Hamlet's language in the past three decades has not only been slim but has also sidelined the pragmatic dimension of his speech. Critics have noted with admiration the expansive range of Hamlet's language: his ability to encompass diverse tropes and schemes in his speech, such as intertextual allusions, aphorisms, metaphors, hendiadys, synecdoches and equivocation, typify and reflect the prince's protean adoption of roles as various as a jaded lover, a melancholic son and the introspective scholar of a newly Protestant Wittenberg. Hamlet is commonly lauded as a gifted rhetorician and actor who is able to imitatively hold 'the mirror up to Nature to show Virtue her feature' (3.2.22) by impersonating those characters in the play with whom he interacts. Since Hamlet is 'a theatrical personality', as Sanford Sternlicht has claimed, the theatricality of his histrionic impersonations rests on and presupposes his linguistic agency.[8] In 1992, Lars Engle addressed critics' censure of Hamlet's inaction by rehabilitating his agency. Hamlet, claimed Engle, possesses a discursive agency that consists of 'the overt manipulation of discourses to produce representations which will, he hopes, reform the agency of others' by showing them 'what they are doing and invit[ing] them to react'.[9] In appropriating and re-contextualizing others' speaking habits in his own speech, Hamlet becomes a 'Bakhtinian discursive agent' whose 'method is a theatrically pragmatic one which involves continual performance with therapeutic ends'.[10] Engle's observations are taken up by Philip Collington, who reads the plurivocality of 2.2 as an instantiation of the play's display of Bakhtinian heteroglossia. Collington argues that the overlapping social speech genres peppering Hamlet's speech are a testament to his 'allusive sarcasm' and to 'the superior mental agility of a prince conversant in many literary forms'.[11] Aside from noting the dialogism of Hamlet's speech and his performative agency as a speaker, neither Collington nor Engle explore what Hamlet does on a pragmatic level with his speech.

Focusing on Hamlet's pragmatic use of language vis-à-vis his self-appointed role as madman, I explore how the contradictory message conveyed by his utterances produces his inscrutability as a character. A careful inspection of Hamlet's pragmatic strategies reveals that his performative utterances constantly undo the antic disposition he performs and make the offstage audience question whether Hamlet is in full control of the discourses he uses. The aura of mystery shrouding Hamlet as a character has been synonymous with his notorious interiority, whose inaccessibility renders him a psychologically 'real' and idiosyncratically complex person.[12]

However, while the unplumbed depths towards which Hamlet himself constantly gestures seem to define his ontological reality, his unfathomable inwardness is extraneous to the anteriority that makes its glinting presence known through his performative utterances. I want to suggest that Hamlet's inscrutability as a character is not due to his interiority or to the hermeneutic impossibility of plucking out the 'heart of [his] mystery' (3.2.357–8) but is instead due to the undecidability arising from the questionable anteriority produced by his utterances. I will demonstrate that Hamlet is an adept pragmatist who controls his conversational encounters with other characters in the play and reveals that there is an anterior 'I' shaping his intentions and controlling his speech. I contend that in performing his role as madman, Hamlet creates conversational implicatures to indirectly convey his scathing critique of Claudius, Gertrude, Polonius and Ophelia's hypocrisy to them and thereby highlights his anteriority. However, Hamlet's implied critique is easily compromised by his obsessive misogyny, which erupts into his utterances and throws into doubt the offstage audience's impression that Hamlet has anteriority by making it seem as if he is mad in earnest. It is this tension between concealment and self-disclosure afforded by Hamlet's antic disposition, coupled with his onstage auditors' inability to grasp the pragmatic import of his implicatures and the dramatic framing of these conversations, that produces our impression of Hamlet's undecidability as a character. A pragmatic reading of Hamlet's utterances as a madman, which foregrounds his failure to produce consistent messages, is congenial to a play riddled with uncertainties and contradictions that preclude a unitary reading or linear interpretation of its protagonist. If *Hamlet* either is or coexists alongside what Terence Hawkes calls '*Telmah*', or a play-text that doubles back on itself to offer readers and audiences 'an ever-present potential challenge and contradiction *within* and *implied by* the text', then this intricate counterpointing of progress and regress is embodied in Hamlet's speech.[13]

Hamlet's implicatures in his opening response to Claudius, which indirectly criticize the king's hypocrisy and reveal to his onstage and offstage audiences the truth of the murder that Claudius strives to hide, produce the impression of his anteriority. Addressing Hamlet as 'my cousin Hamlet, and my son –' (1.2.64), Claudius repeats the possessive pronoun 'my' to highlight the close bond they share. While Hamlet's response affirms that they are indeed kinsmen, his pun on kin/kind violates Grice's maxim of manner ('avoid obscurity of expression' and 'avoid ambiguity') to produce an implicature that records his dissent: 'A little more than kin, and less than kind' (1.2.65).[14] While affirming that he is more than a kinsman to Claudius, Hamlet is also implying that he is less than 'kind' or not his natural son, given Claudius's usurpation of his deceased father's throne. The pun also entails a secondary meaning whereby Hamlet expresses a bitter hostility or unkindness ('less than kind') towards his stepfather, which is motivated by his knowledge of Claudius's vile deed and his scheming. Claudius's unkindness – his callous disregard of his brother and his hasty marriage to Gertrude – spawns and justifies Hamlet's retort. Hamlet's implicature conveys that he is able to see through Claudius's self-righteous veneer and underscores Hamlet's anterior and moralizing voice in the play. Claudius, who either purposefully ignores or altogether fails to understand the pragmatic intent behind Hamlet's pun, proceeds to inquire into the reason for Hamlet's prolonged mourning: 'How is it that the clouds still hang on you?' (1.2.66). Hamlet's second pun on sun/son allows him to further his critique of Claudius under the pretence of flattering him: 'Not so much, my lord, I am too much in the "son"' (1.2.67). Picking up on Claudius's nature imagery, Hamlet satirically flatters the newly crowned king by claiming that his melancholy has dissipated, now that he is in the king's favour (the 'sun') as his son; while seeming to honour Claudius, Hamlet bitterly mocks Claudius's sense of self-importance. The reference to the sun may also be an intertextual allusion to François de Belleforest's Hamblet in his *Histoires Tragiques* (c.1570). In

Belleforest's highly moralized reworking of Saxo's legend of Amleth, Hamblet clandestinely confronts Geruth (Gertrude) and explains the necessity for his dissimulation. He compares his right reason or wits to the sun, which he is impelled to forcefully 'hide vnder this shadow of dissimulation, as the sun doth hir beams vnder some great cloud, when the wether in sommer time ouercasteth'.[15] Shakespeare's either intentional or unintentional allusion to the sun's metaphorical association with good sense in Belleforest's work nevertheless highlights that Hamlet's pun possibly conveys that he is 'too much' in his senses or right wits to allow melancholy and its twin, madness, to overpower him. In appropriating Claudius's words and extending his use of images, Hamlet signals to his auditors that he is aware of the crime that Claudius glosses over. Registering a threat that Claudius fails to detect, Hamlet's implicatures produce his anteriority.

The implicatures produced by Hamlet in response to his mother similarly reveal his moral critique of her actions and reinforce the impression of his anteriority. Urging her son to doff what seems to her to be excessive grief, Gertrude makes the lackadaisical statement that 'Thou knowst 'tis common all that lives must die' (1.2.72). Hamlet, seizing on her use of the word 'common' to mean usual, creates a pun by inserting an additional meaning that registers his condemnation of her overhasty remarriage: 'Ay, madam, it is common' (1.2.74). While serving to convey his agreement with her, Hamlet's pun on 'common' to signify vulgar undermines his agreement and produces an implicature that rebounds back to accuse his mother of vulgarity in marrying his uncle without giving grievance its natural due (see his first soliloquy, which follows [1.2.147–51]). Hamlet not only insinuates that Gertrude's unnatural coupling with Claudius is distastefully incestuous but also criticizes her hypocritical behaviour. Gertrude's question 'Why seems [mourning] so particular with thee?' (75) launches Hamlet into a tirade hinging on the word 'seems,' which he takes to signify the pretence or theatricality that she possesses:

> 'Seems', madam – nay it is, I know not 'seems'.
> 'Tis not alone my inky cloak, cold mother,
> Nor customary suits of solemn black,
> Nor windy suspiration of forced breath,
> No, nor the fruitful river in the eye,
> Nor the dejected haviour of the visage,
> Together with all forms, moods, shapes of grief,
> That can denote me truly. These indeed 'seem',
> For they are actions that a man might play,
> But I have that within which passes show,
> These but the trappings and the suits of woe.
>
> (1.2.76–86)

Violating the maxim of quantity ('make your contribution as informative as is required'), Hamlet enumerates the gestures, actions, facial expressions and costume adopted by an actor impersonating melancholy to deny that his melancholy is feigned.[16] Claiming that his melancholic moping is authentic rather than a mere performance, Hamlet dissevers his outward expression of melancholy from an inner feeling of grief and gestures towards an authentic being. In so doing, Hamlet implies and indirectly condemns not only Gertrude's 'seeming' or feigned mourning for her deceased husband but also censures the moral emptiness and the vacuity of feeling that shape her words. By contending that his actions, like his words, are signifiers that originate in an ontologically prior emotion, Hamlet is showing Gertrude that he is aware of the mere performativity of her and Claudius's words. However, in painting the verbal picture of an actor and drawing attention to the very theatricality he denies, Hamlet precisely does what he denies doing. He asserts that his 'seeming' is authentic – his outward signs of melancholy are truthful expressions of his inner emotion – while contending at the same time that his exterior 'forms, moods, and shapes of grief' (82) cannot denote him 'truly' since he has inwardness or 'that within which passes show' (85). While Hamlet denies that he performs his melancholy as an actor, the meta-dramatic irony of his words highlights that Hamlet the melancholic prince is, in fact, a role played by an actor and makes us question the truthfulness of his words. Hamlet thus denies the possibility of expressing what he claims so truthfully to express. The dramatic irony of Hamlet's retort foregrounds the character bleeding into the actor playing the character, who usurps Hamlet's voice and leads the audience to question *who* is speaking – the character or the actor. This vertiginous effect works to erase Hamlet's anteriority as a pragmatic speaker and illuminates instead that the playwright, rather than the character himself, is in control of Hamlet's enunciation. While Hamlet strives to insert alternative meanings into his speech that point to Claudius and Gertrude's sinful incest, his anteriority undoes itself in the very act of enunciation.

Hamlet's first soliloquy (1.2.129–59), which quickly follows in the wake of his response to Gertrude, reveals that his criticism of his mother is motivated by a misogynistic disgust of her feminine 'frailty' (1.2.146) and corrupt nature.[17] Although his subsequent soliloquies address both offstage and onstage audiences, Hamlet's first soliloquy – uttered as an 'aside' – is self-addressed yet overheard by the offstage audience. It provides insight into Hamlet's perception of his father as well as his reaction to Gertrude's marriage to Claudius. The soliloquy, which harps on Gertrude's unnaturalness and serves as a misogynistic exclamation against the innate fickleness, immorality and practised deception of the female sex in general, is spoken out of Claudius's and Gertrude's earshot to give the impression that Hamlet's speech is private and confessional. Hamlet, the offstage audience learns, suppresses his disgust: 'But break, my heart, for I must hold my tongue' (1.2.159). It is the furtive misogyny expressed in this soliloquy that signals Hamlet's real madness, which excessively encroaches on his performed madness by breaking through his implicatures to compromise the force of his implicit critique.

In his conversation with Polonius, Hamlet's implicatures openly convey his hostility and contemptuous critique of Polonius's (and, by extension, Ophelia's) dishonesty even as he attempts to persuade the old courtier that his utterances are symptomatic of his melancholic madness. Hamlet's utterances thus produce a contradictory message: his implicatures are intended to deceive Polonius into thinking that he is truly mad while indirectly telling him that he is not essentially mad. Polonius's opening question about whether Hamlet knows him leads Hamlet to answer Polonius not with his name or profession but with the eccentric statement 'Excellent well, you are a fishmonger' (2.2.171). Flouting both the maxim of relation ('be relevant') and the maxim of manner ('avoid obscurity of expression' and 'avoid ambiguity'),[18] Hamlet not only denigrates the aristocratic old courtier by reducing him to a low-class labourer but also sardonically delivers his censure of the courtier's deviousness. In calling him a fishmonger, Hamlet invites Polonius to construe his utterance as a mark of his lunacy while also conveying to Polonius that he is aware of the old man's plan, which he had previously divulged to Claudius (159–64), to 'loose [his] daughter' (2.2.159) on Hamlet or to bait him with her. Since the fish, as Karl P. Wentersdorf suggests, is a symbol for sexuality, Hamlet is accusing Polonius of being a procurer who panders his daughter to gain increased favour at court. The fishmonger reference also allusively echoes Polonius's instructions to his servant Reynaldo, whom he charges to cunningly spy on Laertes in order to uncover the truth behind his son's dealings in France:

> Your bait of falsehood take this carp of truth,
> And thus do we of wisdom and of reach,
> With windlasses and with assays of bias,
> By indirections find directions out.
>
> (2.1.60–3)

Hamlet's implicature mocks Polonius's secret scheming. However, it is Hamlet who ironically pre-empts Polonius by baiting *him* with implicatures that he cannot understand. Responding to Polonius's denial of the truth of Hamlet's words (172), Hamlet adds insult to injury by stating 'Then

I would you were so honest a man' (173). Hamlet's wish, whose meaning remains incomprehensible to Polonius (174), is a speech act that serves to accuse Polonius of being more morally corrupt and deceitful than the lowest of social classes. Hamlet, however, quickly tempers his mad performance with a semblance of sanity in pronouncing an aphorism that wins him Polonius's agreement: 'To be honest as this world goes is to be one man picked out of ten thousand' (175–6). By producing a truism that comments on the nature of humanity in order to display a grain of his wisdom, Hamlet diffuses the illocutionary force of his censure and makes Polonius second-guess whether his verbally performed madness is authentic.

The aphorism, nevertheless, also proleptically extends Hamlet's criticism of Polonius's dishonesty to Claudius and, more significantly, to Ophelia herself. This is highlighted by Hamlet's subsequent analogy, which is intended as a warning to Polonius to guard his daughter:

HAMLET
For if the sun breed maggots in a dead dog,
being a good kissing carrion – have you a daughter?
POLONIUS
I have, my lord.
HAMLET
Let her not walk i' th' sun: conception is
a blessing but as your daughter may conceive, friend
– look to't.

(2.2.178–83)

While Hamlet reinforces the impression of his madness by violating the maxim of relation ('be relevant')[19] in using an outlandish comparison that is completely unrelated to his aphorism, he also resurrects the sun metaphor first used in his retort to Claudius to underline the latter's corrupt nature. The grotesque imagery of the decomposing carcass of a dog being kissed by the sun which impregnates it with an oxymoronic life-in-death underlines the extent, and the unnaturalness, of

Claudius's lustful and predatory nature. As the royal 'sun', Claudius's illicit sexual relations with Gertrude breed or give birth to the 'rotten' state of Denmark, a political death-in-life itself. Implying the king's sexual promiscuity, Hamlet's analogy cautions Polonius against exposing his daughter to the king for fear that she would quickly fall prey to him. However, the analogy casts not only Gertrude but also Ophelia as agents, rather than victims, of their own downfalls. Tracing the dog imagery back to Plutarch, Wentersdorf deems that the dog likely represents 'disgusting or defiling uncleanliness' as well as 'uninhibited sexuality'.[20] In having the dog thus possibly connote rampant female sexuality, Hamlet denigrates Ophelia by suggesting that it is her promiscuity – rather than Claudius's sexual prowess – that leads her to 'conceive' by walking in the sun and thus reveals himself to be at the mercy of his misogynistic thoughts. Hamlet may, as Wentersdorf claims, be using the grotesque analogy to express his 'anger at Ophelia's seeming infidelity, his revulsion at the thought of sex, and his intention to satirize the idea of romantic love', but to read Hamlet's words as solely indicative of his raw emotion is to overlook the fact that Hamlet performs his madness at the same time as he expresses it through his speech.[21] The deliberate ambiguity surrounding Hamlet's intention and the meaning of his implicature lead the audience to question the prince's anteriority. If Hamlet's analogy serves as a warning to Polonius to safeguard Ophelia's chastity, then his implicature signals that Hamlet is merely baiting Polonius with his feigned madness while conveying to him moral advice that denotes his anteriority. If the analogy serves as a prescriptive punishment for the lascivious Ophelia whom he implicitly berates, however, then the implicature reveals that Hamlet's misogyny obsessively intrudes upon his performed madness and undermines the anteriority that the speech would otherwise produce as Hamlet slides into real madness. Polonius's ability to notice that Hamlet still 'harps' on his daughter, but his failure to understand the import of Hamlet's implicatures, leads him to deduce that Hamlet is indeed lovesick (186–7).

Hamlet continues to toy with Polonius by producing another conversational implicature that enables him to both ridicule Polonius and to reinforce the impression of his insanity, of which Polonius already suspects him. In responding to Polonius's inquiry into what he reads simply with 'words, words, words' (189), Hamlet violates both the maxim of manner (be clear and brief) and the maxim of quantity (be as informative as needed). Although Hamlet's reply is clear, concise and truthful, it is too curt – albeit ironically redundant – and hence not informative enough. Interpreting Polonius's question literally, Hamlet accentuates his performed madness by underlining that he is incapable of understanding Polonius. This feigned incomprehension occurs again in Hamlet's response to Polonius's question about the 'matter' of his reading ('Between who?' [191]). Nevertheless, the threefold repetition of 'words' in Hamlet's utterance registers his criticism of Polonius. Serving as an echoic utterance of Polonius's copious rhetoric – see Gertrude's protestation that Polonius use 'more matter with less art' (2.2.95) – Hamlet's pregnant words ridicule Polonius's empty use of words, which lack substance or pith and thus fail to communicate their speaker's intended meaning.[22] Hamlet thus draws Polonius's attention to his linguistic flaws by showing the old courtier what he is doing with his utterances: deceiving and mocking him. Not only does Hamlet mock the superfluity of Polonius's speech but he also mocks his lack of cleverness or his inability to fathom the intention behind Hamlet's words. In claiming to read about 'slanders' (193) in his book, Hamlet may be informing Polonius that he is aware of the courtier's attempt to slander him or damage his reputation while at the same time showing Polonius that he is slandering *him* by referring to him as an old man with a grey beard, wrinkled face, amber-oozing eyes and 'a plentiful lack of wit' (196). However, Hamlet cautiously distances himself from this criticism by referring to the author of his book as the 'satirical rogue' (193). He urges Polonius to decipher the meaning behind his words while making it impossible for him to do so by constantly shifting his linguistic footing. In doing so, Hamlet foregrounds himself as the superior interpreter who is in full control of the pragmatic game of chess he plays with Polonius. Hamlet, nevertheless, instantly undercuts his critique of Polonius and cancels the anteriority it produces by reasserting his madness through a seemingly senseless implicature: 'For yourself, sir, shall grow old as I am – if, like a crab, you could go backward' (199–201). Breaking the maxim of relation ('be relevant')[23] by digressing from the 'matter' of his reading to address Polonius's old age, Hamlet hypothetically compares Polonius to a crab walking backward to imply that Polonius is, ironically, as young – and therefore as witless – as Hamlet pretends to be. The 'plentiful lack of wit' with which he has just slandered Polonius is an ill-expressed or impolite (not 'honest') truth, which he revises in his conditional comparison only to show Polonius's foolishness to him while concealing it at the same time through an implicature that Polonius cannot grasp and that makes Hamlet seem mad. While Polonius's aside exhibits his belief in Hamlet's madness, he is nevertheless able to sense that 'though this be madness, yet there is method in't' (202–3). He detects that Hamlet intends to convey a certain message ('How pregnant sometimes his replies are' [205–6]) yet is unable to decipher the meaning of this message. Polonius's musing proves ironic, for he is only able to partially see that Hamlet's love for Ophelia makes Hamlet mad, without noticing Hamlet's feigned madness as a disguise. Appropriating Polonius's strategy of using 'indirections [to] find directions out' (2.1.63), Hamlet's deceitful disguise serves to convey to Polonius the truth of his sanity and his self-control as he pre-empts Polonius from comprehending what he yearns to know by persuading the old courtier of his (seeming) madness.

While Polonius's failure of pragmatic uptake largely generates the dramatic irony that augments the audience's impression of Hamlet's anteriority, it is the dramatic framing of their conversation that unsettles this anteriority by making the audience suspect the existence of an enunciating subject animating Hamlet's speech. Despite Hamlet's performance of his antic disposition, Ophelia's report of Hamlet's erratic behaviour gives rise to the impression that Hamlet's madness intrudes upon and usurps his antic disposition. Frightened by Hamlet's haggard appearance and his peculiar behaviour, Ophelia reports Hamlet's physical actions and gestures to her father (2.1.74–81, 84–97). Her report, which provides an insider's view of Hamlet's actions in the privacy of her chamber, portrays Hamlet as a madman which, according to Polonius, directly results from the 'ecstasy of love' (99) that overwhelms him due to Ophelia's inaccessibility (106–8). The poetic lines that Hamlet writes to Ophelia (2.2.108–9, 114–21) and that Polonius seizes and delivers to Claudius and Gertrude as evidence of their son's lovesick lunacy further cast doubt on Hamlet's feigned performance of madness by suggesting that he may truly be mad. Ophelia's report thus throws into doubt the presence of a stable, speaking subject that predates and controls Hamlet's pragmatic strategies. Nevertheless, just as Ophelia's report drives the audience to question the pragmatic value of Hamlet's verbal performance in his conversation with Polonius, the opening scene of the play compels the audience to be leery of the truthfulness of report and reported speech. Horatio refuses to believe the sentinels' report of the ghost's visitation 'without the sensible and true avouch / Of [his] own eyes' (1.1.56–7). For Horatio, seeing is believing, but even witnessing the ghost first-hand does not necessarily bring about certainty regarding its meaning: 'In what particular thought to work, I know not, / But in the gross and scope of mine opinion / This bodes some strange eruption to our state' (1.1.66–8). Horatio's scepticism regarding Marcellus's report of the ghost on the ramparts, which is evoked by but juxtaposed against Polonius's response to Ophelia's report, throws into relief Polonius's gullibility and his blind trust in the truth of Ophelia's words without confronting visual evidence. The counterpointing of Polonius's and Horatio's differing reactions, which Shakespeare orchestrates to guide audience response, fosters our uncertainty regarding Hamlet's verbal performances by directing us to simultaneously doubt and trust what we see and hear of Hamlet. This only exacerbates our confusion. Just as the visual evidence required by Horatio to believe in the ghost's existence does not help him interpret what its appearance signifies, and just as Polonius's lack of critical acumen prevents him from grasping the meaning of Hamlet's words or what he does with them, so too is the offstage audience placed in an interpretive limbo, unable to ascertain with any certainty when and if Hamlet's 'antic disposition' slides from adopted to real.

The audience's uncertainty is further compounded during Hamlet's confrontation with Ophelia. His conversational implicatures serve to criticize Ophelia for her plotted deception of him while at the same time betraying his contempt for women, which erupts into and melds with his performed madness to undercut his anteriority. Suspecting that Ophelia's return of his tokens of love is insincere, Hamlet asks Ophelia whether she is 'honest' (3.1.102) and 'fair' (3.1.104). Hamlet's pun on 'honest' to mean chaste and truthful creates an implicature that allows him both to convey his madness and to imply that he knows of Polonius's and Ophelia's strategy to manipulate him. In offering Ophelia counsel that 'if [she] be honest and fair [she] should admit no discourse to [her] beauty' (106–7) since 'the power of Beauty will sooner transform Honesty from what it is to a bawd than the force of Honesty can translate Beauty into his likeness' (110–12), Hamlet conveys two different messages through his implicature. First, Hamlet warns Ophelia that her beauty will corrupt her 'honesty' (truthfulness) or make her deceitful, since beauty enables women to deceive and manipulate others. Under the guise of counselling Ophelia to guard against deceit and insincerity, Hamlet is in fact subtly accusing Ophelia of manipulating him and communicating to her his awareness of her ploy – and perhaps even his awareness of Polonius's presence as an eavesdropper. Secondly, he warns Ophelia that her beauty will corrupt her 'honesty' (chastity) and turn her into a strumpet: since beauty makes a woman sexually desirable to men, it poorly protects her chastity. While seeming to utter an instructive apothegm, Hamlet is in fact insinuating that Ophelia is lascivious due to her beauty; the audience can register Hamlet's troubling misogyny, which makes his performed madness seem real. Terminating his moralizing discourse by claiming that time has brought to light the truth of his truism, followed by the almost wistful assertion 'I did love you once' (114), Hamlet implies that Ophelia has become both unchaste and deceptive. He accuses her of lecherous behaviour, of which she is clearly innocent. Hamlet's contempt fuses with his performed lunacy in a way that defeats his moral critique of Ophelia and cancels his anteriority. Yet in signalling to Ophelia that he knows she is deceiving him, Hamlet reveals his sanity and pragmatic astuteness as a speaker and actor who remains in control of his antic disposition.

The oscillation between sanity and insanity that Hamlet's implicatures enable is more clearly exacerbated in his 'nunnery' speech to Ophelia. Even as Hamlet uses an implicature to morally educate Ophelia about the dangers of trusting others and covertly suggests that he still loves her, his mad performance, underwritten by a berating of her sexuality, ironically demonstrates that she should not trust him. After explaining to Ophelia that she should not have believed his pronouncements of love because men are innately sinful and deceitful (116–18), he orders Ophelia: 'Get thee to a nunnery! Why wouldst thou be a breeder of sinners?' (120–1). Hamlet's pun on 'nunnery' creates another implicature that conveys his misogynistic disgust alongside his honourable concern for his erstwhile beloved. Using 'nunnery' to connote a convent, Hamlet commands Ophelia to take refuge in a holy sanctuary that can protect her and her chastity from corrupt and devious men like himself who, he claims, would selfishly use her. However, in also using the term to connote a brothel, Hamlet expresses his revulsion towards Ophelia's putative sexual promiscuity in an attempt to foreground his feigned madness into which he, nevertheless, seems to disappear. In performing the role of madman, Hamlet attempts to persuade Ophelia to believe what he says while simultaneously showing her why she should not believe his mad ravings ('We are arrant knaves – believe none of us' [127–8]). Hamlet denies that he loves Ophelia in order to show her how much he loves her; his performance both reveals and conceals his communicative intentions. In pragmatic terms, the illocutionary force of Hamlet's utterances (his intention to make Ophelia believe that he is mad) coheres with the perlocutionary effect of his words (she believes that he is mad). However, in using his performed madness as a disguise, Hamlet also intends to implicitly communicate to Ophelia that he still loves her by warning her of the corrupt dealings of men, including those of her father. This second illocutionary force does not produce the intended perlocutionary effect of recognition on Ophelia's part but instead strengthens her – as well as the audience's – suspicion of his authentic rather than feigned madness. Hamlet ends his instruction to Ophelia with a question, 'Where's your father?' (129), that serves to introduce an order: 'Let the doors be shut upon him that he may play the fool nowhere but in's own house' (131–2). Although Hamlet implies that Polonius is an 'arrant knave[]' (128) who is as sinful and devious as any man, and conveys to Ophelia that he is aware that her deception of him is her father's ploy, Ophelia fails to see that the intention behind Hamlet's utterance issues from a moralizing and cunning speaker in control of his speech. Instead, taking Hamlet's utterance to be disjointed from the rest of his speech, Ophelia interprets his words as a sign of his mad rambling as she prays for divine intervention on his behalf not once ('O help him, you sweet heavens!' [133]) but twice ('Heavenly powers restore him' [140]). Even though Hamlet seems to proffer Ophelia sound advice, he quickly undoes this semblance of sanity by criticizing Ophelia for her attempted deceit towards him, which revives the obsessive misogyny to which Hamlet's speech is inevitably subjected: 'Or, if thou wilt needs marry, marry a fool, for wise men know well enough what monsters you make of them' (137–9). Hamlet's continual oscillation prevents the audience from determining whether the angry speaker of these lines – who implies that he is not the 'fool' that Ophelia and Polonius make him out to be but rather a 'wise' man who can see through their pretence – regulates his speech or falls prey to his contempt of women that underlies it. Hamlet's verbal performance dupes Ophelia at the same time as it shows her that she has already been duped by others.

Hamlet's oscillation between his real and feigned antic disposition and his criticism of Ophelia are brought to a standstill in his diatribe on female hypocrisy, which reveals that the moralizing voice marking his anteriority dissolves into his disguise of lunacy (141–8). Enumerating the cosmetics ('paintings' [141]), actions ('jig and amble' [143]) and manner of speech (lisping and nicknaming [43–4]) employed by women to deceive men, Hamlet groups Ophelia with women in general to criticize their collective hypocrisy. In claiming that female hypocrisy is the cause of his madness ('Go to, I'll no more on't. It hath made me mad' [145–6]) and in ending his rant with the declaration 'I say we will have no more marriage' (146), Hamlet alludes to his mother's betrayal of his deceased father and associates the innocent and virtuous Ophelia with the guilty and unrighteous Gertrude as an agent of deception in a manner that underscores his misogyny. While the elision of Ophelia and Gertrude is in keeping with Hamlet's mad berating of Ophelia, it nevertheless reveals that Hamlet's disgust towards his mother's actions, divulged in his first soliloquy, also colours his treatment of Ophelia. Terminating his diatribe with the threat that 'those that are married already – all but one – shall live' (146–7), Hamlet seems to become a melancholic madman bent on murder rather than an actor who performs this role, as his raw emotion breaks through and overpowers his speech. Hamlet's rant throws into doubt his ability to produce the divergent messages conveyed by his conversational implicatures as the audience witnesses the possible erasure of an enunciating 'I' that controls Hamlet's speech from a position of anteriority.

The audience's impression of Hamlet's undecidability is framed and further accentuated by his eavesdroppers' responses as well as by his 'to be or not to be' soliloquy which precedes his encounter with Ophelia (3.1.55–89).[24] While critics have often read Hamlet's soliloquy as a vehicle for sincere self-expression, in which the prince philosophically premeditates suicide, both James Hirsh and Phillip Arrington have demonstrated that Hamlet's speech is a feigned soliloquy that registers his awareness of his surveillance by Polonius and Claudius.[25] His speech, claims Arrington, is a 'sophistic performance' that designates Hamlet as a 'consummate sophistic rhetor'.[26] Hamlet intentionally performs his meditation on suicide within earshot of his auditors so as to persuade them that he is indeed mad. That Hamlet contemplates his own death hinges on interpreting the verb 'to be' as signifying 'to exist', which evokes Hamlet's first soliloquy where he expresses his yearning either for a passive death akin to decomposition ('O that this too too sallied flesh would melt, / Thaw and resolve itself into a dew' [1.2.129–30]) or an active death brought about by himself as agent ('Or that the Everlasting had not fixed / His canon 'gainst self-slaughter' [1.2.131–2]). This reading is strengthened by the parting wish Hamlet makes to Ophelia that his 'sins' be remembered in her 'orisons' (3.1.88–9), which eerily anticipates his self-slaughter despite his soliloquizing that death is forestalled by conscience that makes one question the 'undiscovered country' (3.1.78) beyond life. In this light, Hamlet's conversation with Ophelia is staged for the sole purpose of bidding her a feigned farewell, which he intends Claudius and Polonius to hear in order to deceive them into believing that he is on the verge of committing suicide. Nevertheless, Hamlet's pun on 'to be' as signifying 'to act' – both to perform and to take action or rather, to take action by performing his scripted role as avenger – invites a reading of the soliloquy where Hamlet seems to be contemplating not his suicide but the murder of Claudius. It thus registers a threat which Claudius only vaguely senses. By this token, Hamlet initiates his conversation with Ophelia in order to caution her against the rampant corruption of the state and its dangerous political players while urging her departure from Elsinore. Hamlet's implicatures in his conversation with Ophelia thus target two different audiences: addressing Ophelia, Hamlet berates her for her duplicity and warns her against being its victim while performing his feigned madness so as to safely disguise his message to her in an atmosphere taut with surveillance, even as his performance of feigned madness is intended to persuade both Polonius and Claudius of his true madness – into which Hamlet inevitably slides – so as to dupe his eavesdroppers rather than allow them to dupe him. The self-debate that Hamlet stages in his soliloquy – which can be taken to mark either a mind unmoored by emotion or the rational clarity of a speaker in full charge of his verbal performance – sets up the contradiction witnessed by the audience in his conversation with Ophelia and reinforces our undecidability about whether Hamlet possesses anteriority. The divergent responses of Polonius and Claudius as onstage auditors only serve to further promulgate our uncertainty. Agreeing with Ophelia who exclaims that Hamlet's 'noble mind is here o'erthrown!' (3.1.149), Polonius persists in his belief that 'the origin and commencement of his grief / Sprung from neglected love' (3.1.176–7). Claudius, however, maintains that neither Hamlet's speech nor his affections resemble madness arising from thwarted love, and suspects that the prince possesses a certain 'something in his soul / O'er which his melancholy sits on brood' (163–4), whose 'hatch and [] disclose / Will be some danger' (165–6) to his state. Claudius's scepticism, contrasted against Polonius's credulousness, betokens a wilier and more verbally adept auditor who detects an undecipherable threat in Hamlet's performance that makes him suspect the truthfulness of the insanity staged by the prince. By framing Hamlet's linguistic manoeuvring with not only Hamlet's 'to be or not to be' soliloquy but also with Claudius's and Polonius's juxtaposing responses, Shakespeare heightens the audience's doubt about whether it is Hamlet-the-madman or Hamlet-the-pragmatist who speaks.

If *Hamlet* constantly asks us to question, to use Barnardo's opening words, 'Who's there?' (1.1.1) or who Hamlet is, it precludes a cogent answer by demonstrating the impossibility of any interpretive attempt to ascertain 'who' exactly Hamlet is. Rather than ask 'who' Hamlet is, the play more pressingly urges us to ask *where* Hamlet is while showing us that he is 'there', anterior to his utterances, as a speaker with performative agency, at the same time as underlining that Hamlet cannot be found within or behind utterances consumed by fits of madness that obliterate traces of his moralizing voice. This undecidability experienced by the offstage audience is an effect generated by Hamlet's implicatures in conversational contexts with his interlocutors. In conveying to Ophelia, Polonius, Gertrude and Claudius his sharp censure of their hypocrisy and corruption, Hamlet displays a moralizing voice that invokes his anteriority as a character. However, in having his misogynistic attitude intrude upon his performance of madness, Hamlet cancels the impression of the anteriority he linguistically produces as the audience witnesses an enunciating subject inundated with and overpowered by unresolved emotion. While the narrative of revenge linearly marches forward and draws to an eventual close as Fortinbras stands in for Hamlet and visually completes his embodiment as a scripted avenger, Hamlet's presence disconcertingly persists to haunt the action of the play and drives the audience to consider whether Hamlet's verbal performativity is commensurable with the performance of vengeance that he could neither intend nor carry out. As a character in old Hamlet's scripted play of revenge, Hamlet desperately wants to be an actor in his own but is ultimately defeated by a script that he cannot re-script to suit his pragmatic goals; the play stages Hamlet's pragmatic failure to produce consistent anteriority. In urging his audience to find Hamlet in utterances that tend to self-implode, Shakespeare reveals that it is he, himself an old Hamlet of sorts, who sets the play in motion and is the controlling agent of Hamlet's utterances and actions.[27] It is the playwright's authorial anteriority that precedes Hamlet's flickering anteriority.

NOTES

Introduction

1 William Jackson, 'Letter XIV', in *Thirty Letters on Various Subjects*, 3rd edn (London: T. Cadell, 1795), 93. Eighteenth-Century Collections Online.

2 See, for instance, A. C. Bradley, 'Introduction', in *Shakespearean Tragedy: Lectures on Hamlet, Othello, King Lear, Macbeth* (1904; repr., London: Macmillan, 1960), xxv–xxvii.

3 L. C. Knights, 'How Many Children Had Lady Macbeth? An Essay in the Theory and Practice of Shakespeare Criticism', in *Hamlet and Other Shakespearean Essays* (Cambridge: Cambridge University Press, 1979), 273.

4 Ibid., 279.

5 See, for instance, Catherine Belsey, *The Subject of Tragedy: Identity and Difference in Renaissance Drama* (London: Methuen, 1985), and Jonathan Dollimore, *Radical Tragedy: Religion, Ideology and Power in the Drama of Shakespeare and His Contemporaries* (Chicago: University of Chicago Press, 1984).

6 Stephen Greenblatt, *Renaissance Self-Fashioning: From More to Shakespeare* (Chicago: University of Chicago Press, 1980), 3.

7 Ibid., 9, 2.

8 Michel Foucault, 'Rarity, Exteriority, Accumulation', in *The Archaeology of Knowledge*, trans. A. M. Sheridan Smith (London: Tavistock Publications, 1972), 119.

9 See Karen Newman, *Shakespeare's Rhetoric of Comic Character* (New York: Methuen, 1985), and Christy Desmet, *Reading Shakespeare's Characters: Rhetoric, Ethics, and Identity* (Amherst: University of Massachusetts Press, 1992). Newman is interested in uncovering the origins of an ideology of being. She contends that a comic character's lifelikeness – what she

calls 'residue or excess' – results from the friction between the linguistic conventions of the soliloquy, which 'endow' characters 'with motive and intention, conflict and complexity', and the dramatic conventions of comic characterization (*Shakespeare's Rhetoric*, 2, 4). See also Alan Sinfield, who argues that Cultural Materialism need not dispose of the concept of character along with its disposal of the Bradleyan essentialism underpinning it ('When Is a Character Not a Character? Desdemona, Olivia, Lady Macbeth, and Subjectivity', in *Faultlines: Cultural Materialism and the Politics of Dissident Reading* [Berkeley: University of California Press, 1992]).

10 Paul Yachnin and Jessica Slights, 'Introduction', in *Shakespeare and Character: Theory, History, Performance, and Theatrical Persons*, eds Yachnin and Slights (Basingstoke: Palgrave Macmillan, 2009), 6–7.

11 Ibid., 1.

12 William Dodd, 'Character as Dynamic Identity: From Fictional Interaction Script to Performance', in *Shakespeare and Character: Theory, History, Performance, and Theatrical Persons*, eds Paul Yachnin and Jessica Slights (Basingstoke: Palgrave Macmillan, 2009), 62.

13 Illocutionary force is the speaker's intention in making an utterance. Austin divides performative utterances into illocutionary and perlocutionary acts: an illocutionary act is an action that is performed *in* uttering X, which entails a change in state or condition, whereas a perlocutionary act is an action that is performed *by* uttering X, which registers the effect that the action has on the hearer.

14 Jacob L. Mey, *Pragmatics: An Introduction* (Cambridge, MA: Blackwell, 1993), 35.

15 Jenny Thomas, *Meaning in Interaction: An Introduction to Pragmatics* (London and New York: Longman, 1995), 22.

16 Mey, *Pragmatics: An Introduction*, 10. The pragmatic emphasis on context can be traced back to the discipline of social anthropology and, more specifically, to Malinowski; see Wataru Koyama, 'The Rise of Pragmatics: A Historiographic Overview', in *Foundations of Pragmatics*, eds Wolfram Bublitz and Neal R. Norrick (Berlin: De Gruyter Mouton, 2011), 139–66, at 144–5.

17 Stanley Fish, 'How to Do Things with Austin and Searle: Speech Act Theory and Literary Criticism', *Modern Language Notes* 91, no. 5 (October 1976): 1024.

18 See Joseph A. Porter, *The Drama of Speech Acts: Shakespeare's Lancastrian Tetralogy* (Berkeley: University of California Press, 1979).

19 See John Kerrigan, *Shakespeare's Binding Language* (Oxford: Oxford University Press, 2016).

20 See also Roman Kopytko's quantitative study of negative and positive politeness strategies in Shakespeare's comedies and tragedies: 'Linguistic Politeness Strategies in Shakespeare's Plays', in *Historical Pragmatics: Pragmatic Developments in the History of English*, ed. Andreas Jucker (Amsterdam: John Benjamins, 1995), 515–40. The versatile and ever-evolving field of historical pragmatics, which studies the pragmatic use of language in historical settings, took flight in the 1990s. More recent work in historical pragmatics vis-à-vis Shakespeare neither discusses, nor makes explicit assumptions about, character; see, for instance, Minako Nakayasu's study of the modal system in Shakespeare's plays, *The Pragmatics of Modals in Shakespeare* (Frankfurt, Germany: Peter Lang, 2009), and Raymond F. Person's historical examination of the discourse marker 'O' in the quarto and Folio versions of Shakespeare's play-texts: '"Oh" in Shakespeare: A Conversation Analytic Approach', *Journal of Historical Pragmatics* 10, no. 1 (2009): 84–107.

21 Roger Brown and Albert Gilman, 'Politeness Theory and Shakespeare's Four Major Tragedies', *Language in Society* 18, no. 2 (June 1989): 171, 159.

22 Juhani Rudanko, *Pragmatic Approaches to Shakespeare: Essays on Othello, Coriolanus, and Timon of Athens* (Lanham, MD: University Press of America, 1993), 9.

23 Ibid., 28. Adjacency pairs are conversational sequences where both speakers take turns speaking. For example, a question and an answer are considered to be an adjacency pair. On adjacency pairs, see Stephen C. Levinson, *Pragmatics* (Cambridge: Cambridge University Press, 1983), 303–8.

24 Keir Elam, *Shakespeare's Universe of Discourse: Language – Games in the Comedies* (Cambridge and New York: Cambridge University Press, 1984), 7.

25 See Andrew Kennedy, *Dramatic Dialogue: The Duologue of Personal Encounter* (Cambridge: Cambridge University Press, 1983).

26 Simon Palfrey and Tiffany Stern, *Shakespeare in Parts* (Oxford: Oxford University Press, 2007), 47.

27 Ibid., 110.

28 The term 'character effect' is first employed by Magnusson and then by Dodd as 'character-effects'; see Lynne Magnusson, *Shakespeare and Social Dialogue: Dramatic Language and Elizabethan Letters* (Cambridge: Cambridge University Press, 1999), 34, and Dodd, 'Character as Dynamic Identity', 63.

29 Magnusson, *Shakespeare and Social Dialogue*, 27, 34.

30 Dodd, 'Character as Dynamic Identity', 62.

31 William Dodd, 'Destined Livery? Character and Person in Shakespeare', *Shakespeare Survey* 51 (1998): 156.

32 Dodd, 'Character as Dynamic Identity', 69.

33 See Jonathan Culpeper, *Language and Characterisation: People in Plays and Other Texts* (Harlow: Longman, 2001). With the exception of Culpeper, cognitive approaches to Shakespeare promote an understanding of characters as real, psychologically embodied entities. Raphael Lyne's rhetoric-oriented cognitive study of characterization, *Shakespeare, Rhetoric and Cognition* (Cambridge: Cambridge University Press, 2011), and Neema Parvini's character-based cognitive study, *Shakespeare and Cognition: Thinking Fast and Slow through Character* (Basingstoke: Palgrave Macmillan, 2015), both suggest that characters have essential and coherent selves that pre-date language.

34 Thomas, *Meaning in Interaction*, 22.

35 I borrow the term from Laura M. Ahearn, 'Language and Agency', *Annual Review of Anthropology* 30, no. 1 (October 2001): 130.

36 Kennedy, *Dramatic Dialogue*, 11.

37 Mick Short, 'Discourse Analysis and the Analysis of Drama', in *Language, Discourse and Literature: An Introductory Reader in Discourse Stylistics*, eds Ronald Carter and Paul Simpson (London: Unwin Hyman, 1989), 146.

38 Duncan Salkeld, 'Shakespeare and "the I-word"', *Style* 44, no. 3 (Fall 2010): 338; see also 329.
39 David Schalkwyk, 'Giving Intention Its Due?' *Style* 44, no. 3 (Fall 2010): 316.
40 Peter J. Rabinowitz, 'Shakespeare's Dolphin, Dumbo's Feather, and Other Red Herrings: Some Thoughts on Intention and Meaning', *Style* 44, no. 3 (Fall 2010): 352.
41 See, most notably, Jean E. Howard, 'Figures and Grounds: Shakespeare's Control of Audience Perception and Response', *SEL: Studies in English Literature 1500–1900* 20, no. 2 (Spring 1980): 185–99, and her book *Shakespeare's Art of Orchestration: Stage Technique and Audience Response* (Urbana: University of Illinois Press, 1984); Kent Cartwright, *Shakespearean Tragedy and Its Double: The Rhythms of Audience Response* (University Park, PA: Pennsylvania State University Press, 1991); E. A. J. Honigmann, *Shakespeare: Seven Tragedies Revisited: The Dramatist's Manipulation of Response* (1976; repr., Basingstoke: Palgrave, 2002); and, more recently, Jeremy Lopez, *Theatrical Convention and Audience Response in Early Modern Drama* (Cambridge: Cambridge University Press, 2003).

Chapter 1

1 Samuel Johnson, 'Notes' on *2 Henry IV*, in *Johnson on Shakespeare: Essays and Notes*, ed. Walter Raleigh (Oxford: Oxford University Press, 1925), 125.
2 Barbara Everett makes a similar comment that Falstaff's material presence marks his greatness as a character ('The Fatness of Falstaff: Shakespeare and Character', *Proceedings of the British Academy* 76 [1990]: 109–28); David Womersley, by contrast, takes up the question of Falstaff's portliness but ascribes it to a phrase in Foxe's *Actes and Monuments* to signify his ungodliness ('Why Is Falstaff Fat?' *Review of English Studies* 47, no. 185 [February 1996]: 1–22). Noteworthy examples of critics who read Falstaff as a real person include Corbyn Morris, 'An Essay towards Fixing the True Standards of Wit, Humour, Raillery, Satire, and Ridicule' (London: J. Roberts and W. Bickerton, 1744); A. C. Bradley,

'The Rejection of Falstaff', in *Henry the Fourth, Parts I and II: Critical Essays*, ed. David Bevington (1902; repr., New York and London: Garland Publishing, 1986), 77–98; and E. K. Chambers, *Shakespeare: A Survey* (London: Sidgwick and Jackson, 1925).

3   Maurice Morgann, *An Essay on the Dramatic Character of Sir John Falstaff* (London: T. Davies, 1777; repr. New York: AMS Press, 1970), 13.

4   Ibid., 177, 28.

5   Ibid., 4–5, fn. 62.

6   I label Falstaff's character effect as roundness; Morgann attributes 'roundnefs' to Shakespearean characters generally rather than to Falstaff specifically (see footnote 58). Morgann claims that Shakespeare 'boldly makes a character act and fpeak from thofe parts of the compofition, which are *inferred* only, and not diftinctly fhewn' and that characters 'which are feen only in part, are yet capable of being unfolded and underftood in the whole; every part being in fact relative, and inferring all the reft' (fn. 62, 61).

7   Richard A. Levin, *Shakespeare's Secret Schemers: The Study of an Early Modern Dramatic Device* (Newark, DE: University of Delaware Press, 2001), 15.

8   Ibid., 132, 133–6.

9   The twentieth-century trend of source study was inspired in large part by John Dover Wilson's contextualization of Falstaff as an allegorical Vanity figure within the morality play tradition; see Dover Wilson's *The Fortunes of Falstaff* (Cambridge: Cambridge University Press, 1943). Other notable critics engaged in source study include Bernard Spivack, *Shakespeare and the Allegory of Evil: The History of a Metaphor in Relation to His Major Villains* (New York: Columbia University Press, 1958); Kristen Poole, 'Saints Alive! Falstaff, Martin Marprelate, and the Staging of Puritanism', *Shakespeare Quarterly* 46, no. 1 (Spring 1995): 47–75; and C. L. Barber, *Shakespeare's Festive Comedy: A Study of Dramatic Form and Its Relation to Social Custom* (Princeton, NJ: Princeton University Press, 1959). Barber's identification of Falstaff as the Lord of Misrule, coupled with Bakhtin's theory of the carnival grotesque, inspired a number of readings in the 1990s and early 2000s that evaluated Falstaff within the

socio-historical contours of early modern popular culture and the festival tradition. See, for instance, David A. Ruiter's *Shakespeare's Festive History: Feasting, Festivity, Fasting, and Lent in the Second Henriad* (Aldershot: Ashgate, 2003) and the collection of essays edited by Ronald Knowles, *Shakespeare and Carnival: After Bakhtin* (Basingstoke: Macmillan Press, 1998).

10 Mark Van Doren, '*Henry IV*', in *Henry the Fourth, Parts I and II: Critical Essays*, ed. David Bevington (1939; repr., New York and London: Garland Publishing, 1986), 109.

11 Ibid., 110.

12 Roy W. Battenhouse, 'Falstaff as Parodist and Perhaps Holy Fool', *PMLA* 90, no. 1 (January 1975): 36.

13 See Poole, 'Saints Alive!', 70.

14 Harry J. Berger, 'The Prince's Dog: Falstaff and the Perils of Speech-Prefixity', *Shakespeare Quarterly* 49, no. 1 (Spring 1998): 62.

15 Although pragmatic theories have been used by literary critic Joseph A. Porter in the 1970s and, more recently, by linguist Derek Bousfield in their respective studies of *1 Henry IV*, both critics sideline Falstaff to focus on Prince Hal. Porter uses Austin's speech act theory to briefly identify Falstaff's speech acts of naming, summoning and denying but separates these acts from the particular speech contexts in which Falstaff uses them, while Derek Bousfield applies impoliteness theory to the banter between Hal and Falstaff during the parodic role-playing of 2.4 to make a case for Hal's depth as a character. See Joseph A. Porter, '*Henry V*', in *The Drama of Speech Acts: Shakespeare's Lancastrian Tetralogy* (Berkeley, CA: University of California Press, 1979), 116–50, and Derek Bousfield, '"Never a Truer Word Said in Jest": A Pragmastylistic Analysis of Impoliteness as Banter in *Henry IV, Part I*', in *Contemporary Stylistics*, eds Marina Lambrou and Peter Stockwell (London: Continuum, 2007), 209–20.

16 All references to the play follow *King Henry IV, Part1*, ed. David Scott Kastan, The Arden Shakespeare 3rd series (London: Bloomsbury, 2002).

17 Wayne A. Davis, 'Irregular Negations: Implicature and Idiom Theories', in *Meaning and Analysis: New Essays on Grice*, ed. Klaus Petrus (London: Palgrave Macmillan, 2010), 111. Grice uses the verb 'implicate' to denote 'imply' and its synonyms; see

Grice, 'Utterer's Meaning and Intentions', in *Studies in the Way of Words* (Cambridge, MA: Harvard University Press, 1989; repr. 1991), 86. ACLS Humanities E-Book. My use of 'implicate' mirrors that of Grice.

18 Grice, 'Logic and Conversation', in *Studies in the Way of Words* (Cambridge, MA: Harvard University Press, 1989; repr. 1991), 26. ACLS Humanities E-Book.

19 Ibid., 26, 27.

20 Ibid., 30. Grice identified flouting, violating and opting out as three principal ways a speaker can fail to observe a maxim; Jenny Thomas notes that Grice and contemporary pragmatists use the terms interchangeably. For the difference between the terms, see Thomas, *Meaning in Interaction: An Introduction to Pragmatics* (London and New York: Longman, 1995), 65–74. An example of an implicature that flouts the maxim of quantity would be if A asks B for the time, and B responds by saying 'It's exactly the same time as it was yesterday at this hour'. B's response is not as informative as it should be and does not answer A's question in a precise manner: B uses circumlocution to imply more than is needed. An implicature flouting the maxim of relevance would occur if A asks B what B thinks of Shakespeare, and B responds by saying 'It's a gorgeous day today'. B's response is not relevant to A's question and implies that B changes the topic to avoid having to share his or her opinion. An example of an implicature that flouts the maxim of quality would be if an exasperated A exclaims 'This is the sixth week in a row that we're studying *Macbeth*!' and B sarcastically responds with 'Yes, it's another fantastic week'. The irony of B's response indicates that B implies and believes that what he or she says is not true. Finally, an example of an implicature flouting the maxim of manner would be if A asks B what the secret to making a perfect chocolate cake is, and B responds with an overly detailed description of the process using foreign words that A does not understand (B is not being brief). Other instances of flouting the maxim of manner may involve exaggeration or a certain ambiguity in the choice of words. Implicatures may flout more than one maxim.

21 Jennifer M. Saul, 'Speaker Meaning, What Is Said, and What Is Implicated', *Noûs* 36, no. 2 (2002): 229. Distinguishing speaker

implicatures ('utterer-implicatures') from hearer implicatures ('audience-implicatures'), Saul holds that a speaker's claim is successfully communicated if the implicature is implied by the speaker and acknowledged as such by the audience or hearer (243). Neo-Griceans deem that implicatures need not be intended or 'meant' in order to be construed as implicatures. Charles Lassiter, for instance, holds that conversational implicatures can be unintentional: 'A hearer may attribute a belief to the speaker – one which the speaker actually holds – on the basis of the speaker's utterance without the speaker's intending to implicate anything. That is to say, one may construct cases in which a speaker's utterance implicates but the speaker does not intend to implicate anything by her utterance' ('Implicating without Intending on the Gricean Account of Implicature', *Empedocles: European Journal for the Philosophy of Communication* 4, no. 2 [2012]: 204). For the purpose of my argument, I assume that Falstaff's implicatures are intentional rather than unintentional or accidental.

22 Penelope Brown and Stephen C. Levinson, *Politeness: Some Universals in Language Usage* (Cambridge: Cambridge University Press, 1987), 61.

23 Ibid., 61, 62.

24 Ibid., 101–29. Brown and Levinson note that joking may also indicate an 'exploitation of politeness strategies' or the desire to threaten the hearer's face (124).

25 Ibid., 70. Brown and Levinson list the following as positive FTAs: 'expressions of disapproval, criticism, contempt or ridicule, complaints and reprimands, accusations, insults' and 'contradictions or disagreements, challenges' in addition to 'expressions of violent… emotions' and 'blatant non-cooperation' such as disruptions or a lack of attention (66–7). An example of positive politeness would be the utterance 'Sweetie, can I borrow your pen?' while an example of negative politeness would be 'I sincerely apologize for bothering you, Sir, but could you please shut the door?'

26 Ibid., 211.

27 The hearer's inference of the speaker's intended meaning is contingent on the hearer's awareness of the speaker's transgression of Gricean maxims in accordance with the Cooperative Principle, along with his or her 'knowledge of face-preserving strategies' (ibid., 6).

28 See Brown and Levinson, *Politeness*, 107–9.
29 Grice, 'Logic and Conversation', 27.
30 Ibid.
31 Ibid.
32 Ibid.
33 See Herbert Weil and Judith Weil, eds, *The First Part of King Henry IV* (Cambridge: Cambridge University Press, 1997), 73 (fn. 11).
34 Derek Bousfield, *Impoliteness in Interaction* (Amsterdam: John Benjamins, 2008), 95.
35 Grice, 'Logic and Conversation', 27.
36 Lopez, *Theatrical Convention*, 49.
37 *Oxford English Dictionary Online*, s.v. 'credit', 5b.
38 Grice, 'Logic and Conversation', 27.
39 See Hal's eulogy to Falstaff at Shrewsbury: 'O, I should have a heavy miss of thee / If I were much in love with vanity' (5.4.104–5).
40 Jack R. Sublette, 'Time's Fool: A Reading of *I Henry IV*', *The Aligarh Journal of English Studies* 8, no. 1 (1983): 68–78, at 69.
41 For resonances between Falstaff and Henry Bolingbroke, see James Black, '*Anon, Anon, Sir*: Discourse of Occasion in *Henry IV*', *Cahiers élisabéthains* 37 (April 1990): 27–42, especially 29–31. See also James L. Calderwood, who claims that Falstaff is a burlesque of King Henry (*Metadrama in Shakespeare's Henriad: Richard II to Henry V* [Berkeley, CA: University of California Press, 1979]), especially 44–9.
42 See definitions 1a and 5a, *Oxford English Dictionary Online*, s.v. 'true'.
43 Poole notes that Falstaff's style of speech is highly reminiscent of Puritan preaching in its use of cant terms like 'saint', 'vocation' and 'wicked', and is 'repetitive, pedagogic, and laced with abundant biblical exegesis' ('Saints Alive!', 66, 65).
44 Grice, 'Logic and Conversation', 27.
45 Poole observes that we laugh both with and at Falstaff, but at him because he is 'a satiric representation of a famous Lollard martyr' (68).

46 Grice, 'Logic and Conversation', 27.
47 Bousfield, 'Never a Truer Word Said in Jest', 211–13, 218.
48 J. McLaverty, 'No Abuse: The Prince and Falstaff in the Tavern Scenes of *Henry IV*', *Shakespeare Survey* 34 (1981): 106–7.
49 Robert Weimann and Douglas Bruster, 'Personation and Playing: "Secretly Open" Role-Playing', in *Shakespeare and the Power of Performance: Stage and Page in the Elizabethan Theatre* (Cambridge: Cambridge University Press, 2008), 153.
50 Although I allude to Kemp playing Falstaff, I am not here making a historical argument about Kemp's relationship to the audience in the Globe theatre. Instead, I use Kemp as an example to demonstrate that the meta-theatricality written into Falstaff's part can be – and usually is – activated and exploited by an actor in non-Elizabethan contexts.
51 Robert Weimann, 'Playing with a Difference', in *Author's Pen and Actor's Voice: Playing and Writing in Shakespeare's Theatre* (Cambridge: Cambridge University Press, 2000), 97.
52 Calderwood, *Metadrama in Shakespeare's Henriad*, 40.
53 *Oxford English Dictionary Online*, s.v. 'counterfeit', 4.
54 Arden editor David Scott Kastan adds a stage direction [*He drops Hotspur's body*] in line 139 but notes that no stage direction appears in extant play-texts.

Chapter 2

1 All quotes follow *Antony and Cleopatra*, ed. John Wilders, The Arden Shakespeare 3rd series (London: Bloomsbury, 1995).
2 L. T. Fitz, 'Egyptian Queens and Male Reviewers: Sexist Attitudes in *Antony and Cleopatra* Criticism', *Shakespeare Quarterly* 28, no. 3 (Summer 1977): 306. For a survey of what Sara Munson Deats calls 'moralistic' and 'romantic' criticism on Cleopatra, see her 'Shakespeare's Anamorphic Drama: A Survey of *Antony and Cleopatra* in Criticism, on Stage, and on Screen', in *Antony and Cleopatra: New Critical Essays*, ed. Sara Munson Deats (New York: Routledge, 2005), 7–8 and 15–18. The bifurcated

judgements of Cleopatra have, in large part, been informed by the early critical treatment of Rome and Egypt as irreconcilable binaries in the play: Egypt, a feminized space dominated by Cleopatra, is perceived as the Eastern 'Other' whereas Rome is defined as the civilized masculine West. Critics like Howard Felperin (*Shakespearean Representation: Mimesis and Modernity in Elizabethan Tragedy* [Princeton, NJ: Princeton University Press, 1977]) and Michael Payne ('Erotic Irony and Polarity in *Antony and Cleopatra*', *Shakespeare Quarterly* 24, no. 3 [Summer 1973]: 265–79) have demonstrated the play's ambivalences and, most recently, James Hirsh has deconstructed the Rome-Egypt binary by arguing for the existence of four, rather than two, locales; see Hirsh, 'Rome and Egypt in *Antony and Cleopatra* and in Criticism of the Play', in *Antony and Cleopatra: New Critical Essays*, ed. Sara Munson Deats (New York: Routledge, 2005), 175–91.

3   Theodora A. Jankowski, *Women in Power in the Early Modern Drama* (Urbana and Chicago, IL: University of Chicago Press, 1992), 153; Mary Ann Bushman, 'Representing Cleopatra', in *In Another Country: Feminist Perspectives on Renaissance Drama*, eds Dorothea Kehler and Susan Baker (Metuchen, NJ: Scarecrow Press, 1991), 43; Linda Charnes, 'Spies and Whispers: Exceeding Reputation in *Antony and Cleopatra*', in *Notorious Identity: Materializing the Subject in Shakespeare* (Cambridge, MA: Harvard University Press, 1993), 127; Catherine Belsey, 'Cleopatra's Seduction', in *Alternative Shakespeares*, vol. 2, ed. Terence Hawkes (London and New York: Routledge, 1996), 42.

4   Cristina León Alfar, *Fantasies of Female Evil: The Dynamics of Gender and Power in Shakespearean Tragedy* (Newark, DE: University of Delaware Press, 2003), 137. Alfar's analysis is centred on Cleopatra's use of her material (sexual) and metaphorical (political), but also racialized, body 'as an object of desire' (139).

5   Alfar, *Fantasies of Female Evil*, 151.

6   Russ McDonald, 'Late Shakespeare: Style and the Sexes', *Shakespeare Survey* 46 (1993): 101; see also David Schalkwyk, *Speech and Performance in Shakespeare's Sonnets and Plays* (Cambridge: Cambridge University Press, 2002). See, for instance, Benjamin T. Spencer, '*Antony and Cleopatra* and the Paradoxical Metaphor', *Shakespeare Quarterly* 9, no. 3 (Summer 1958): 373–8; Robert D. Hume, 'Individuation and Development of Character through Language in *Antony and*

Cleopatra', *Shakespeare Quarterly* 24, no. 3 (Summer 1973): 280–300; and Janet Adelman, who identifies paradox (for Cleopatra) and hyperbole (for Antony) as the protagonists' defining linguistic traits as well as the tropes which shape character and structure the play (*The Common Liar: An Essay on* Antony and Cleopatra [New Haven, CT: Yale University Press, 1973], 111–13). See also Carol Cook, who claims that the language of the play 'locates or creates Cleopatra in linguistic and logical gaps, in puns that tease us out of sense and paradoxes that tease us out of thought'('The Fatal Cleopatra', in *Shakespearean Tragedy and Gender*, eds Shirley Nelson Garner and Madelon Sprengnether [Bloomington, IN: Indiana University Press, 1996], 246). Katherine Eggert notes that Cleopatra's language is a site where 'betrayal, fecundity, and startling invention interwrap themselves inextricably both as modes of speaking and as metaphors in which to speak' (*Showing Like a Queen: Female Authority and Literary Experiment in Spenser, Shakespeare, and Milton* [Philadelphia, PA: University of Pennsylvania Press, 2000], 149).

7   Linda Charnes claims that 'the word "report" occurs more frequently in this play than in any other' ('Spies and Whispers', 106). See also Michael Goldman, *Acting and Action in Shakespearean Tragedy* (Princeton, NJ: Princeton University Press, 1985): 116–17, and Leo G. Salingar, 'Uses of Rhetoric: *Antony and Cleopatra*', *Cahiers élisabéthains* 55 (April 1999): 17–26, at 20.

8   Early Elizabethans viewed Cleopatra and Antony as 'shameless voluptuaries' who were 'notorious for their lust and extravagance'; see Franklin M. Dickey, *Not Wisely but Too Well: Shakespeare's Love Tragedies* (San Marino, CA: Huntington Library, 1957), 152. See also the Prologue in G. B. Giraldi Cinthio's 1583 play, *Cleopatra Tragedia*, extracted in *Narrative and Dramatic Sources of Shakespeare*, vol. 5, ed. Geoffrey Bullough (London: Routledge and Kegan Paul and New York: Columbia University Press, 1964), 343–57, especially 344–5.

9   Flavius Josephus, '*The Antiquities of the Jews*', in *Narrative and Dramatic Sources of Shakespeare*, vol. 5, ed. Geoffrey Bullough (London: Routledge and Kegan Paul and New York: Columbia University Press, 1964), 331, 332.

10 Lucan, *Pharsalia*, trans. Jane Wilson Joyce (Ithaca, NY and London: Cornell University Press, 1993), bk. 10, lines 60, 65.

11 Ibid., bk. 10, lines 61 and 104–6.

12 Plutarch, 'The Life of Antonius', in *Selected Lives from the Lives of the Noble Grecians and Romans*, vol. 2, ed. Paul Turner (Carbondale, IL: Southern Illinois University Press, 1963), 119, 120–1.

13 Lisa Jardine claims that despite her agency, Sidney's Cleopatra embodies stereotypical female passivity; see *Still Harping on Daughters: Women and Drama in the Age of Shakespeare* (Sussex: Harvester Press, 1983). See also Mimi Still Dixon, '"Not Know Me Yet?": Looking at Cleopatra in Three Renaissance Tragedies', in *The Female Tragic Hero in English Renaissance Drama*, ed. Naomi Conn Liebler (New York: Palgrave, 2002), 84–5.

14 Act and line numbers follow Mary Herbert Sidney's *The Tragedie of Antonie*, in *Narrative and Dramatic Sources of Shakespeare*, vol. 5, ed. Geoffrey Bullough (London: Routledge and Kegan Paul and New York: Columbia University Press, 1964).

15 Act and line number follow Samuel Daniel's *The Tragedie of Cleopatra*, in *Narrative and Dramatic Sources of Shakespeare*, vol. 5, ed. Geoffrey Bullough (London: Routledge and Kegan Paul and New York: Columbia University Press, 1964).

16 The term 'reported speech' lacks consistency in linguistics. On terminology, see Matylda Włodarczyk, *Pragmatic Aspects of Reported Speech: The Case of Early Modern English Courtroom Discourse* (Frankfurt: Peter Lang, 2007), 30–3; see also Elizabeth Holt, 'Reported Speech', in *The Pragmatics of Interaction*, eds Sigurd D'hondt, Jan-Ola Östman and Jef Verschueren (Amsterdam: John Benjamins, 2009): 190–205, at 192. I use the term to signify speech that is reported either indirectly *or* directly. I also opt for the term 'reportage' with reference to Cleopatra to signify not only variegated instances of reported discourse (i.e. speech that is direct, indirect or hypothetical) but also reported thought, reported occurrences and the use of reports themselves. On the inseparability of reported thoughts, feelings and perceptions from reported speech, see Anna Wierzbicka, 'The Semantics of Direct and Indirect Discourse', *Papers in Linguistics* 7, no. 3–4 (September 1974): 297–9.

17 Daniel E. Collins, *Reanimated Voices: Speech Reporting in a Historical-Pragmatic Perspective* (Amsterdam: John Benjamins, 2001), 11; see also Włodarczyk, *Pragmatic Aspects of Reported Speech*, 39–40.

18 Collins, *Reanimated Voices*, 11. For example, linguists would examine how the meaning of the direct report in the sentence 'He said "it's raining"' is altered by its transposition to the syntactic unit of a *that*-clause which characterizes indirect speech: 'He *said that* it *was* raining' (italics mine). The syntactic transposition of direct to indirect speech would also entail an examination of 'pronoun shift, tense shift, mood shift, [and] embedding of the reported clause in a matrix sentence dominated by a verb of saying or communication' (Mike Baynham, 'Direct Speech: What's It Doing in Non-Narrative Discourse?', *Journal of Pragmatics* 25, no. 1 [January 1996]: 62).

19 Collins, *Reanimated Voices*, 11; Alessandro Duranti and Charles Goodwin, 'Re-Thinking Context: An Introduction', in *Re-Thinking Context: Language as an Interactive Phenomenon*, eds Duranti and Goodwin (Cambridge: Cambridge University Press, 1992), 3. Duranti and Goodwin mount a detailed defence of context from the perspective of linguistic anthropology. See Collins for a linguistic critique of the syntactic approach to reported speech (*Reanimated Voices*, 11–16).

20 Collins, *Reanimated Voices*, 3.

21 Valentin N. Vološinov, *Marxism and the Philosophy of Language*, trans. Ladislav Matejka and I. R. Titunik (New York: Seminar Press, 1986), 115, 119.

22 Ibid., 118.

23 In Austin's speech act theory, a performative is a speech act that 'does' something. Illocutionary and perlocutionary acts are both performatives: an illocutionary utterance, according to Austin, entails a change in state or condition immediately upon its utterance, whereas a perlocutionary utterance registers the effect of the utterance on its hearers.

24 See Vološinov, *Marxism*, 116.

25 Charnes, 'Spies and Whispers', 110, 107.

26 Antony's intention to thank Pompey for his 'strange courtesies and great' (2.2.163) prior to waging war against him, for

example, is motivated by his desire to uphold his reputation among his countrymen as an honourable Roman lest 'remembrance suffer ill report' (2.2.165).

27 See Charnes, 'Spies and Whispers', 108.

28 Andrew Hiscock, '"Here is my Space": The Politics of Appropriation in Shakespeare's *Antony and Cleopatra*', *English: The Journal of the English Association* 47, no. 189 (October 1998): 196. See also Charnes, who observes that reporters are not just messengers but also the main characters who discursively recreate other characters' words or actions ('Spies and Whispers', 106).

29 Caesar's preoccupation with public display is evident at a number of points throughout the play, but perhaps most significantly when he learns of Antony's suicide. Caesar not only weeps but also draws his council's attention to his weeping as a means of persuading them of his sincere love for his rival: 'Look you, sad friends. / The gods rebuke me' (5.1.27–8). In the same scene, Caesar urges the council to read or bear witness to the written reports he sent to Antony (5.1.73–7) in order to display his pacifism in war. His concern for visual display or theatrical 'showing' – witness his intention to later showcase Cleopatra as an Egyptian 'puppet' on the Roman political stage – is a means of consolidating his power. William Junker makes a similar point; see 'The Image of Both Theaters: Empire and Revelation in Shakespeare's *Antony and Cleopatra*', *Shakespeare Quarterly* 66, no. 2 (Summer 2015): 167–87, at 175.

30 Alexander Leggatt, implying a similar point, notes that Caesar's 'imagination lingers over foul images' (*Shakespeare's Political Drama: The History Plays and The Roman Plays* [London: Routledge, 1988], 166).

31 Heather James, *Shakespeare's Troy: Drama, Politics, and the Translation of Empire* (Cambridge and New York: Cambridge University Press, 1997), 128.

32 Vološinov, *Marxism*, 120. Indirect reported speech, for Vološinov, also includes mixed forms of speech reporting such as quasi indirect and quasi direct discourse (see *Marxism*, 122).

33 Hiscock, '"Here is my Space"', 194.

34 Robert Lipscomb, noting that food and sexuality are frequently intertwined in the play, claims that 'strange flesh' refers to both

Cleopatra's excess and to Caesar's temperance; see 'Caesar's Same-Sex-Food-Sex Dilemma', *Early English Studies* 2 (2009): 1–13, at 4–6.

35 Charnes, 'Spies and Whispers', 107.

36 Ibid., 108. While Charnes claims that 'mimetic subversion' is not essentially anti-discursive since 'it filches from and poaches on existing discourses', she nevertheless views mimesis and narrative as opposite ends on a spectrum rather than as complementary modes of representation (107).

37 Patricia Mayes, 'Quotation in Spoken English', *Studies in Language* 14, no. 2 (1990): 346.

38 On indirect speech, see Florian Coulmas, 'Reported Speech: Some General Issues', in *Direct and Indirect Speech*, ed. Coulmas (Amsterdam: Mouton, 1986), 1–28, especially 5–6.

39 Vološinov, *Marxism*, 120, 119.

40 Mayes, 'Quotation in Spoken English', 348. Direct reported speech is neither factual nor an authentic reconstruction of a previous utterance but a form of creatively 'constructed dialogue' as Deborah Tannen explains; see *Talking Voices: Repetition, Dialogue, and Imagery in Conversational Discourse* (New York: Cambridge University Press, 2007), 112.

41 Collins, *Reanimated Voices*, 69. Direct report can create a 'sense of objectivity' (71).

42 Ania Loomba, *Shakespeare, Race, and Colonialism* (Oxford: Oxford University Press, 2002), 133.

43 Wierzbicka, 'Semantics', 272.

44 Mayes, 'Quotation in Spoken English', 338. Mayes observes that direct speech often conveys 'affective elements' of meaning in addition to factual information (358); Vološinov contends that indirect speech cannot register emotion (see *Marxism*, 128).

45 Plutarch, 'The Life of Antonius', 127. For the connection between motion and sexual copulation, see the gloss on 'go' in *Antony and Cleopatra: A New Variorum Edition of Shakespeare*, ed. Martin Spevack (New York: MLA, 1990), 23–4, fn. 141.

46 She is called a 'ribaudred nag of Egypt' (3.10.10) by Scarus and is mocked by Enobarbus, who insinuates that she is a horse (whore) (3.7.8–10).

47 Adelman, *Common Liar*, 135.
48 *Oxford English Dictionary Online*, s.v. 'murmur', 1a.
49 Caesar similarly compares Pompey to a snake that 'thrives in our idleness' (1.4.77).
50 Loomba suggests that Antony's love for Cleopatra is mixed with political self-interest; see *Shakespeare, Race, and Colonialism*, 134.
51 Palfrey and Stern, *Shakespeare in Parts*, 329, 364.
52 Dan Sperber and Deirdre Wilson, 'Irony and the Use-Mention Distinction', in *Radical Pragmatics*, ed. Peter Cole (New York: Academic Press, 1981), 302.
53 Ibid., 303.
54 Ibid.
55 The ouroboros dates back to the ancient papyrus called the *Chrysopoeia of Cleopatra*, which depicts a black-headed snake devouring its white tail. The image is symbolic of eternity.
56 Adelman, *Common Liar*, 66.
57 Heather James, 'The Politics of Display and the Anamorphic Subjects of *Antony and Cleopatra*', in *Shakespeare's Late Tragedies: A Collection of Critical Essays*, ed. Susanne L. Wofford (Upper Saddle River, NJ: Prentice Hall, 1996), 212.
58 See also Antony's tautological description of Cleopatra as a crocodile, which reinforces Cleopatra's circular self-identity (2.7.42–3). Cleopatra exceeds narrative frameworks of description and report.
59 Collins, *Reanimated Voices*, 74.
60 Hypothetical, because Cleopatra imagines what Caesar would say.
61 Marvin Rosenberg, *The Masks of Antony and Cleopatra*, ed. Mary Rosenberg (Newark, DE: University of Delaware Press, 2006), 58.
62 María Luisa Dañobeitia Fernández, 'Cleopatra's Role-Taking: A Study of *Antony and Cleopatra*', in *Spanish Studies in Shakespeare and His Contemporaries*, ed. José Manuel González (Newark, DE: University of Delaware Press, 2006), 173 (italics mine).
63 Paul Yachnin, 'Shakespeare's Politics of Loyalty: Sovereignty and Subjectivity in *Antony and Cleopatra*', *SEL: Studies in English Literature 1500–1900* 33, no. 2 (Spring 1993): 347.

64 Jan H. Blits, *New Heaven, New Earth: Shakespeare's* Antony and Cleopatra (Lanham, MD: Lexington Books, 2009), 175.
65 On how Cleopatra stimulates desire through absence, see Catherine Belsey, 'Cleopatra's Seduction'.
66 Goldman makes the same observation; see *Acting and Action*, 119.
67 Charnes, 'Spies and Whispers', 121.
68 Caesar's remark that Cleopatra 'looks like sleep, / As she would catch another Antony / In her strong toil of grace' (5.2.345–7) heralds his successful uptake of her intention to display her sexual power through performance.

Chapter 3

1 All quotes follow *King Henry V*, ed. T. W. Craik, The Arden Shakespeare 3rd series (London: Bloomsbury, 1995).
2 See Gerald Gould, 'A New Reading of *Henry V*', *The English Review* 29 (July 1919): 42–55. Critics who perceive Henry as a Christian king include E. M. W. Tillyard, *Shakespeare's History Plays* (London: Chatto & Windus, 1944); Moody Prior, *The Drama of Power: Studies in Shakespeare's History Plays* (Evanston, IL: Northwestern University Press, 1973); and Sherman H. Hawkins, 'Virtue and Kingship in Shakespeare's *Henry IV*', *English Literary Renaissance* 5, no. 3 (September 1975): 313–43. Critics who perceive Henry as a Machiavellian politician include Harold C. Goddard, *The Meaning of Shakespeare*, vol. 1 (Chicago, IL: University of Chicago Press, 1951); Roy W. Battenhouse, '*Henry V* as Heroic Comedy', in *Essays on Shakespeare and the Elizabethan Drama in Honor of Hardin Craig*, ed. Richard Hosley (Columbia, MO: University of Missouri Press, 1962), 163–82, and Honor Matthews, *Character & Symbol in Shakespeare's Plays: A Study of Certain Christian and Pre-Christian Elements in Their Structure and Imagery* (Cambridge: Cambridge University Press, 1962). Phyllis Rackin traces this critical partisanship to the 'ideological conflict' between 'providential and Machiavellian theories of historical causation' in Shakespeare's history plays;

see *Stages of History: Shakespeare's English Chronicles* (Ithaca, NY: Cornell University Press, 1990), 45, 43.

3   Norman Rabkin, 'Rabbits, Ducks, and Henry V', *Shakespeare Quarterly* 28, no. 3 (Summer 1977): 279. For a critique of Rabkin's binary paradigm, see Graham Bradshaw, *Misrepresentations: Shakespeare and the Materialists* (Ithaca, NY: Cornell University Press, 1993), 77–80, and Maurice Hunt, 'The "Breaches" of Shakespeare's *The Life of King Henry the Fifth*', *College Literature* 41, no. 4 (Fall 2014): 7–24.

4   Rabkin, 'Rabbits, Ducks, and Henry V', 296.

5   Ayers's observation, however, is nevertheless scaffolded on the assumption that Henry's rhetorical performances 'conceal' his self. See P. K. Ayers, '"Fellows of Infinite Tongue": Henry V and the King's English', *SEL: Studies in English Literature 1500–1900* 34, no. 2 (Spring 1994): 258.

6   Paola Pugliatti, 'The Strange Tongues of *Henry V*', *The Yearbook of English Studies* 23 (January 1993): 243, 246; Michael Neill, 'Broken English and Broken Irish: Nation, Language, and the Optic of Power in Shakespeare's Histories', *Shakespeare Quarterly* 45, no. 1 (Spring 1994): 1–32. See also Janette Dillon, *Language and Stage in Medieval and Renaissance England* (Cambridge: Cambridge University Press, 1998).

7   Stephen Greenblatt, 'Invisible Bullets', in *Shakespearean Negotiations: The Circulation of Social Energy in Renaissance England* (Berkeley, CA: University of California Press, 1988), 21–65; Claire McEachern, *The Poetics of English Nationhood, 1590–1612* (Cambridge: Cambridge University Press, 1996), 86. See also Alison A. Chapman who, in a New Historicist vein, argues that in making his St Crispin's Day speech commemorate 'monarchical instead of artisanal power' rather than the social advancement of his men, Henry is able to contain and prevent the 'subversive holidays' associated with the patron saint of shoemakers ('Whose Saint Crispin's Day Is It?: Shoemaking, Holiday Making, and the Politics of Memory in Early Modern England', *Renaissance Quarterly* 54, no. 4 [Winter 2001]: 1482).

8   Peter Parolin, for instance, explores Henry's 'godly self-presentation' through rhetoric but claims that this self-presentation is undermined by rhetoric itself, which has the

'power to misrepresent persuasively' ('Figuring the King in *Henry V*: Political Rhetoric and the Limits of Performance', *Journal of the Wooden O Symposium* 9 [2009]: 49, 50).

9   Roger D. Sell, '*Henry V* and the Strength and Weakness of Words: Shakespearean Philology, Historicist Criticism, Communicative Pragmatics', in *Shakespeare and Scandinavia: A Collection of Nordic Studies*, ed. Gunnar Sorelius (Newark, DE: University of Delaware Press, 2002), 126; Urszula Kizelbach, *The Pragmatics of Early Modern Politics: Power and Kingship in Shakespeare's History Plays* (Amsterdam: Rodopi, 2014); David Schalkwyk, 'Proto-Nationalist Performatives and Trans-Theatrical Displacement in *Henry V*', in *Transnational Exchange in Early Modern Theater*, eds Robert Henke and Eric Nicholson (Burlington, VT: Ashgate, 2008), 197–213.

10 Schalkwyk, 'Proto-Nationalist Performatives', 204, 200. In Austin's terminology, an illocutionary act is an utterance that, once pronounced, causes a change in state or condition (Austin gives the example of 'I do' uttered during a wedding ceremony, which instantaneously turns the speaker into husband or wife) whereas a perlocutionary act is an utterance that has either intended or unintended effects on the hearer (the utterance can persuade, deter, mislead, etc.). Both illocutionary and perlocutionary acts are performative utterances since they 'do' things or act upon reality. See J. L. Austin, *How to Do Things with Words: The William James Lectures*, eds J. O. Urmson and Marina Sbisà, 2nd edn (Oxford: Clarendon Press, 1975), 5, 99–100, and 107–8.

11 Constative statements 'describe' reality or 'report' a fact that may be true or untrue; see Austin, *How to Do Things*, 5.

12 Henry's shortened speeches and interactions with his interlocutors in the quarto do not lend themselves to ambivalent readings. The quarto also omits the Chorus, Canterbury and Ely, Henry's speech at Harfleur and other aspects that are crucial in constructing a morally complex portrait of the monarch.

13 Edward Hall, *The Victorious Actes of Kyng Henry the Fifth*, in *The Vnion of the Two Noble and Illustre Famelies of Lancastre and Yorke* (1548; repr. in *Hall's Chronicle; Containing the History of England, during the Reign of Henry the Fourth, and*

the Succeeding Monarchs, to the End of the Reign of Henry the Eighth [London: J. Johnson, 1809]), 46. Page references are to the 1809 edition.

14 Ibid., 46, 47.

15 Raphael Holinshed, 'Henry V', in *Holinshed's Chronicle as Used in Shakespeare's Plays*, eds Allardyce and Josephine Nicoll (London: Dent, 1965), 88.

16 Ibid., 89.

17 Scene and line numbers for *The Famous Victories of Henry the Fifth* follow those in Seymour M. Pitcher's *The Case for Shakespeare's Authorship of* The Famous Victories, *with the Complete Text of the Anonymous Play* (New York: State University of New York, 1961).

18 Larry S. Champion, '"What Prerogatives Meanes": Perspective and Political Ideology in *The Famous Victories of Henry V*', *South Atlantic Review* 53, no. 4 (November 1988): 14.

19 Ibid. Shakespeare's play also adopts the structural juxtaposition of acts and scenes found in *The Famous Victories*.

20 Rhetorical treatises after Aristotle divorced rhetoric from dialectic and isolated it as an art of persuasion or style. Cicero, for instance, stripped rhetoric down to *elocutio* or eloquence and it was this conception of rhetoric that infiltrated the early modern English grammar school. The institutionalization of rhetoric as a subject of study under Tudor pedagogues, in addition to the pedagogical reforms of Ramism, further reinforced the ornamental function of rhetoric. See, for instance, Sister Miriam Joseph's *Shakespeare's Use of the Arts of Language* (New York: Hafner Publishing, 1966) and Brian Vickers, 'The Recovery of Rhetoric: Petrarch, Erasmus, Perelman', in *The Recovery of Rhetoric: Persuasive Discourse and Disciplinarity in the Human Sciences*, eds R. H. Roberts and J. M. M. Good (London: Bristol Classical Press, 1993), 25–48.

21 Chaïm Perelman, *The New Rhetoric and the Humanities: Essays on Rhetoric and Its Applications* (Dordrecht, the Netherlands: Reidel, 1979), 5. Italics mine.

22 Ibid., 3.

23 On the distinction between logic and argumentation, see Michel Meyer, 'Toward a Rhetoric of Reason', *Rhetoric Society Quarterly* 19, no. 2 (Spring 1989): 131–9, especially 131–2. Although Perelman and Olbrechts-Tyteca disassociate their 'New Rhetoric' from formal logic, they nevertheless hold that rhetoric is 'complementary to formal logic' and argumentation is 'complementary to demonstrative proof' (Perelman, *The New Rhetoric and the Humanities*, 31).

24 Chaïm Perelman and Lucie Olbrechts-Tyteca, *The New Rhetoric: A Treatise on Argumentation*, trans. John Wilkinson and Purcell Weaver (Notre Dame, IN: University of Notre Dame Press, 1969), 1; Perelman, *The New Rhetoric and the Humanities*, 10.

25 Not all tropes and schemes are argumentative. Perelman and Olbrechts-Tyteca note that a trope is argumentative only 'if it brings about a change of perspective' and 'the adherence of the hearer' (*The New Rhetoric*, 169).

26 Jésus M. Larrazabal and Kepa Korta, 'Pragmatics and Rhetoric for Discourse Analysis: Some Conceptual Remarks', *Manuscrito* 25, no. 2 (2002): 244.

27 Marcelo Dascal and Alan G. Gross, 'The Marriage of Pragmatics and Rhetoric', *Philosophy and Rhetoric* 32, no. 2 (1999): 109.

28 Ibid., 117.

29 Ibid., 110.

30 Ibid., 109.

31 Ibid., 110.

32 See Quentin Skinner's gloss on *virtù* in *The Foundations of Modern Political Thought, Volume I* (Cambridge: Cambridge University Press, 1978), 138; see also 130–1. Although Machiavelli declares that the ruler 'should not deviate from the good, if possible', he qualifies this counsel by saying that the ruler should nevertheless know how to practise deception 'if necessary': 'It is unnecessary for a prince to have all the good qualities…, but it is very necessary to *appear* to have them…. *to appear to have them is useful*; to appear merciful, faithful, humane, religious, upright, and to be so, but with a

mind so framed that should you require not to be so, you may be able and know how to change to the opposite' (Niccolò Machiavelli, chap. 18, in *The Prince*, trans. W. K. Marriott [London: Dent, 1940], 139). Italics mine.

33 See Ronald Knowles, who claims that Shakespeare's history plays are informed by various forms of argument (*Shakespeare's Arguments with History* [Basingstoke: Palgrave, 2002]), and Russ McDonald, who charts how rhetorical training involving the *in utramque partem* model in the early modern grammar schoolroom infiltrated and complicated Shakespeare's plays ('Rhetoric and Theater', in *The Oxford Handbook of Rhetorical Studies*, ed. Michael J. MacDonald [New York: Oxford University Press, 2015], 1–15).

34 See James S. Baumlin, 'Introduction: Positioning *Ethos* in Historical and Contemporary Theory', in *Ethos: New Essays in Rhetorical and Critical Theory*, eds James S. Baumlin and Tita French Baumlin (Dallas, TX: Southern Methodist University Press, 1994), xv. James L. Kinneavy and Susan C. Warshauer disambiguate Aristotle's use of 'ethos', showing it to be both a rhetorical appeal and 'the qualities of character that audiences find persuasive' ('From Aristotle to Madison Avenue: *Ethos* and the Ethics of Argument', in *Ethos: New Essays*, eds Baumlin and Baumlin, 183).

35 It should be noted that Aristotle's emphasis on the orator's appearance of ethos is not Machiavellian, since rhetorical ethos is intertwined with his idea of the 'Good'; see Nan Johnson, 'Ethos and the Aims of Rhetoric', in *Essays on Classical Rhetoric and Modern Discourse*, eds Robert J. Connors, Lisa S. Ede, and Andrea A. Lunsford (Carbondale, IL: Southern Illinois University Press, 1984), 98–114, at 101–3. Aristotle differs from Plato and Isocrates, who hold discourse to be expressive of the speaker's moral character while character itself incarnates truth (see Baumlin, 'Introduction: Positioning *Ethos*', xiii).

36 Kinneavy and Warshauer, 'From Aristotle to Madison Avenue', 175, 176, 179, 178.

37 Ibid., 180.

38 For example, a speaker who explicitly says 'I worked as a diplomat for twenty years' directly enhances his or her credibility (ethos) but may not necessarily be successful in persuading his or her hearers or making them believe that the speaker is a credible authority. If the speaker enhances this statement with an argument that displays his or her knowledge of international relations (logos) or delivers a touching anecdote about the sacrifices his or her family endured because of his or her career (pathos), then the speaker would indirectly strengthen his or her ethos.

39 The *enthymeme* is the rhetorical variant of the syllogism in logic, with the difference that one of its premises is usually omitted or implied. An example from Shakespeare is the Fourth Plebeian's utterance following Antony's funeral oration for Caesar: 'Mark ye his words? [Caesar] would not take the crown; / Therefore 'tis certain he was not ambitious' (*Julius Caesar*, 3.2.113–14). The omitted premise is that only ambitious men take the crown.

40 Eugene Garver, *Aristotle's Rhetoric: An Art of Character* (Chicago, IL: University of Chicago Press, 1994), 195, 175.

41 Erasmus, quoting Julius Pollux, enumerates the God-like qualities of a Christian king: 'mild, peaceful, lenient, foresighted, just, humane, magnanimous, frank ... rational ... sound in his advice, ... sensible, mindful of religious matters ... slowly moved to vengeance; ... true, constant, unbending, prone to the side of justice' (*The Education of a Christian Prince*, trans. Lester K. Born [New York: Octagon Books, 1965], 171). The king establishes his authority through 'wisdom, then integrity, self-restraint' (209; see also 162–3 for a description of a good king).

42 Henry nevertheless conflates legal right with moral right. After Canterbury's excursus on the Salic Law, Henry's equivocation on 'right' in his question 'May I with right and conscience make this claim?' (1.2.96) renders his injunction to Canterbury that the latter avoid 'titles miscreate' absurd, for if these titles are morally right then they are also already true. Henry decides the matter even as he poses the question.

43 Lynne Magnusson, 'A Play of Modals: Grammar and Potential Action in Early Shakespeare', *Shakespeare Survey* 62 (2009): 69;

John Lyons, *Semantics Vol. 2* (Cambridge: Cambridge University Press, 1977), 823.

44 The sentence 'John may come tomorrow', for example, can have both epistemic and deontic modality: the speaker may be expressing belief in the possibility of John's arrival (epistemic) or granting permission for John's arrival (deontic). In *Othello*, for example, the verb 'may' in Iago's warning to Roderigo exemplifies epistemic modality: 'Sir, he's rash and very sudden in choler, and haply with his truncheon may strike at you' (2.1.270–1). Desdemona's use of 'must' and 'will' in her exchange with Cassio, on the other hand, instantiates deontic modality: 'You must awhile be patient: / What I can do I will' (3.4.130–1).

45 Modality here overlaps with the future tense. On the evolution of modal verbs as auxiliaries of futurity, see Maurizio Gotti, 'Pragmatic Uses of Shall and Will for Future Time Reference in Early Modern English', in *English Modality in Context: Diachronic Perspectives*, ed. David Hart (Bern: Peter Lang, 2003), 109–70, and Merja Kytö, 'Shall or Will? Choice of the Variant Form in Early Modern English, British and American', in *Historical Linguistics 1987*, eds Henning Andersen and Konrad Koerner (Amsterdam: John Benjamins, 1990), 275–88.

46 Leslie K. Arnovick, *The Development of Future Constructions in English: The Pragmatics of Modal and Temporal 'Will' and 'Shall' in Middle English* (New York: Peter Lang, 1990), 6. Arnovick deems that the Wallis paradigm teaches speakers 'how to perform ... illocutionary acts' with modal verbs 'in certain declarative and interrogative sentences' (1). While the Wallis Rules may seem anachronistic, Arnovick shows that they are historically grounded in late Middle English and early modern English utterances.

47 Magnusson, 'A Play of Modals', 69, 76. Magnusson's study focuses on Marcus's equivocal use of 'must' in *Titus Andronicus* and on Richard's use of 'may' in *Richard III*.

48 *King Henry IV, Part 2*, ed. A. R. Humphreys, The Arden Shakespeare (London: Methuen & Co., 1966).

49 The recurrent strategy of foisting responsibility onto others so as to absolve himself of guilt is characteristic of Henry's rhetoric

throughout the play. See Bradley Greenburg, '"O for a Muse of Fire": *Henry V* and Plotted Self-Exculpation', *Shakespeare Studies* 36 (2008): 182–206.

50 The comparison is an analogy rather than a simile because it is functionally argumentative. Perelman and Olbrechts-Tyteca outline the argumentative structure of the analogy as follows: 'A is to B as C is to D'. This is the four-term structure that Henry's analogies follow, even though analogies can also be comprised of three terms: 'B is to A as C is to B' or 'A is to B as A is to C' (*The New Rhetoric*, 372, 375, 376).

51 John R. Searle, 'The Structure of Illocutionary Acts', in *Speech Acts: An Essay in the Philosophy of Language* (Cambridge: Cambridge University Press, 1969), 58, 59.

52 A fallacy arises from the unsound use of reasoning.

53 Aristotle identifies ambiguity in language as a material fallacy. According to Sister Miriam Joseph, a material fallacy 'vitiates an argument which on the surface appears to be formally correct'; the material fallacy may arise from ambiguity either in a single word or in a series of words (*Shakespeare's Use of the Arts of Language*, 367–8).

54 Camille Wells Slights, 'The Conscience of the King: *Henry V* and the Reformed Conscience', *Philological Quarterly* 80, no. 1 (Winter 2001): 38.

55 *Oxford English Dictionary Online*, s.v. 'credit'.

56 Judith Mossman, '*Henry V* and Plutarch's *Alexander*', *Shakespeare Quarterly* 45, no. 1 (Spring 1994): 61. Mossman recognizes that the comparison between Alexander and Henry 'has the potential for equal polyvalency' (63).

57 Janet M. Spencer, 'Princes, Pirates, and Pigs: Criminalizing Wars of Conquest in *Henry V*', *Shakespeare Quarterly* 47, no. 2 (Summer 1996): 169. Spencer explains that Canterbury 'suppresses the guile of the one version [of the Gordian knot episode] and the violence of the other' through his gloss on 'unloose' (169).

58 See also lines 263–4: 'We will in France, by God's grace, play a set / Shall strike his father's crown into the hazard'.

59 Perelman and Olbrechts-Tyteca, *The New Rhetoric*, 117. Presence is confidently used by Henry again in his speech at

Harfleur to vividly describe the ravage he could cause in France (3.3.1–43).

60 Joseph defines *epiplexis* or *percontatio* as figures of 'accusations and reprehensions' in which 'one asks questions, not in order to know, but to chide or reprehend' (*Shakespeare's Use of the Arts of Language*, 256).

61 See Karl P. Wentersdorf, 'The Conspiracy of Silence in *Henry V*', *Shakespeare Quarterly* 27, no. 3 (Summer 1976): 286.

62 Post hoc fallacies posit a definite causation between two events where there may only be a correlation between them; see Douglas Walton, *Informal Logic: A Pragmatic Approach*, 2nd edn (Cambridge: Cambridge University Press, 2008), 260.

63 Henry later, similarly, attributes the minimal loss of his men at Agincourt to God: 'O God, thy arm was here, / And not to us, but to thy arm alone / Ascribe we all' (4.8.106–8).

64 In Austin's speech act theory, 'uptake' refers to the hearer's ability to grasp the intended meaning behind the speaker's utterance. While 'uptake' is commonly used with reference to illocutionary utterances, I use it here with reference to Henry-as-soldier's dutiful and patriotic sentiment, which is an emotional effect that Henry-the-king fully intends his speech to have.

65 A syllogism explicitly contains a major premise (which must be a universal proposition), a minor premise and a conclusion, whereas the *enthymeme* usually implies a major or a minor premise. Henry's implicit premise is that all men are equal. Translated into a syllogism, Henry's *enthymeme* would read: (A) All men are equal; (B) the king is a man, like his soldiers; (C) therefore if Henry's soldiers are seized by fear, so is Henry. For an explanation of the rules governing the syllogism, see Joseph, *Shakespeare's Use of the Arts of Language*, 356–7.

66 Erasmus compares the ideal ruler to a 'father' of the state:

> There is the same difference between a prince and a tyrant as there is between a conscientious father and a cruel master. The former is ready and willing to give even his life for his children; the latter thinks of nothing else than his own gain, or indulges his caprices to his own taste, with no thought to the welfare of his subjects.
>
> (*Education*, 152, 161)

67 See Erasmus, *Education*, 180.

68 The French tongue, like France itself, is consistently feminized throughout the play. France is envisioned as the *hortus conclusus*, symbolized by Princess Katherine, that Henry metaphorically invades and deflowers in taking her as his wife. In doing so, Henry achieves a prelapsarian paradise or 'the world's best garden' (Epilogue, 7).

Chapter 4

1 All quotations of the play follow *The Taming of the Shrew*, ed. Barbara Hodgdon, The Arden Shakespeare 3rd series (London: Bloomsbury, 2010).

2 Critics who endorse a patriarchal view include Shirley Nelson Garner, '*The Taming of the Shrew*: Inside or Outside of the Joke?', in '*Bad' Shakespeare: Revaluations of the Shakespeare Canon*, ed. Maurice Charney (Rutherford, NJ: Fairleigh Dickinson University Press, 1988): 105–19 and Maureen Quilligan, 'Staging Gender: William Shakespeare and Elizabeth Cary', in *Sexuality and Gender in Early Modern Europe: Institutions, Texts, Images*, ed. James Grantham Turner (Cambridge: Cambridge University Press, 1993), 208–32. Critics who endorse a feminist view include, most prominently, Coppélia Kahn, '*The Taming of the Shrew*: Shakespeare's Mirror of Marriage', *Modern Language Studies* 5, no. 1 (Spring 1975): 88–102.

3 See, for instance, Marion D. Perret, 'Petruchio: The Model Wife', *SEL: Studies in English Literature 1500–1900* 23, no. 2 (Spring 1983): 223–35; Margie Burns, 'The Ending of the *Shrew*', *Shakespeare Studies* 18 (1986): 41–64; Jay L. Halio, 'The Induction as Clue in *The Taming of the Shrew*', in '*A Certain Text': Close Readings and Textual Studies on Shakespeare and Others*, eds Linda Anderson and Janis Lull (Newark, DE: University of Delaware Press, 2002), 94–106; and Corinne S. Abate, 'Neither a Tamer nor a Shrew Be: A Defense of Petruchio and Katherine', in *Privacy, Domesticity, and Women in Early Modern England*, eds Corinne S. Abate and Elizabeth Mazzola (Aldershot: Ashgate, 2003), 31–44.

4   For an account of Kate as a farcical character, see, most notably, Robert B. Heilman, 'The Taming Untamed, or, The Return of the Shrew', *Modern Language Quarterly* 27, no. 2 (June 1966): 147–61.

5   Wayne A. Rebhorn, 'Petruchio's "Rope Tricks": *The Taming of the Shrew* and the Renaissance Discourse of Rhetoric', *Modern Philology* 92, no. 3 (February 1995): 324; Kahn, '*The Taming of the Shrew*', 99; and Halio, 'The Induction as Clue', 98. See also Helga Ramsey-Kurz, 'Rising above the Bait: Kate's Transformation from Bear to Falcon', *English Studies* 88, no. 3 (June 2007): 262–81.

6   See Geoffrey Bullough, who claims that the play 'shows that Shakespeare was already moving from the outer world of appearances and situation to the inner world of character and ethical implications' ('Introduction', in *Narrative and Dramatic Sources of Shakespeare*, vol. 1, ed. Bullough [London: Routledge and Kegan Paul and New York: Columbia University Press, 1964], 68). John C. Bean, 'Comic Structure and the Humanizing of Kate in *The Taming of the Shrew*', in *The Woman's Part: Feminist Criticism in Shakespeare*, eds Carolyn Ruth Swift Lenz, Gayle Greene and Carol Thomas Neely (Urbana, IL: University of Illinois Press, 1980), 66.

7   Barbara Hodgdon, 'Katherina Bound; or, Play(K)ating the Strictures of Everyday Life', *PMLA* 107, no. 3 (May 1992): 541.

8   Tita French Baumlin, 'Petruchio the Sophist and Language as Creation in *The Taming of the Shrew*', *SEL: Studies in English Literature 1500–1900* 29, no. 2 (Spring 1989): 242.

9   Karen Newman, 'Renaissance Family Politics and Shakespeare's *The Taming of the Shrew*', *English Literary Renaissance* 16, no. 1 (Winter 1986): 99.

10 Rebhorn, 'Petruchio's "Rope Tricks"', 327.

11 Ibid., 324.

12 Elizabeth Hutcheon similarly explores Kate's speech in relation to educational practices but claims that Kate's monologue illustrates Petruccio's success as a humanist educator since he enables Kate to master the declamation and publicly demonstrate her rhetorical prowess as a school boy. See 'From Shrew to Subject: Petruchio's Humanist Education of Katherine

in *The Taming of the Shrew*', *Comparative Drama* 45, no. 4 (Winter 2011): 315–37.

13 Elizabeth Ann Mackay, 'Good Grammar, Possessive Pronouns, and Preposterous Possessions in *The Taming of the Shrew*', *Journal for Early Modern Cultural Studies* 17, no. 1 (Winter 2017): 32, 60.

14 Megan D. Little, 'The Persuasion of "The Poor Informal Women": The Problem of Rhetorical Training in *The Taming of the Shrew* and *Measure for Measure*', *Explorations in Renaissance Culture* 33, no. 1 (Summer 2007): 96.

15 Ibid., 98.

16 Ibid., 104.

17 See Marilyn M. Cooper, 'Implicature, Convention, and *The Taming of the Shrew*', *Poetics: International Review for the Theory of Literature* 10, no. 1 (February 1981): 1–14. For a discussion of Grice's theory of conversational implicature, see Chapter 1 on Falstaff.

18 Eleanor Hubbard has suggested that the court case of Christopher Percy and Margery Gore may have served as a possible source for Kate's shrewishness; see '"I Will Be Master of What Is Mine Own"': Fortune Hunters and Shrews in Early Modern London', *Sixteenth Century Journal* 46, no. 2 (Summer 2015): 331–58. Critics have detected a note of clandestine admiration of the shrew alongside the traditional, misogynistic condemnation of her in early modern texts: Pamela Allen Brown claims that the jest tradition challenges the depiction of the shrew in tracts, sermons and polemical pamphlets by portraying her as a clever, resourceful and hence more desirable woman to the sheepish Griselda type (*Better a Shrew than a Sheep: Women, Drama, and the Culture of Jest in Early Modern England* [Ithaca, NY: Cornell University Press, 2003]), while Anna Bayman and George Southcombe contend that the pamphlets in the later years of Elizabeth's reign, which condemn shrewish behaviour, also invite readers to admire this same behaviour since it enables women to negotiate city streets and their place in patriarchal society ('Shrews in Pamphlets and Plays', in *Gender and Power in Shrew-Taming Narratives, 1500–1700*, eds David Wootton and Graham Holderness [London: Palgrave, 2010], 11–28).

19 *A merry Ieste of a shrewde and curst Wyfe*, c. 1580, ed. Risa S. Bear, Renascence Editions (University of Oregon, 2001). http://www.luminarium.org/renascence-editions/jest.html.

20 Leah Marcus makes the case for intertextuality; see 'The Shakespearean Editor as Shrew Tamer', *English Literary Renaissance* 22, no. 2 (Spring 1992): 198. I agree with Marcus that the anonymous play may have an earlier date of composition and that it may be a source text for Shakespeare's play.

21 All scene and line references to *A Shrew* are from *The Taming of a Shrew: The 1594 Quarto*, ed. Stephen Roy Miller (Cambridge: Cambridge University Press, 1998).

22 Brown, *Better a Shrew than a Sheep*, 206.

23 Grice, 'Logic and Conversation', 26.

24 Ibid., 27.

25 Kate's ironic reference to herself in the third person also occurs in her earlier retort to Hortensio's warning that she shall not get a husband unless she curbs her unruliness:

> Iwis it is not half-way to her heart,
> But if it were, doubt not her care should be
> To comb your noddle with a three-legged stool,
> And paint your face, and use you like a fool.
>
> (1.1.62–5)

Kate distances herself from the role of mild and gentle maid scripted for her by men to mock the passivity required of her as an object of male possession.

26 Lucentio epitomizes the Petrarchan lover in the play. He claims that he will 'burn', 'pine' and 'perish' (1.1.144) if he does not win Bianca's hand in marriage; see his rejoinders to Tranio (1.1.168-70 and 1.1.212-14).

27 See Sperber and Wilson, 'Irony', 306–10.

28 Ibid., 310.

29 Ibid., 309, 306. In this way, Sperber and Wilson distinguish reported speech (or indirect quotation) from echoic mention.

30 Grice, 'Logic and Conversation', 27. That irony arises from a speaker's violation of the Gricean maxim of quality is a

presupposition that also underwrites Brown and Levinson's theory of politeness. Brown and Levinson classify irony as an off-record strategy used by a speaker who performs a face-threatening act on a hearer. I discuss Brown and Levinson's politeness theory in relation to Falstaff in Chapter 1.

31 Deirdre Wilson and Dan Sperber, 'Explaining Irony', in *Meaning and Relevance* (Cambridge: Cambridge University Press, 2012), 129; see also 141. Wilson and Sperber provide the example of Mary who, after a boring party, exclaims 'That was fun'. Mary's statement does not imply the opposite of what she explicitly states – that the party was boring – but rather expresses 'an attitude of scorn towards (say) the general expectation among the guests that the party would be fun' (125). Wilson and Sperber note that dissociative attitudes can range from 'amused tolerance through various shades of resignation or disappointment to contempt, disgust, outrage or scorn' (130).

32 Richard Madelaine, '"He Speaks Very Shrewishly": Apprentice-Training and *The Taming of the Shrew*', in *Gender and Power in Shrew-Taming Narratives, 1500–1700*, eds David Wootton and Graham Holderness (London: Palgrave, 2010), 70–83; Juliet Dusinberre, '*The Taming of the Shrew*: Women, Acting, and Power', in *The Taming of the Shrew: Critical Essays*, ed. Dana E. Aspinall (New York: Routledge, 2002), 168–85.

33 Madelaine, 'He Speaks Very Shrewishly', 70. The age of the apprentice actor would have been between 14 – which, according to David Kathman, is typically when puberty starts in boys – and 21. See David Kathman, 'How Old Were Shakespeare's Boy Actors?', *Shakespeare Survey* 58 (2005): 220–46. Richard Madelaine notes that boy apprentices aspired to play male rather than female parts and thereby assert their status as adults; see 'Material Boys: Apprenticeship and the Boy Actors' Shakespearean Roles', in *Shakespeare Matters: History, Teaching, Performance*, ed. Lloyd Davis (Newark, DE: University of Delaware Press, 2003), 225–38, at 230. See also the earlier work of Robertson Davies, *Shakespeare's Boy Actors* (London: Dent, 1939).

34 In Perelman and Olbrechts-Tyteca's theory of rhetoric as persuasive argumentation, comparisons carry argumentative

weight and thus constitute an orator's logos or logical reasoning. Logos, ethos and pathos are rhetorical appeals that must be kept in balance if the orator is to produce a speech that successfully persuades his or her audience. Persuasive argumentation is the focus of Chapter 3 on *Henry V*.

35 Grice, 'Logic and Conversation', 27.

Coda

1 All quotations follow *Hamlet, The Revised Edition*, eds Ann Thompson and Neil Taylor, The Arden Shakespeare 3rd series (London: Bloomsbury, 2016).

2 Jacqueline Rose, similarly noting the performativity of Hamlet's speech, observes that in both *Hamlet* and *Measure for Measure* 'words either fail to complete themselves in action or else they reach their destination too fast' ('Sexuality in the Reading of Shakespeare: *Hamlet* and *Measure for Measure*', in *Alternative Shakespeares*, 2nd edn, ed. John Drakakis [New York: Routledge, 2002], 120). See also John Paterson, who observes that the play portrays the 'word' as having lost 'its correspondence with the deed, thought, feeling' ('The Word in Hamlet', *Shakespeare Quarterly* 2, no.1 [January 1951]: 50).

3 Saxo Grammaticus, bk. 3, in *The First Nine Books of the Danish History of Saxo Grammaticus*, trans. Oliver Elton (London: David Nutt, 1894), 107.

4 Ibid., 109.

5 Ibid., 110.

6 Ibid., 117.

7 Ibid.

8 Sanford Sternlicht, '*Hamlet*: Six Characters in Search of a Play', *College English* 27, no. 7 (April 1966): 528.

9 Lars Engle, 'Discourse, Agency, and Therapy in *Hamlet*', *Exemplaria* 4, no. 2 (January 1992): 451, 452.

10 Ibid., 453.

11 Philip D. Collington, '"Sallets in the Lines to Make the Matter Savoury": Bakhtinian Speech Genres and Inserted Genres in *Hamlet* 2.2', *Texas Studies in Literature and Language* 53, no. 3 (Fall 2011): 262.

12 Margreta de Grazia holds that Hamlet's famed interiority is a product of eighteenth-century critical attempts to distinguish Shakespeare from the ancients; see 'When Did Hamlet Become Modern?', *Textual Practice* 17, no. 3 (Winter 2003): 485–503.

13 Terence Hawkes, 'Telmah: To the Sunderland Station', *Encounter* (April 1983): 58.

14 Grice, 'Logic and Conversation', 27.

15 François de Belleforest, *The Hystorie of Hamblet, Prince of Denmark,* trans. anon. (London, *c.* 1608), chap. III, 24, Literature Online – ProQuest E-book.

16 Grice, 'Logic and Conversation', 26.

17 The soliloquy is consistently placed first in Q1, Q2, and in the Folio. In Q1, however, Hamlet's speech on 'seeming' is addressed to Claudius rather than to his mother.

18 Grice, 'Logic and Conversation', 27.

19 Ibid., 27.

20 Karl P. Wentersdorf, 'Animal Symbolism in Shakespeare's *Hamlet*: The Imagery of Sex Nausea', *Comparative Drama* 17, no. 4 (Winter 1983–1984): 355.

21 Ibid., 356.

22 For a plethora of other possible interpretations of Hamlet's phrase, see Bill Delaney, 'Shakespeare's *Hamlet*', *The Explicator* 63, no. 2 (Winter 2005): 66–8.

23 Grice, 'Logic and Conversation', 27.

24 This is true for all three extant texts of the play.

25 James Hirsh, 'The "To Be or Not to Be" Speech: Evidence, Conventional Wisdom, and the Editing of *Hamlet*', *Medieval and Renaissance Drama in England: An Annual Gathering of Research, Criticism and Reviews* 23 (2010): 34–62; Phillip Arrington, 'Feigned Soliloquy, Feigned Argument: Hamlet's "To Be or Not to Be" Speech as Sophistic *Dissoi Logoi*', *Ben Jonson Journal* 22, no. 1 (May 2015): 101–18.

26 Arrington, 'Feigned Soliloquy', 108, 107.
27 On authorial intention and the delegation of scripted action, see Luke Wilson, '*Hamlet*: Equity, Intention, Performance', *Studies in the Literary Imagination* 24, no. 2 (Fall 1991): 91–113. Wilson similarly notes a parallel between the ghost's and Shakespeare's intention.

BIBLIOGRAPHY

Adelman, Janet. *The Common Liar: An Essay on* Antony and Cleopatra. New Haven, CT: Yale University Press, 1973.

Ahearn, Laura M. 'Language and Agency'. *Annual Review of Anthropology* 30, no. 1 (October 2001): 109–37.

Alfar, Cristina León. *Fantasies of Female Evil: The Dynamics of Gender and Power in Shakespearean Tragedy*. Newark, DE: University of Delaware Press, 2003.

Arnovick, Leslie. *The Development of Future Constructions in English: The Pragmatics of Modal and Temporal 'Will' and 'Shall' in Middle English*. New York: Peter Lang, 1990.

Arrington, Phillip. 'Feigned Soliloquy, Feigned Argument: Hamlet's "To Be or Not to Be" Speech as Sophistic *Dissoi Logoi*'. *Ben Jonson Journal* 22, no. 1 (May 2015): 101–18.

Austin, J. L. *How to Do Things with Words: The William James Lectures*, 2nd edn. Edited by J. O. Urmson and Marina Sbisà. Oxford: Clarendon Press, 1975.

Ayers, P. K. '"Fellows of Infinite Tongue": Henry V and the King's English'. *SEL: Studies in English Literature 1500–1900* 34, no. 2 (Spring 1994): 253–77.

Battenhouse, Roy W. 'Falstaff as Parodist and Perhaps Holy Fool'. *PMLA* 90, no. 1 (January 1975): 32–52.

Baumlin, James S. 'Introduction: Positioning *Ethos* in Historical and Contemporary Theory'. In *Ethos: New Essays in Rhetorical and Critical Theory*, edited by James S. Baumlin and Tita French Baumlin, xi–xxxi. Dallas, TX: Southern Methodist University Press, 1994.

Baumlin, Tita French. 'Petruchio the Sophist and Language as Creation in *The Taming of the Shrew*'. *SEL: Studies in English Literature 1500–1900* 29, no. 2 (Spring 1989): 237–57.

Baynham, Mike. 'Direct Speech: What's It Doing in Non-Narrative Discourse?' *Journal of Pragmatics* 25, no. 1 (January 1996): 61–81.

Bean, John C. 'Comic Structure and the Humanizing of Kate in *The Taming of the Shrew*'. In *The Woman's Part: Feminist Criticism of Shakespeare*, edited by Carolyn Ruth Swift Lenz, Gayle Greene, and Carol Thomas Neely, 65–78. Urbana, IL: University of Illinois Press, 1980.

Belleforest, François de. *The Hystorie of Hamblet, Prince of Denmark*. London, *c*. 1608. Literature Online–ProQuest.

Belsey, Catherine. 'Cleopatra's Seduction'. In *Alternative Shakespeares*. Vol. 2, edited by Terence Hawkes, 38–62. London and New York: Routledge, 1996.

Berger, Harry J. 'The Prince's Dog: Falstaff and the Perils of Speech-Prefixity'. *Shakespeare Quarterly* 49, no. 1 (Spring 1998): 40–73.

Blits, Jan H. *New Heaven, New Earth: Shakespeare's* Antony and Cleopatra. Lanham, MD: Lexington Books, 2009.

Bousfield, Derek. *Impoliteness in Interaction*. Amsterdam: John Benjamins, 2008.

Bousfield, Derek. '"Never a Truer Word Said in Jest": A Pragmastylistic Analysis of Impoliteness as Banter in *Henry IV, Part I*'. In *Contemporary Stylistics*, edited by Marina Lambrou and Peter Stockwell, 209–20. London: Continuum, 2007.

Brown, Pamela Allen. *Better a Shrew than a Sheep: Women, Drama, and the Culture of Jest in Early Modern England*. Ithaca, NY: Cornell University Press, 2003.

Brown, Penelope and Stephen C. Levinson. *Politeness: Some Universals in Language Usage*. Cambridge: Cambridge University Press, 1987.

Brown, Roger and Albert Gilman. 'Politeness Theory and Shakespeare's Four Major Tragedies'. *Language in Society* 18, no. 2 (June 1989): 159–212.

Bullough, Geoffrey. 'Introduction'. In *Narrative and Dramatic Sources of Shakespeare*. Vol. 1, edited by Bullough, 57–68. London: Routledge and Kegan Paul and New York: Columbia University Press, 1964.

Bushman, Mary Ann. 'Representing Cleopatra'. In *In Another Country: Feminist Perspectives on Renaissance Drama*, edited by Dorothea Kehler and Susan Baker, 36–49. Metuchen, NJ: Scarecrow Press, 1991.

Calderwood, James L. *Metadrama in Shakespeare's Henriad: Richard II to Henry V*. Berkeley, CA: University of California Press, 1979.

Champion, Larry S. '"What Prerogatives Meanes": Perspective and Political Ideology in *The Famous Victories of Henry V*'. *South Atlantic Review* 53, no. 4 (November 1988): 1–19.

Chapman, Alison A. 'Whose Saint Crispin's Day Is It?: Shoemaking, Holiday Making, and the Politics of Memory in Early Modern England'. *Renaissance Quarterly* 54, no. 4 (Winter 2001): 1467–94.

Charnes, Linda. 'Spies and Whispers: Exceeding Reputation in *Antony and Cleopatra*'. In *Notorious Identity: Materializing the Subject in Shakespeare*, 103–47. Cambridge, MA: Harvard University Press, 1993.

Collington, Philip D. '"Sallets in the Lines to Make the Matter Savoury": Bakhtinian Speech Genres and Inserted Genres in *Hamlet* 2.2'. *Texas Studies in Literature and Language* 53, no. 3 (Fall 2011): 237–72.

Collins, Daniel E. *Reanimated Voices: Speech Reporting in a Historical-Pragmatic Perspective*. Amsterdam: John Benjamins, 2001.

Cook, Carol. 'The Fatal Cleopatra'. In *Shakespearean Tragedy and Gender*, edited by Shirley Nelson Garner and Madelon Sprengnether, 241–67. Bloomington, IN: Indiana University Press, 1996.

Daniel, Samuel. 'The Tragedie of Cleopatra'. 1599 edn. In *Narrative and Dramatic Sources of Shakespeare*. Vol. 5, edited by Geoffrey Bullough, 406–49. London: Routledge and Kegan Paul and New York: Columbia University Press, 1964.

Dascal, Marcelo and Alan G. Gross. 'The Marriage of Pragmatics and Rhetoric'. *Philosophy and Rhetoric* 32, no. 2 (1999): 107–29.

Davis, Wayne A. 'Irregular Negations: Implicature and Idiom Theories'. In *Meaning and Analysis: New Essays on Grice*, edited by Klaus Petrus, 103–37. London: Palgrave Macmillan, 2010.

Deats, Sara Munson. 'Shakespeare's Anamorphic Drama: A Survey of *Antony and Cleopatra* in Criticism, on Stage, and on Screen'. In *Antony and Cleopatra: New Critical Essays*, edited by Sara Munson Deats, 1–94. New York: Routledge, 2005.

Dickey, Franklin M. *Not Wisely but Too Well: Shakespeare's Love Tragedies*. San Marino, CA: Huntington Library, 1957.

Dodd, William. 'Character as Dynamic Identity: From Fictional Interaction Script to Performance'. In *Shakespeare and Character: Theory, History, Performance, and Theatrical Persons*, edited by Paul Yachnin and Jessica Slights, 62–79. Basingstoke: Palgrave Macmillan, 2009.

Dodd, William. 'Destined Livery? Character and Person in Shakespeare'. *Shakespeare Survey* 51 (1998): 147–58.

Duranti, Alessandro and Charles Goodwin. 'Re-Thinking Context: An Introduction'. In *Re-Thinking Context: Language as an Interactive Phenomenon*, edited by Duranti and Goodwin, 1–42. Cambridge: Cambridge University Press, 1992.

Eggert, Katherine. *Showing Like a Queen: Female Authority and Literary Experiment in Spenser, Shakespeare, and Milton*. Philadelphia, PA: University of Pennsylvania Press, 2000.

Elam, Keir. *Shakespeare's Universe of Discourse: Language-Games in the Comedies*. Cambridge and New York: Cambridge University Press, 1984.

Engle, Lars. 'Discourse, Agency, and Therapy in *Hamlet*'. *Exemplaria* 4, no. 2 (January 1992): 441–53.

Erasmus, Desiderius. *The Education of a Christian Prince*. 1516. Translated by Lester K. Born. New York: Octagon Books, 1965.

The Famous Victories of Henry the Fifth. 1598. Reprinted by Seymour M. Pitcher in *The Case for Shakespeare's Authorship of* The Famous Victories, *with the Complete Text of the Anonymous Play* (New York: State University of New York, 1961).

Fernández, María Luisa Dañobeitia. 'Cleopatra's Role-Taking: A Study of *Antony and Cleopatra*'. In *Spanish Studies in Shakespeare and His Contemporaries*, edited by José Manuel González, 171–95. Newark, DE: University of Delaware Press, 2006.

Fish, Stanley. 'How to Do Things with Austin and Searle: Speech Act Theory and Literary Criticism'. *Modern Language Notes* 91, no. 5 (October 1976): 983–1025.

Fitz, L. T. 'Egyptian Queens and Male Reviewers: Sexist Attitudes in *Antony and Cleopatra*'. *Shakespeare Quarterly* 28, no. 3 (Summer 1977): 297–316.

Foucault, Michel. 'Rarity, Exteriority, Accumulation'. In *The Archaeology of Knowledge*, 118–25. Translated by A. M. Sheridan Smith. London: Tavistock Publications.

Garver, Eugene. *Aristotle's Rhetoric: An Art of Character*. Chicago, IL: University of Chicago Press, 1994.

Grammaticus, Saxo. Book Three. *The First Nine Books of the Danish History of Saxo Grammaticus*, 83–117. Translated by Oliver Elton. London: David Nutt, 1894.

Greenblatt, Stephen. *Renaissance Self-Fashioning: From More to Shakespeare*. Chicago, IL: University of Chicago Press, 1980.

Grice, H. P. 'Logic and Conversation'. In *Studies in the Way of Words*, 22–40. Cambridge, MA: Harvard University Press, 1989; repr. 1991. ACLS Humanities E-Book.

Grice, H. P. 'Utterer's Meaning and Intentions'. In *Studies in the Way of Words*, 86–116. Cambridge, MA: Harvard University Press, 1989; repr. 1991. ACLS Humanities E-Book.

Halio, Jay L. 'The Induction as Clue in *The Taming of the Shrew*'. In *"A Certain Text": Close Readings and Textual Studies on Shakespeare and Others*, edited by Linda Anderson and Janis Lull, 94–106. Newark, DE: University of Delaware Press, 2002.

Hall, Edward. *The Victorious Actes of Kyng Henry the Fifth*. In *The Vnion of the Two Noble and Illustre Famelies of Lancastre and Yorke*. 1548. Reprinted in *Hall's Chronicle; Containing the History of England, during the Reign of Henry the Fourth, and the Succeeding Monarchs, to the End of the Reign of Henry the Eighth*, 46–114. London: J. Johnson, 1809.

Hawkes, Terence. 'Telmah: To the Sunderland Station'. *Encounter* (April 1983): 50–60.

Hiscock, Andrew. '"Here Is My Space": The Politics of Appropriation in Shakespeare's *Antony and Cleopatra*'. *English: The Journal of the English Association* 47, no. 189 (October 1998): 187–212.

Hodgdon, Barbara. 'Katherina Bound; or, Play(K)ating the Strictures of Everyday Life'. *PMLA* 107, no. 3 (May 1992): 538–53.

Holinshed, Raphael. 'Henry V'. In *Holinshed's Chronicle as Used in Shakespeare's Plays*, edited by Allardyce and Josephine Nicoll, 71–89. London: Dent, 1965.

Jackson, William. 'Letter XIV'. In *Thirty Letters on Various Subjects*, 3rd edn. London: T. Cadell, 1795. Eighteenth-Century Collections Online.

James, Heather. 'The Politics of Display and the Anamorphic Subjects of *Antony and Cleopatra*'. In *Shakespeare's Late Tragedies: A Collection of Critical Essays*, edited by Susan L. Wofford, 208–34. Upper Saddle River, NJ: Prentice Hall, 1996.

James, Heather. *Shakespeare's Troy: Drama, Politics, and the Translation of Empire*. Cambridge and New York: Cambridge University Press, 1997.

Jankowski, Theodora A. *Women and Power in the Early Modern Drama*. Urbana and Chicago, IL: University of Chicago Press, 1992.

Johnson, Samuel. 'Notes' on *2 Henry IV*. In *Johnson on Shakespeare: Essays and Notes*, edited by Walter Raleigh, 119–25. Oxford: Oxford University Press, 1925.

Joseph, Sister Miriam. *Shakespeare's Use of the Arts of Language*. New York: Hafner Publishing, 1966.

Josephus, Flavius. *The Antiquities of the Jews*. In *Narrative and Dramatic Sources of Shakespeare*. Vol. 5, edited by Geoffrey Bullough, 331–6. London: Routledge and Kegan Paul and New York: Columbia University Press, 1964.

Kahn, Coppélia. '*The Taming of the Shrew*: Shakespeare's Mirror of Marriage'. *Modern Language Studies* 5, no. 1 (Spring 1975): 88–102.

Kinneavy, James L. and Susan C. Warshauer. 'From Aristotle to Madison Avenue: *Ethos* and the Ethics of Argument'. In *Ethos: New Essays in Rhetorical and Critical Theory*, edited by James S. Baumlin and Tita French Baumlin, 171–90. Dallas, TX: Southern Methodist University Press, 1994.

Knights, L. C. 'How Many Children Had Lady Macbeth? An Essay in the Theory and Practice of Shakespeare Criticism'. 1933. In *Hamlet and Other Shakespearean Essays*, 270–308. Cambridge: Cambridge University Press, 1979.

Larrazabal, Jésus M. and Kepa Korta. 'Pragmatics and Rhetoric for Discourse Analysis: Some Conceptual Remarks'. *Manuscrito* 25, no. 2 (2002): 233–48.

Lassiter, Charles. 'Implicating without Intending on the Gricean Account of Implicature'. *Empedocles: European Journal for the Philosophy of Communication* 4, no. 2 (2012): 199–215.

Leggatt, Alexander. *Shakespeare's Political Drama: The History Plays and The Roman Plays*. London: Routledge, 1988.

Levin, Richard A. *Shakespeare's Secret Schemers: The Study of An Early Modern Dramatic Device*. Newark, DE: University of Delaware Press, 2001.

Little, Megan D. 'The Persuasion of "The Poor Informal Women": The Problem of Rhetorical Training in *The Taming of the Shrew* and *Measure for Measure*'. *Explorations in Renaissance Culture* 33, no. 1 (Summer 2007): 83–108.

Loomba, Ania. *Shakespeare, Race, and Colonialism*. Oxford: Oxford University Press, 2002.

Lopez, Jeremy. *Theatrical Convention and Audience Response in Early Modern Drama*. Cambridge: Cambridge University Press, 2003.

Lucan. *Pharsalia*. Translated by Jane Wilson Joyce. Ithaca, NY and London: Cornell University Press, 1993.

Lyons, John. *Semantics*. Vol. 2. Cambridge: Cambridge University Press, 1977.

Machiavelli, Niccolò. *The Prince*. 1513. Translated by W. K. Marriott. London: Dent, 1940.

Mackay, Elizabeth Ann. 'Good Grammar, Possessive Pronouns, and Preposterous Possessions in *The Taming of the Shrew*'. *Journal for Early Modern Cultural Studies* 17, no. 1 (Winter 2017): 31–67.

Madelaine, Richard. '"He Speaks Very Shrewishly"': Apprentice-Training and *The Taming of the Shrew*'. In *Gender and Power in Shrew-Taming Narratives, 1500–1700*, edited by David Wootton and Graham Holderness, 70–83. London: Palgrave Macmillan, 2010.

Magnusson, Lynne. 'A Play of Modals: Grammar and Potential Action in Early Shakespeare'. *Shakespeare Survey* 62 (2009): 69–80.

Magnusson, Lynne. *Shakespeare and Social Dialogue: Dramatic Language and Elizabethan Letters*. Cambridge: Cambridge University Press, 1999.

Marcus, Leah. 'The Shakespearean Editor as Shrew Tamer'. *English Literary Renaissance* 22, no. 2 (Spring 1992): 177–200.

Mayes, Patricia. 'Quotation in Spoken English'. *Studies in Language* 14, no. 2 (1990): 325–63.

McDonald, Russ. 'Late Shakespeare: Style and the Sexes'. *Shakespeare Survey* 46 (1993): 91–106.

McEachern, Claire. *The Poetics of English Nationhood, 1590–1612*. Cambridge: Cambridge University Press, 1996.

McLaverty, J. 'No Abuse: The Prince and Falstaff in the Tavern Scenes of *Henry IV*'. *Shakespeare Survey* 34 (1981): 105–10.

A merry Ieste of a shrewde and curst Wyfe. c. 1580. Transcribed by Risa S. Bear. Renascence Editions. University of Oregon, 2001. http://www.luminarium.org/renascence-editions/jest.html.

Mey, Jacob L. *Pragmatics: An Introduction*. Cambridge, MA: Blackwell, 1993.

Morgann, Maurice. *An Essay on the Dramatic Character of Sir John Falstaff*. London: T. Davies, 1777; repr. New York: AMS Press, 1970.

Mossman, Judith. '*Henry V* and Plutarch's *Alexander*'. *Shakespeare Quarterly* 45, no. 1 (Spring 1994): 57–73.

Newman, Karen. 'Renaissance Family Politics and Shakespeare's *The Taming of the Shrew*'. *English Literary Renaissance* 16, no. 1 (Winter 1986): 86–100.

Newman, Karen. *Shakespeare's Rhetoric of Comic Character: Dramatic Convention in Classical and Renaissance Comedy*. New York: Methuen, 1985.

Palfrey, Simon and Tiffany Stern. *Shakespeare in Parts*. Oxford: Oxford University Press, 2007.

Parolin, Peter. 'Figuring the King in *Henry V*: Political Rhetoric and the Limits of Performance'. *Journal of the Wooden O Symposium* 9 (2009): 43–60.

Paterson, John. 'The Word in *Hamlet*'. *Shakespeare Quarterly* 2, no. 1 (January 1951): 47–55.

Perelman, Chaïm. *The New Rhetoric and the Humanities: Essays on Rhetoric and Its Applications*. Dordrecht, the Netherlands: D. Reidel, 1979.

Perelman, Chaïm and Lucie Olbrechts-Tyteca. *The New Rhetoric: A Treatise on Argumentation*. 1958. Translated by John Wilkinson and Purcell Weaver. Notre Dame: University of Notre Dame Press, 1969.

Plutarch. 'The Life of Antonius'. In *Selected Lives from the Lives of the Noble Grecians and Romans*. Vol. 2, edited by Paul Turner, 104–61. Carbondale, IL: Southern Illinois University Press, 1963.

Poole, Kristen. 'Saints Alive! Falstaff, Martin Marprelate, and the Staging of Puritanism'. *Shakespeare Quarterly* 46, no. 1 (Spring 1995): 47–75.

Pugliatti, Paola. 'The Strange Tongues of *Henry V*'. *The Yearbook of English Studies* 23 (January 1993): 235–53.

Rabinowitz, Peter J. 'Shakespeare's Dolphin, Dumbo's Feather, and Other Red Herrings: Some Thoughts on Intention and Meaning'. *Style* 44, no. 3 (Fall 2010): 342–64.

Rabkin, Norman. 'Rabbits, Ducks, and *Henry V*'. *Shakespeare Quarterly* 28, no. 3 (Summer 1977): 279–96.

Rackin, Phyllis. *Stages of History: Shakespeare's English Chronicles*. Ithaca, NY: Cornell University Press, 1990.

Rebhorn, Wayne A. 'Petruchio's "Rope Tricks": *The Taming of the Shrew* and the Renaissance Discourse of Rhetoric'. *Modern Philology* 92, no. 3 (February 1995): 294–327.

Rose, Jacqueline. 'Sexuality in the Reading of Shakespeare: *Hamlet* and *Measure for Measure*'. In *Alternative Shakespeares*, 2nd edn. Edited by John Drakakis, 97–120. New York: Routledge, 2002.

Rosenberg, Marvin. *The Masks of Anthony and Cleopatra*. Edited by Mary Rosenberg. Newark, DE: University of Delaware Press, 2006.

Rudanko, Juhani. *Pragmatic Approaches to Shakespeare: Essays on Othello, Coriolanus, and Timon of Athens*. Lanham, MD: University Press of America, 1993.

Salkeld, Duncan. 'Shakespeare and "the I-word"'. *Style* 44, no. 3 (Fall 2010): 328–41.

Saul, Jennifer M. 'Speaker Meaning, What Is Said, and What Is Implicated'. *Noûs* 36, no. 2 (2002): 228–48.

Schalkwyk, David. 'Giving Intention Its Due?' *Style* 44, no. 3 (Fall 2010): 311–27.

Schalkwyk, David. 'Proto-Nationalist Performatives and Trans-Theatrical Displacement in *Henry V*'. In *Transnational Exchange in Early Modern Theater*, edited by Robert Henke and Eric Nicholson, 197–213. Burlington, VT: Ashgate, 2008.

Searle, John R. 'The Structure of Illocutionary Acts'. In *Speech Acts: An Essay in the Philosophy of Language*, 54–71. Cambridge: Cambridge University Press, 1969.

Sell, Roger D. '*Henry V* and the Strength and Weakness of Words: Shakespearean Philology, Historicist Criticism, Communicative Pragmatics'. In *Shakespeare and Scandinavia: A Collection of Nordic Studies*, edited by Gunnar Sorelius, 108–41. Newark, DE: University of Delaware Press, 2002.

Shakespeare, William. *Antony and Cleopatra*. Edited by John Wilders. Arden Shakespeare, 3rd ser. London: Bloomsbury, 1995.

Shakespeare, William. *Hamlet, The Revised Edition*. Edited by Ann Thompson and Neil Taylor. Arden Shakespeare, 3rd ser. London: Bloomsbury, 2016.

Shakespeare, William. *Julius Caesar*. Edited by David Daniell. Arden Shakespeare, 3rd ser. London: Bloomsbury, 1998.

Shakespeare, William. *King Henry IV, Part 1*. Edited by David Scott Kastan. Arden Shakespeare, 3rd ser. London: Bloomsbury, 2002.

Shakespeare, William. *King Henry IV, Part 2*. Edited by A. R. Humphreys. Arden Shakespeare. London: Methuen & Co., 1966.

Shakespeare, William. *King Henry V*. Edited by T. W. Craik. Arden Shakespeare, 3rd ser. London: Bloomsbury, 1995.

Shakespeare, William. *Othello*. Edited by E. A. J. Honigmann. Arden Shakespeare. London: Bloomsbury, 1997.

Shakespeare, William. *The Taming of the Shrew*. Edited by Barbara Hodgdon. Arden Shakespeare, 3rd ser. London: Bloomsbury, 2010.

Short, Mick. 'Discourse Analysis and the Analysis of Drama'. In *Language, Discourse and Literature: An Introductory Reader in Discourse Stylistics*, edited by Ronald Carter and Paul Simpson, 137–68. London: Unwin Hyman, 1989.

Sidney, Mary Herbert, trans. 'The Tragedie of Antonie'. 1595. In *Narrative and Dramatic Sources of Shakespeare*. Vol. 5, edited by Geoffrey Bullough, 358–406. London: Routledge and Kegan Paul and New York: Columbia University Press, 1964.

Slights, Camille Wells. 'The Conscience of the King: *Henry V* and the Reformed Conscience'. *Philological Quarterly* 80, no. 1 (Winter 2001): 37–55.

Spencer, Janet M. 'Princes, Pirates, and Pigs: Criminalizing Wars of Conquest in *Henry V*'. *Shakespeare Quarterly* 47, no. 2 (Summer 1996): 160–77.

Sperber, Dan and Deirdre Wilson. 'Irony and the Use-Mention Distinction'. In *Radical Pragmatics*, edited by Peter Cole, 295–318. New York: Academic Press, 1981.

Sternlicht, Sanford. '*Hamlet*: Six Characters in Search of a Play'. *College English* 27, no. 7 (April 1966): 528–31.

The Taming of a Shrew: The 1594 Quarto. Edited by Stephen Roy Miller. Cambridge: Cambridge University Press, 1998.

Tannen, Deborah. *Talking Voices: Repetition, Dialogue, and Imagery in Conversational Discourse*. 2nd edn. New York: Cambridge University Press, 2007.

Thomas, Jenny. *Meaning in Interaction: An Introduction to Pragmatics*. London and New York: Longman, 1995.

Van Doren, Mark. '*Henry IV*'. 1939. Reprinted in *Henry the Fourth, Parts I and II: Critical Essays*, edited by David Bevington, 99–116. New York: Garland Publishing, 1986.

Vološinov, Valentin N. *Marxism and the Philosophy of Language*. 1930. Translated by Ladislav Matejka and I. R. Titunik. New York and London: Seminar Press, 1973.

Weimann, Robert. 'Playing with a Difference'. In *Author's Pen and Actor's Voice: Playing and Writing in Shakespeare's Theatre*, 79–108. Cambridge: Cambridge University Press, 2000.

Weimann, Robert and Douglas Bruster. 'Personation and Playing: "Secretly Open" Role-Playing'. In *Shakespeare and the Power of Performance: Stage and Page in the Elizabethan Theatre*, 139–59. Cambridge: Cambridge University Press, 2008.

Wentersdorf, Karl P. 'Animal Symbolism in Shakespeare's *Hamlet*: The Imagery of Sex Nausea'. *Comparative Drama* 17, no. 4 (Winter 1983–1984): 348–82.

Wentersdorf, Karl P. 'The Conspiracy of Silence in *Henry V*'. *Shakespeare Quarterly* 27, no. 3 (Summer 1976): 264–87.

Wierzbicka, Anna. 'The Semantics of Direct and Indirect Discourse'. *Papers in Linguistics* 7, no. 3–4 (September 1974): 267–307.

Wilson, Deirdre and Dan Sperber. 'Explaining Irony'. In *Meaning and Relevance*, 123–45. Cambridge: Cambridge University Press, 2012.

Yachnin, Paul. 'Shakespeare's Politics of Loyalty: Sovereignty and Subjectivity in *Antony and Cleopatra*'. *SEL: Studies in English Literature 1500–1900* 33, no. 2 (Spring 1993): 343–63.

Yachnin, Paul and Jessica Slights, eds. 'Introduction'. In *Shakespeare and Character: Theory, History, Performance, and Theatrical Persons*, edited by Yachnin and Slights, 1–18. Basingstoke: Palgrave Macmillan, 2009.

INDEX

Note: Page references with the letter 'n' denote note numbers.

Adelman, Janet, 74, 78
agency
   of character, 11–12
   Falstaff, 24–5
   Hamlet, 190
   of intention, 14–15
   Katherine (*The Taming of the Shrew*), 138–9
Alfar, Cristina León, 60
analogy
   in *Hamlet,* 179–80
   in *Henry V,* 112–18, 125
   Katherine (*The Taming of the Shrew*), 159–62
anamorphic ambiguity, 139
anteriority, 16–19
   Antony and Cleopatra, 91–2
   Falstaff, 41, 46, 53, 57–8
   Hamlet, 169–90, 173, 182–3, 187–90
   Katherine (*The Taming of the Shrew*), 18–19, 156–7
Antony
   and Atlas, compared, 74–5
   Caesar's tribute to, 67–70
   emasculation by Cleopatra, 84
   as great Egyptian, 86
Antony and Cleopatra, 17, 59, 61, 66-67, 95. *See also* Antony; Cleopatra

arete, 107, 109, 117, 121, 135
Aristotle
   plot over character, 4
   rhetorical appeals, 107–8
   rhetoric as pragma-rhetoric, 103–6
Arnovick, Leslie, 110
Arrington, Phillip, 188
audience
   assumptions of, 27–8
   'authorial', 15
   direct address to, 40–3, 50
   Elizabethan, 35–6, 45
   female, 18, 72, 142, 158, 161–6, 188–9
   inferences, 28, 34–7, 54, 73, 105, 111, 141–2
   as interlocutor, 13–14, 18–19, 28, 50–7, 92–5
   interpretations by, 102–7, 129–31
   male, 18, 142, 158, 162, 164–7
   offstage, 2, 79–80, 137, 139, 155–7, 170, 172–4, 177
   onstage, 18, 74, 80–3, 85, 88, 95, 142, 155, 165–6
   perceptions of, 5–6, 45, 123–4, 150, 180, 182–7, 190

INDEX

response, 15–16
role, 13–16, 19–20
Austin, J.L., 6–7, 8, 10, 66, 100
How to Do Things with Words, 6
Ayers, P.K., 98

Bakhtin, Mikhail, 65–6, 172
Bakhtinian dialogism, 11, 98–9, 172
Battenhouse, Roy W., 24
Baumlin, Tita French, 139
Bean, John C., 139
Belleforest, François de
Hamblet in *Histoires Tragiques*, 174–5
Belsey, Catherine, 60
Berger, Harry J., 24
Blits, Jan H., 85
Bousfield, Derek, 34, 49–50
boy actors
Cleopatra, 83, 86, 88, 91–2, 95
Katherine (*The Taming of the Shrew*), 18, 138–9, 142, 151, 156–7, 163–5, 167
Bradley, A.C., 1–2, 5, 9, 98
Brown, Roger
face, 28–58 (*see also* face)
and Gilman, Albert, 'Politeness Theory and Shakespeare's Four Major Tragedies', 9
politeness theory, 12, 17, 28–31, 33–4, 37–8, 99
Bushman, Mary Ann, 60

Caesar (*Antony and Cleopatra*)
Cleopatra's mockery of, 81–3
reports by, 64–5, 67–70, 80, 93–4
tribute to Antony, 67–70
Calderwood, James L., 54
Chambers, E.K., 22
Champion, Larry S., 102–3
character, life-likeness of. *See* reality effect
character effect, 10, 12–13, 16–19
Falstaff, 23
Katherine (*The Taming of the Shrew*), 167
character studies, 4, 10–11, 13, 23–5
charisma, sexual, 59–95. *See also* Cleopatra
Charnes, Linda, 60, 66–7, 70
Chomsky, Noam, 7
Cleopatra, 16–18, 59–95
ambivalence of, 61
Antony, relationship to (*see* Antony)
audience, 72–3, 79–83, 88, 92–5
barge-scene report, 86–7, 89
boy actor, 83, 86, 88, 91–2, 95
Caesar, mockery of, 81–3
Caesar, relationship to, 89–91, 93–4
Caesar's reports, 64–5, 67–70, 80, 93–4
commanding of report, 61, 67, 82–4, 89–90
as courtesan, 17, 91
death of, 84–5, 90, 93–4
direct reported speech, 73–5, 81–3

dream-vision report, 85–6, 89, 95
echoic mention, 77
as Egyptian monarch, 79–80, 82, 89, 92–3, 95
Enobarbus's report, 85–9
feminism and, 59–60, 138–9
final act, 92–4
historical depictions of, 62–4
histrionic strategies, 60–1, 70
indirect reported speech, 68–70, 72, 93–4
irony, dramatic, 74, 91–2
irony, verbal, 68–9, 76–80, 77, 82–3
meta-theatre, 18, 83, 88, 91–2, 95
monologue, 63–4, 70–1, 73, 76, 79–80
narrative imperative, 66–7, 70
perlocutionary effect, 81, 83–4, 87–8
personal imaginings, 17, 61, 72, 75, 79–81, 83, 87–8, 91–3
political role, 59–60
powerlessness/power oscillation, 61, 73–5, 80, 85
prosodic switches, 76–7
reported speech, 61–4, 84–5, 94–5 (*see also* reported speech)
as reporter, 70–95
report of others' speech, 17, 61, 66–7, 73, 83, 85
Roman discourse, 66–70
Roman report, 17–18, 64, 70, 88, 91–2, 94–5
self-dramatization, 78–9
self-praise, 74–5, 80, 85–8
sexual power, 17, 59, 74–5, 77–80, 89, 91–5
Shakespeare's report, 92
as subject of Roman Empire, 60–1, 81, 95
as woman in love, 59, 71–3, 84, 93, 95
Collington, Philip D., 172
Collins, Daniel E., 65, 79
constative statements, 100, 114–15, 129–30, 135
conversational implicatures, 26–58, 141, 146–50, 173. *See also* Falstaff
Cooper, Marilyn M., 141
Cooperative Principle, 27–8, 31–2, 50
Culpeper, Jonathan, 13

Daniel, Samuel, 63–4
 The Tragedie of Cleopatra, 63
Dascal, Marcelo, 105–6
Davis, Wayne A., 27
deliberative rhetoric, 157–8, 165
Desmet, Christy, 3–4
dialectic/logic, 104, 120–4
dialogues, stichomythic, 146, 150, 154
direct reported speech. *See* reported speech
discourse biography, 12–13
Dodd, William, 4, 11–13
doubleness, 55–6
double personation, 52–3
dramatic irony. *See* irony

INDEX

Duranti, Alessandro, 65
Dusinberre, Juliet, 156

echoic mention, 77, 152–5, 160–1
echoic utterances
  Hamlet, 181
  Katherine (*The Taming of the Shrew*), 142, 150–7, 160–1, 166–7
Egyptian values, 59–60, 82, 86
Elam, Keir, 10–11
  Shakespeare's Universe of Discourse, 10
emotion/pathos, 107–8
enargia, 118
Engle, Lars, 172
English and French, compared, 131–4
Enobarbus' report, 85–9
enthymeme, 108, 122–3, 125
epideictic rhetoric, 150–7
ethos
  Henry V, 100–1, 107–27, 132–3, 135
  Katherine, 142, 158, 166–7
eunoia, 107, 113, 115, 117, 122, 133, 135
exteriority/interiority. *See* interiority/exteriority

face
  comic, 32, 38
  and conversational implicatures, 28–58 (*see also* Falstaff; politeness theory)
  damage to, 58
  negative, 29–30, 147–8
  and politeness theory, 28–31
  positive, 29–30, 56
face-threatening acts (FTAs)
  insults, 49
  negative politeness strategies, 29–30, 47
  off-record strategies, 29–30, 34, 37
  positive politeness strategies, 29–30, 33–4, 37
fallacies, logical
  analogy and, 113
  argumentum ad consequentiam, 121–2, 127
  dicto simpliciter, 126
  ethos and, 116–17
  ignoratio elenchi, 123, 125–6
  material, 131
  non causa pro causa, 120–4
  post-hoc inference, 121
Falstaff, 21–58
  apposition, 25, 33-38
  audience, 27–8, 35–6, 40–3, 45, 50–7
  Bolingbroke, criticism of, 17, 25, 36, 38, 39–40, 43
  as braggart, 17, 23, 25–6, 30, 38–9, 41–2, 44–6, 58
  character studies of, 23–4
  as clown, 51, 58
  comic face, 32, 38
  courage and cowardice, 22, 42–3
  as devil, 56
  double implicatures, 43, 46
  doubleness, 55–6
  double personation, 52–3
  dramatic irony, 36–7, 41, 53
  exteriority/interiority, 22–3

face-threatening acts (FTAs), 29–30, 33–4, 37, 47, 49
Falstaff-as-king's speech, 46–9
Gad's Hill robbery, 41–2, 56
Hal, imitation of, 49–50
as hedonist, 25, 31, 41, 45–6, 51
impoliteness theory, 34–5, 42, 49, 197 n.15
irony, dramatic, 17, 36–7, 41, 52–6
irony, verbal, 32–3, 39, 44–5, 48–50
King Henry, critique of, 39–40, 45–7, 52–3
King Henry, imitation of, 46–9, 52
as knight, 23, 38–9, 41, 43, 46, 58
life, symbol of, 55
Machiavellian aspects, 22, 25, 40, 45
meta-theatre, 17, 25, 37, 52–5, 57, 61–2
mockery/self-mockery (*see* mockery, Falstaff)
moral voice, 35, 39–41, 44, 46–8, 51–2, 58
as Oldcastle, 45–6
perlocutionary effect, 24–5, 35
play extempore, 46–8, 50, 52–5
politeness theory, 28–31, 33–4, 37–8
as Puritan, 17, 23–5, 35, 44–6, 50, 58
reality effect, 21–2, 25–6, 36, 54, 57
roundness of, 17, 21–3, 25–6, 52, 55, 57
self-inflation and self-deflation, 25, 31, 38–9, 46, 57
self-praise, 31, 33, 38, 40, 46, 48–9
soliloquies, 36, 41, 50–1, 53–4, 57
as thief, 17, 25, 30–3, 36, 38–43, 48
undermining of own roles, 17, 42–4
as Vice/Vanity, 51, 56, 196 n.9
visual representation, 17, 25, 53–5, 57
The Famous Victories of Henry the Fifth, 102–3
feminism, 59–60, 138–9
Fernández, María Luisa Dañobeitia, 81
Fish, Stanley, 8–9
French language, *Henry V,* 131–4

Garver, Eugene, 108
Goffman, Erving, 28
Goodwin, Charles, 65
Gould, Gerald, 97–8
Grammaticus, Saxo, 175
  Vita Amlethi, 170–1
Greenblatt, Stephen, 3, 99
Grice, H.P., 6–7, 10, 21–58, 57–8, 141, 147–8, 152, 164, 174
Gricean implicatures. *See* conversational implicatures
Gross, Alan, 105–6

INDEX

Hal (*1 Henry IV*), 21–58. *See also* Falstaff
Halio, Jay L., 138
Hall, Edward
  The Union of the Two Noble and Illustrious Families of Lancaster and York, 101
Hamlet, 19, 169–90
  agency of, 172, 190
  anteriority, 19, 170, 187–9
  antic disposition, 170, 173, 182–5
  as avenger, 170
  Claudius, opening response to, 174–5
  female hypocrisy, tirade on, 187–9
  final utterance of, 169–70
  Gertrude, response to, 175–7
  inner feeling/outer expression, 164, 176, 183–4
  inscrutability of, 19
  interiority, 172–3
  irony, dramatic, 176–7, 182
  irony, verbal, 176–9, 181–2
  as madman, 19, 172–3, 177–80, 182–3, 185–9
  misogyny of, 19, 177, 180, 185–6, 187–9
  Ophelia, conversation with, 184–5
  Ophelia, nunnery speech to, 185–7
  Ophelia's report of, 182–3
  Polonius, conversation with, 177–84
  pragmatic failure, 19, 170, 173, 180, 182, 190
  soliloquy, 'to be or not to be,' 187–9
  sources for, 170–1
  undecidability of, 19, 187–90
Hawkes, Terence, 173
1 Henry IV, 21–50. *See also* conversational implicatures; Falstaff
Henry V, 8–9, 16, 18, 97–135
  analogy, use of, 112–18, 125–6, 216 n.49
  anaphora, use of, 117, 119–20
  arete, 107, 109, 117, 121, 135
  audience, 102–7, 111, 123–4, 129–31
  as Christian monarch, 18, 97, 100, 103, 106, 108, 123–5, 127, 134–5
  enthymeme, 108, 122–3, 125
  Erasmus, 125–6
  ethos, 100–1, 107–27, 132–3, 135
  eunoia, 107, 113, 115, 122, 133, 135
  as historical figure, 101–3
  interiority/exteriority, 98
  irony, dramatic, 18, 97, 100–1, 106, 111, 123–4, 135
  irony, verbal, 114–19, 128–33
  Katherine, speech to, 130–1
  Katherine, wooing of, 127–34
  logical fallacies, 113, 116–17, 120–7

logos, 100, 104–5, 107–8, 116–17, 120–7, 133–5
lords, speech to, 116–22, 129
Machiavellianism, 18, 97–8, 106, 111–12, 114, 125, 128, 133, 135
modality, 109–13, 216 n.44
modal verbs, 102–3, 108–12, 110–11, 135
monologue, 108–9
moral ambivalence, 18, 97–8, 100, 126–7, 135
New Rhetoric, 104–5
as orator, 100–6, 108–9
pathos, 107–8
perlocutionary effect, 104–5, 117
phronesis, 107–8, 127, 135
as plain-speaking soldier, 100, 122, 123–4, 127–35
pragma-rhetoric, 18, 100–1, 103–6
'presence' as rhetorical strategy, 118–19
promise to Canterbury, 112–14
soldiers, speech to, 122–7
syllogism, 108, 122–3, 125
Wallis rules, 110, 112, 116
Hirsh, James, 188
Hiscock, Andrew, 67, 69
Hodgdon, Barbara, 139
Holinshed, Raphael
Chronicles of England, Scotland, and Ireland, 101–2

illocutionary force, 6, 83, 88, 100, 114, 117, 179, 186, 192 n.13

implicatures. *See* conversational implicatures
impoliteness theory. *See also* politeness theory
Bousfield, 34
Falstaff, 34–5, 42, 49
Henry V, 99–100
indirect reported speech. *See* reported speech
intentions of speaker, 14–15, 105–6
interiority/exteriority
Falstaff, 22–3
Hamlet, 172–3
of Henry V, 98
irony, dramatic
Cleopatra, 74, 91–2
Falstaff, 36–7, 41, 52–6
Hamlet, 176–7, 182
Henry V, 18, 97, 100–1, 106, 111, 123–4, 135
Katherine (*The Taming of the Shrew*), 156–7, 165, 167
irony, verbal
Cleopatra, 68–9, 76–80, 82–3
Falstaff, 17, 32–3, 39, 44–5, 48–50
Hamlet, 176–9, 181–2
Henry V, 114–19, 128–33
Katherine (*The Taming of the Shrew*), 18, 148, 151–4, 160–2, 165

Jackson, William, 1
James, Heather, 68, 78–9
Jankowski, Theodora A., 60
Johnson, Samuel, 21–2
Josephus, Flavius, 62

Kahn, Coppélia, 138, 141
Katherine (*The Taming of the Shrew*), 18–19, 137–67
  agency of, 138–9
  ambiguity of, 139, 142, 164–7
  analogy, use of, 159–62
  anteriority, 18–19
  audience, offstage, 137, 139, 155–8, 161–7
  audience, onstage, 142, 155, 165–6
  boy actor, 138–9, 142, 151, 156–7, 163–5, 167
  communicative intentions, 18, 140
  comparisons, argumentative use of, 142, 166–7
  conversational implicatures, 141, 146–50, 147
  courtship scene with Petruccio, 146–50
  critique of patriarchy, 18, 145–54, 156, 158, 160–2, 166–7
  deliberative rhetoric, 157–8, 165
  dialogues, stichomythic, 146, 150, 154
  echoic mention, 152–5, 160–1
  echoic utterances, 142, 150–8, 166–7
  encomium, 140–1
  epideictic rhetoric, 150–7
  historical background, 143–6
  irony, dramatic, 156–7, 165, 167
  irony, verbal, 18, 148, 151–4, 160–2, 165
  meta-theatre, 18–19, 138–9, 142, 154, 156–7, 164–5, 167
  monologue, 138, 157–67
  as obedient wife, 139, 142, 150–7, 154–5, 166–7
  patriarchal view of, 138–43
  perlocutionary effect, 137, 141
  persuasion, 140–2, 151, 154–6, 158, 161, 164–7
  puns, 139, 146–50
  reality effect, 138–9, 157, 166
  semantic ambiguity, 18, 142, 158, 162, 164–6
  as shrew, 142, 143–6, 154, 166–7
  subordination as public façade, 18, 138, 142, 147, 150, 158, 161, 166
  sun/moon scene, 150–7
  wordplay, 139, 146–50
Kemp, Will, 52
Kennedy, Andrew, 10–11, 14
Kerrigan, John, 9
Kinneavy, James L., 107
Kizelbach, Urszula, 99
Knights, L.C., 2
  'How Many Children Had Lady Macbeth?,' 5
Ko, Yu Jin, 4
Korta, Kepa, 105–6

Lancastrian dynasty. *See* mockery, Falstaff
Larrazabal, Jésus M., 105–6
Levin, Richard A., 22–3
Levinson, Stephen C., 28–9
  face, 28–58, 147–8 (*see also* face)

politeness theory, 9, 12, 17, 28–31, 33–4, 37–8, 99
life-likeness. *See* reality effect
Little, Megan D., 140–1
logic/dialectic, 103–4, 120–4
logos, 100–1, 104–5, 107–8, 111, 115–17, 120–7, 133–5
Loomba, Ania, 73
Lopez, Jeremy, 35–6
Lucan, 62
Lyons, John, 110

Machiavellianism
  Falstaff, 22, 25, 40, 45
  Henry V, 18, 97–8, 106, 111–12, 114, 125, 128, 133, 135
Mackay, Elizabeth Ann, 140
Madelaine, Richard, 156
Magnusson, Lynne, 11–13, 110–11
maxims, Cooperative Principle, 57–8, 198 n.20
  of manner, 28, 32, 38, 148, 163–4, 174, 178, 181
  of quality, 27, 31, 45, 152, 198 n.20
  of quantity, 27, 147, 176, 181, 198 n.20
  of relation, 27–8, 31, 178–9
Mayes, Patricia, 72
McDonald, Russ, 61
McEachern, Claire, 99
McLaverty, J., 50
A Merry Jest of a Shrewd and Curst Wife, 143
meta-theatre, 6, 8–9, 15–16
  Cleopatra, 18, 83, 88, 91–2, 95

Falstaff, 17, 25, 37, 52–5, 57, 61–2
Hamlet, 176–7
Katherine (*The Taming of the Shrew*), 18–19, 138–9, 142, 154, 156–7, 164–5, 167
Mey, Jacob L., 8
mockery, Falstaff
  of Hal, 32, 35, 38, 42, 44
  of Lancastrian dynasty, 17, 25–6, 30, 34, 38–41, 44, 47–8, 56, 58
  of Puritanism, 45
  self-mockery, 24–5, 30–1, 33, 38, 41, 44–6, 51
modality, 109–13
  deontic, 110, 216 n.44
  epistemic, 110, 216 n.44
monologues
  Cleopatra, 63–4, 70–1, 73, 76, 79–80
  Henry V, 108–9
  Katherine (*The Taming of the Shrew*), 18, 138–9, 144–5, 157–67
moral ambivalence, 97–135. *See also* Henry V
moral character. *See* ethos
Morgann, Maurice, 22–3
Morris, Corbyn, 22
Mossman, Judith, 115

narrative imperative, 66–7, 70
Neill, Michael, 99
new character criticism, 4
New Historicism, 2–4, 24, 98–9, 140
Newman, Karen, 3, 139
New Rhetoric, 104–5

Olbrechts-Tyteca, Lucie, 103–6, 118
Oldcastle, Sir John, 45–6
Ophelia (*Hamlet*),
  conversation with Hamlet, 184–7
  Hamlet's nunnery speech to, 185–7
  report on Hamlet, 182–3

Palfrey, Simon, 11–12, 76
pathos, 107–8, 120, 215 n.38
patriarchy, critique of, 18, 145–54, 156, 158, 160–2, 166–7
Perelman, Chaïm, 103–6, 118
perlocutionary effect, 6
  Cleopatra, 81, 83–4, 87–8
  Falstaff, 24–5, 35
  Hamlet, 186
  Henry V, 104–5, 117
  Katherine (*The Taming of the Shrew*), 137, 141–2
Petrarchan conventions, 129, 152–3
Petruccio (*The Taming of the Shrew*)
  conversational implicatures, 147
  courtship scene with Katherine, 146–50
  financial motivations of, 146–7
  rhetoric, use of, 139–41
  sun/moon scene, 150–7
phronesis, 107–8, 127, 135
play extempore, 46–8, 50, 52–5
play-within-a-play, 52–3, 156

Plutarch, 180
  Parallel Lives, 62–4
politeness theory
  and conversational implicatures, 17 (*see also* face-threatening acts (FTAs); impoliteness)
  and face, 28–31
  Falstaff, 33–4, 37–8
  Gilman on, 9
  Levinson on, 28–9, 34
  Magnusson on, 12
  negative and positive strategies, 193 n.20
  Penelope Brown on, 28–9, 34
  Roger Brown on, 9
Porter, Joseph A., 8–9
Post-Structuralism, 2–4
pragma-rhetoric
  Henry V, 18, 100–1, 103–6, 111
  Katherine (*The Taming of the Shrew*), 139, 158
pragmatics, 5–20
  failure of, 169–90 (*see also* Hamlet)
  historical, 9
  of reported speech, 64–6
prosodic switches, 76–7
Protestantism, 46, 171
Pugliatti, Paola, 98–9
puns
  'bear' in *The Taming of the Shrew*, 148–9
  'beauty/booty' in *1 Henry IV*, 31, 39
  'common' in *Hamlet*, 175
  'credit/counterfeit' in *1 Henry IV*, 53–4

'credit' in *1 Henry IV*, 36–8
'crown' in *Antony and Cleopatra*, 90
'die' in *Antony and Cleopatra*, 79
'double' in *1 Henry IV*, 55
'government' in *1 Henry IV*, 39–40
'grace' in *1 Henry IV*, 33–6
'here apparent/heir apparent' in *1 Henry IV*, 37–8
'honest' in *Hamlet*, 184–5
'jack' in *1 Henry IV*, 55
by Katherine (*The Taming of the Shrew*), 146–50
'kin/kind' in *Hamlet*, 174
'knight's bawdy' in *1 Henry IV*, 39
'light/weight' in *The Taming of the Shrew*, 149–50
'like' in *Henry V*, 129
'measure' in *Henry V*, 130
'moon and seven stars' in *1 Henry IV*, 32–3
'movable' in *The Taming of the Shrew*, 148–9
'nunnery' in *Hamlet*, 185–6
'part' in *1 Henry IV*, 36
'parts' in *The Taming of the Shrew*, 163–4
'queen' in *1 Henry IV*, 76
'reckoning' in *1 Henry IV*, 36
sexual wordplay in *1 Henry IV*, 36–8
'son/sun' in *Hamlet*, 174–5, 179–80
'sun' in *The Taming of the Shrew*, 154
'to be' in *Hamlet*, 188–9
'true' in *1 Henry IV*, 43
Puritanism, 23–5, 35, 44–5, 50

quotation, direct and indirect. *See* reported speech

Rabinowitz, Peter J., 15
Rabkin, Norman, 98
reality effect, 1–2, 5–6, 11–13, 16–17, 20
  Falstaff, 21–2, 25–6, 36, 54, 57
  Hamlet, 173
  Katherine (*The Taming of the Shrew*), 138–9, 157, 166
Rebhorn, Wayne A., 138–40
reported speech, 59–95
  authorial context, 66
  Caesar's reports, 64–5, 67–70, 80, 93–4
  Cleopatra, 17, 61–4, 70–95, 84–5
  commanding of report, 61, 67, 82–4, 89–90
  direct, 73–5, 81–3
  indirect, 68–70, 72, 93–4
  personal imaginings, 17, 61
  pragmatics of, 64–6
  as public self-display, 67
  Roman discourse, 17–18, 66–70
  and sexual power, 59
  as spectacle, 80
  speech of others, 17, 61, 66–7, 73, 83, 85
  syntactic approach to, 65
  as tool for conquest and domination, 67–8

rhetorical ethos, 107–27. *See also under* Henry V
rhetorical question
  in Cleopatra's reported speech, 71
  in Katherine's monologue (*The Taming of the Shrew*), 162–3
Roman discourse, 66–70
Roman Empire
  Cleopatra as subject of, 60–1
  as locus of narrative imperative, 60
  messengers of, 82
  reported speech and, 95
  Roman values, 17–18, 59–60, 82
Roman reporting, 17–18, 64, 70, 88, 91–2, 94–5
Rosenberg, Marvin, 81
Rudanko, Juhani
  Pragmatic Approaches to Shakespeare, 10

Salkeld, Duncan, 15
Saussure, Ferdinand de, 7, 65
Schalkwyk, David, 15, 61, 99–100
Searle, John R., 6–7, 105, 112
self-image. *See* face
self-praise
  Cleopatra, 74–5, 80, 85–8
  Falstaff, 31, 33, 38, 40, 46, 48–9
Sell, Roger D., 99
sexual charisma, 59–95. *See also* Cleopatra

sexual diplomacy, 60–1
sexual wordplay, 36–8
Short, Mick, 14
Shrewsbury, 53, 56–7
Shurgot, Michael
  Shakespeare's Sense of Character: On the Page and from the Stage, 4
Sidney, Mary Herbert
  The Tragedie of Antonie, 63–4
Sinfield, Alan, 192
Slights, Camille Wells, 113
Slights, Jessica
  Shakespeare and Character: Theory, History, Performance, and Theatrical Persons, 4
soliloquies
  dramatic conventions of, 3
  Falstaff, 41, 53–4, 57
  Hal, 36, 50–1
  Hamlet, 177, 187–9
  purpose, 9–10
speech act theory, 8, 197 n.15
Spencer, Janet M., 115
Sperber, Dan, 77, 152
Stern, Tiffany, 11–12, 76
Sternlicht, Sanford, 172
stichomythic dialogues, 146, 150, 154
Sublette, Jack R., 39
syllogism, 108, 122–3, 125

The Taming of a Shrew, 144–5
Thomas, Jenny, 8, 13–14

undecidability, Hamlet's, 169–90

Van Doren, Mark, 23–4
Virgil, 62
Vološinov, Valentin N., 65–6, 68

Wallis, Bishop John, 110
    Wallis rules, 110, 112, 116
Warshauer, Susan C., 107
Weimann, Robert, 52–3

Wentersdorf, Karl P., 119, 180
Wierzbicka, Anna, 73
Wilson, Deirdre, 77, 152

Yachnin, Paul, 82
    Shakespeare and Character: Theory, History, Performance, and Theatrical Persons, 4

www.ingramcontent.com/pod-product-compliance
Lightning Source LLC
Chambersburg PA
CBHW050348230426
43663CB00010B/2043